PASSPORT TO HELL

How I Survived **SADISTIC PRISON GUARDS** AND **HARDENED CRIMINALS** IN Spain's **TOUGHEST PRISONS**

TERRY DANIELS

summersdale

PASSPORT TO HELL

Summersdale Publishers Ltd
46 West Street
Chichester
West Sussex
PO19 1RP
UK

www.summersdale.com

Printed and bound by CPI Group (UK) Ltd, Croydon

ISBN: 978-1-84953-344-7

Substantial discounts on bulk quantities of Summersdale books are available to corporations, professional associations and other organisations. For details contact Nicky Douglas by telephone: +44 (0) 1243 756902, fax: +44 (0) 1243 786300 or email: nicky@summersdale.com.

DISCLAIMER
The information and views expressed in this book are those of the author and do not necessarily reflect the views and opinions of Summersdale Publishers Ltd.

Lyric from 'Looking Out My Window' by the Rat Pack used with permission.

All images used with permission.

I am dedicating this book to my mum because without her, God only knows where I'd be today. She offered her tireless love and support and never gave up on me. She is my Wonder Mum. I would also like to dedicate it to my dad. I hope he's proud of me.

ABOUT THE AUTHOR

During her time inside, **Terry Daniels'** story was featured in *The Mirror*, *The Sun*, the *Daily Mail* and *The Daily Telegraph*. She appeared on every major news programme. Nowadays her life is a lot less exciting, which is exactly how she likes it. She undertakes charity work on behalf of Fair Trials International and Prisoners Abroad, and volunteers with ex-offenders and drug abusers.

ACKNOWLEDGEMENTS

I would like to thank my sister, who was my best pen pal whilst I was in prison, who is my best friend and who has put up with so much and still loves me; everyone at Prisoners Abroad, everyone at Fair Trials, John Bercow, who was there from start to finish and never gave up, my MEP James Elles, all my media supporters (Tom Walton, Nikki Jenkins, Alex Forest and Amanda Walton, who has given me her continuous support), Bev (my angel in Spain); all the people who wrote letters of support for my pardon (without you I never would have got it), SMART and the Drug and Alcohol Team for their support in my recovery and help in preparing me for my release from jail; my solicitors in England and Northern Ireland, Mari Luz in Spain for believing in me and taking on the case for my pardon; everyone who supported me on my release and gave me a chance (you know who you are and I'll never forget this), friends and family who wrote to me while I was inside (your letters were a great comfort), Ellen, who always appeared when Mum and I needed her, our guardian angel Siv Tunnicliffe for her prayers and support, Linda for being Linda; a big thanks to all my girls at Trendz and also for Jamie Scott for my photos; Danny for always listening even when I bored him to tears, Sabine Zanker, who was not just my legal representative but also became a very close friend, Summersdale for publishing my book and making this all happen and finally to my ghost writer, who took the story on and made my dreams come true... and boy it's some story!

Some of the names of individuals included in this book have been changed to protect their identities. The names of nightclubs have also been changed for legal reasons.

CONTENTS

FOREWORD

Reading this book made my own experiences feel like a stroll in the woods by comparison. In 1993 I was convicted and sent to a Thai prison for attempting to smuggle 90 grams of heroin through Bangkok airport. I was guilty and deserved my sentence, and I knew I had to face the consequences – somehow. Terry was just a young girl, living life to the full and oblivious to the dangers around her. She got caught up in someone else's misdeeds and paid a harsh price for being with the wrong people at the wrong time.

Being convicted and imprisoned for a crime I had committed was bad enough; being wrongly condemned has always been my worst nightmare. I have met women who have been convicted of crimes they have not committed; I have seen how the injustice eats away at them, eroding them of all interests, except the drive to prove their innocence. Guilty people tend to accept their punishments and move on. The innocent do not. After several years in prison it is easy to spot who is innocent.

When I was arrested in Thailand a life sentence was 99.9 years, worse than the death penalty. The best sentence I could hope for was 25 years. In the beginning I felt as though I had no choice but to let go of my life, to forget my family and friends and hope that they would forget me. Terry, knowing in her heart that she did not deserve the sentence she had received, chose to fight from the very beginning, never letting go of her family and the dream of the freedom that was rightfully hers. She suffered greatly in her fight. The fact that she got through it with her sanity intact is an outstanding testament to her strength and something worthy of great admiration.

For anyone going off to warmer climes to party in the sun and to indulge in a little reckless behaviour, Terry's story should be taken as a warning. It reveals the terrible hidden dangers behind the beach-revelling, carefree life abroad that so many young people crave. I hope that it serves to remind everyone who reads it that it's the people you love, and who love you, that really make life worth living.

Sandra Gregory, 2013

'Thoughts of Freedom'
by Terry Daniels

At the moment I may be thinking
Of how things used to be,
Before these trying times
That have brought such misery
But please stop and think a while
About all that I have learned,
Of just how far I've travelled
And all the corners I have turned,
So always try to remember
That this time won't always be,
For then I may look forward
To when I'm home safe and free.

Chapter 1

THE EXPERIMENTAL YEARS

'*¿Qué es esto? ¿Qué es esto? ¡Es cocaína! ¿A quién pertenece?*'

I couldn't speak a word of Spanish but understood the word '*cocaína*' and knew that I was in a lot of trouble. Thick, white clouds of coke billowed around the room as the heavily built Guardia Civil officers tore apart my travel companion's suitcase. I should have been paralysed with fear but it didn't seem real to me. What the hell was going on?

'She's got nothing to do with this,' yelled Antonio as one of the officers thrust the cold, steel nozzle of a gun against my head. 'They're my drugs. She doesn't know a thing; you might as well let her go.'

'No,' the officer replied. 'She stay.'

In spite of all the trouble they had caused, the drugs were still calling out to me. In the midst of everything that was going on, I looked at the piles of cocaine that were spread across the floor and my mouth began to water. Some of it had fallen into a nice, big, fat line and I was mesmerised by it and wished that I could snort it up.

'Let her go,' Antonio repeated. 'She didn't know.'

He was telling the truth as well. Although I was no stranger to cocaine, the last thing that had been going through my mind during my holiday to Brazil was the possibility that he would try to smuggle 4 kilos of the stuff back across to Spain. It was like an episode of *Banged Up Abroad*. But how had I got myself into this situation in the first place? I was only twenty-three, I had a drink and drug problem and I had travelled overseas with one of the slimiest, most untrustworthy people I knew. Where had it all gone wrong?

My early years were a million miles away from the world of hedonistic, cocaine-filled excess that I eventually entered into. I was born in Aylesbury, the county town of Buckinghamshire and grew up in the tiny, rural village of Wingrave, which is your typical slice of idyllic English countryside. The village is surrounded by lush, green fields and has very little crime. It is hardly the type of place that you would expect somebody who has been accused of smuggling a million pounds' worth of cocaine to have been brought up in.

Our house was amongst the first council houses to be built in Wingrave and my parents bought it straightaway. It was a little on the cramped side, but apart from that, it was perfect. We lived on a quiet, relatively trouble-free estate and there were plenty of other children nearby for me to play with. My early surroundings were a far cry from the vice-filled den of iniquity where I would end up living in the months leading up to my arrest.

I was always well behaved as a child and did well at school. I didn't pass my eleven-plus exams but the teachers at Wing County Secondary School, the secondary modern that I attended, coached me through my GCSEs and gave me the attention that I needed to succeed. If I had gone to the local grammar school they would have left me at the back of the class, but as it was, I ended up with nine passes. Aylesbury College, where I did my A levels, wasn't quite as disciplined. I left with two A levels, but could have done a lot better if I had stayed on at Wing County.

I very rarely got into any trouble during my school days, although I started smoking at age twelve. My cousin plied me with cigarettes whenever she came round and I would secretly light up a fag whenever my mum and dad were out. It was all fun and games until my dad caught me taking a drag a few years down the line. He was furious. I think he was secretly devastated that his little girl was gradually losing her innocence and becoming a woman. My mum says she has never seen him as angry as he was that day.

Although I had to hide the fact that I smoked from my parents, drinking was a different matter. My dad's family are Irish and alcohol is a big part of the culture. I was never told that boozing was wrong, although I was never taught that it was a particularly clever thing to do either.

The first time I got drunk was during an exchange trip to France. Wingrave is twinned with La Bouëxière in Brittany and every year the village would arrange for either a French family to come and stay here or a family from Wingrave to travel over there. When our family was chosen to visit Brittany, I decided to single-handedly polish off two bottles of wine and my mum found me heaving my guts up in a forest close to where we were staying. She was mortified.

'Let's get you inside and get you sorted out,' she told me, slapping me around the face to try and sober me up.

Our hosts thought it was hilarious that I was so horribly out of it, but my parents didn't share in their amusement. They were disappointed with my behaviour, but not because I had consumed alcohol. They were more annoyed with me for getting drunk whilst we were relying on somebody else's hospitality. Drinking was regarded as something that I would inevitably do at one point or another. They didn't see it as anywhere near as dirty a habit as smoking.

I may have smoked the occasional cigarette and drunk the odd alcoholic drink but I was still a good kid. I had respect for authority and very rarely fell foul of the law. Funnily enough, I even wanted to be a copper at one point. I was a massive *Cagney and Lacey* fan, which led me to joining the police cadets in the hope that I would one day be able to follow in my heroines' footsteps.

I wanted to be a girl-in-blue right up until I was seventeen when I had my first encounter with a real-life policewoman. A rude, young, female officer came to issue me with a warning after I got into a fight with my next-door neighbour and I thought, 'OK, I could never be like you. You're horrible.' She had very aggressive, authoritarian body language and seemed more concerned with asserting her dominance over me than she was about upholding the law. It was a case of, 'Look at me; I'm in a uniform. I'm going to try and frighten you.'

Apart from that one unfortunate blip, my teenage years were relatively hassle-free. My parents both had full-time jobs, I always had plenty of friends and my folks grafted hard all year so that the family could afford an annual holiday to the Isle of Wight. Our vacations on the island were the highlight of our year. We loved it there. The scenery was beautiful and the weather was a lot hotter than it is on the mainland. Dad wasn't one for change so we always stayed in Ventnor, a large seaside resort on the south coast of the island. We went there so many times, that we ended up in the background of a postcard, which we all thought was hilarious.

The Isle of Wight became a home away from home. We had our own beach hut and spent hour upon hour bronzing ourselves on the sandy beach. It was a magical place and thinking about it conjures up a lot of happy memories.

When I was fifteen, my family decided that it would be cheaper to go abroad. I was sad that we were changing our holiday destination but at the same time excited at the prospect of going somewhere hotter.

'We're off to Tenerife,' my dad announced.

It sounded good to me. As long as there was sun, sea and sand, I would enjoy every single minute of it.

Tenerife was everything the Isle of Wight had been, plus more. It was twice as hot, there was a swimming pool and a beach and all the women looked super-glamorous. I was immediately taken with it. The rest of the family were equally enamoured with the place. My dad loved going for strolls in the countryside and there were plenty of scenic walks. The only downside was the fact that we were staying at an all-inclusive hotel and the catering wasn't all that good. Dad was quite fussy with his food so we spent a lot of time eating out.

Tenerife has a lively nightlife and our hotel was close to Veronicas Strip, a busy 200-metre stretch of clubs and pubs. The strip was patrolled by an army of PR girls, whose job it was to drag passers-by into the bars and persuade them to spend their cash. One of the girls managed to coax us into a cheesy-looking nightclub called Mrs G's and it soon became our regular hangout. It was small and crowded but there was a fun, holiday atmosphere and we went back time and time again.

The following year, we returned to Tenerife and headed straight for Mrs G's. As I said, my dad was never big on change and once he'd found somewhere that he liked, he would usually keep going back. We soon got to know the bar staff and I can remember thinking that they had a cushy little number going on. Working on an island that was as beautiful as that barely constituted work. It was as if they were being paid for taking one long holiday in the sun.

'I could start off as a PR girl and work my way up to a bar job, like theirs,' I thought to myself.

PR work isn't the best job in the world but I figured it would be worth it once I got a job in a club. It was definitely food for thought.

The staff at Mrs G's told us about a block of self-catering apartments called The Optimist in Playa de las Americas, which were ideal for us because Dad was fed up with having to pay for food that nobody wanted to eat. The Optimist was the missing piece of the puzzle. Now our holiday was complete.

After a couple of years of visiting the island, I really got to know the place and made up my mind that I was going to move there at some point in the not-too-distant future. I knew that I was still too young to live abroad, but made a mental note that it was something that I had to do when I got a little bit older. For now, I would just have to make do with holidaying there once a year.

Whenever I got a moment to myself, I would dream of life in Tenerife. It was exotic, it was glamorous and there were plenty of opportunities for adventure; how could rainy, old England ever even hope to compete with a place like that? What was there to do over here that could possibly compare to the levels of excitement that were to be found in Playa de las Americas?

Well, as it turns out, there was one thing that Britain had to offer. My journey into the early stages of adulthood coincided with the birth of underground rave culture. If you came of age during the late 1980s or early 1990s, you would have had to walk round with your eyes shut to avoid the rave scene. It was huge. And from the moment I attended my very first rave, I was hooked.

Had I started my new life in Tenerife the minute I left college, I probably would have missed out on the rave era. As it was, I chose to stay in England because I wasn't ready to move across and I also hadn't saved enough money. I loved to dance and I loved anything with a heavy beat, so rave was the perfect music for me. It was fast, it was energetic and it was uplifting. I liked it all, from the pumping, synthesised beats of Judge Jules and DJ Dougal, to the garage-influenced, electronic rhythms of Jon of the Pleased Wimmin. MC Conrad and LTJ Bukem were another of my favourites. They were drum 'n' bass rather than conventional dance music, but I was into anything that sounded good, regardless of what genre it fitted into. They were originally from Aylesbury and made me proud to be from Bucks.

One of the first ever raves I attended was a warehouse party in Luton, organised by a group of squatters known as 'Exodus'. The Exodus boys threw the biggest illegal events going, drawing crowds of up to 10,000 people. One week they managed to pull in twice the attendance of Luton Town Football Club, which shows you how big rave culture was. So many people went to their raves that it was impossible for the police to shut them down. Their deejays played a mix of jungle and techno with a strong dub influence. It was immense.

A good number of the raves took place in either disused warehouses or abandoned buildings but one of my all-time favourite events had its own purpose-built venue. The Sanctuary in Milton Keynes looked like a big, dirty warehouse but was actually a rave club. It could hold up to 3,000 people and played a mixture of hardcore, drum 'n' bass, hard dance and garage. It was always very loud and very hot in there. You could feel the baseline reverberating throughout your entire body and there was sweat dripping off the ceiling.

There were two main types of ravers in existence at the time; 'chavvy' ravers, who wore designer clothing, and what we referred to as 'smelly' ravers, who had dreadlocks and dressed like hippies. The Sanctuary was more popular with the chavvy type of raver because it cost a lot of money to get in and the smellies didn't like parting with their cash. Some of the venues tended to draw more chavs and some were more hippy-orientated. Although I dressed more chavvy than smelly, I would socialise with anybody, regardless of their style of dress. That was what raves were all about to me; different types of people coming together for the love of the music.

The Rectory, just outside Aylesbury, was another of my favourite clubs. It was around the size of your average living room but usually rammed to capacity and there was always a good crowd. There was never any attitude in the venue itself, but normally a fight occurred outside at closing time, which eventually led to it being shut down. It was a shame because for the most part, everybody got on. One of our mates worked behind the bar and we went there every time we got the chance.

The Rectory was the first place I encountered drugs. Getting off your face was, unfortunately, part and parcel of the rave scene.

The events would go on well into the early hours of the morning and the partygoers would need mountains of drugs to stay awake.

'Try a bit of this,' one of my raving buddies implored me. 'It's good stuff.'

'What is it?' I asked her.

I had never come across amphetamines before. Nobody at our school had taken any kind of drugs so it was something completely new.

'It's whiz. Take some.'

It would be easy for me to pass the blame onto my peers and say that they pressured me into taking speed but that would be a lie. I took it because I wanted to take it. I didn't even think about the dangers of consuming a completely unknown substance. It could have been anything for all I knew, but yet there I was, dabbing my finger into the powder and putting it in my mouth.

The first bag of amphetamines didn't seem to do anything, so I had another. The moment the second lot had entered my body, I got a sudden rush of adrenaline and couldn't stop talking. I had a strange, tingling sensation in my head and felt completely energised from top to toe. It was phenomenal.

I was working at Tesco at the time and the following morning was gruelling to say the least. I hadn't slept a wink and kept falling asleep behind the till. That was the downside to taking speed. It kept you awake all night and you ended up feeling worn down and exhausted the next day. I couldn't help thinking that I should have stuck to just the one bag.

Ecstasy was the other ravers' drug of choice. The first time I took an E was at a night called Dreamscape at The Sanctuary. The pills back then weren't all cut with heroin and rat poison like they are nowadays. They were pure MDMA and cost between £15 and

£20. I took a quarter of a pill and was rushing all night. My skin felt ultra-sensitive and whenever anybody brushed past me, it sent shivers down my spine. I had the time of my life.

Es and speed soon became a routine part of my nights out, although I usually stuck to the speed because Ecstasy was a lot more expensive. We went to rave events all over the south of England. Some of them were in warehouses, some were in aircraft hangars and disused quarries and some were in your regular, run-of-the-mill nightclubs. The Paradise Club in Islington, North London was one of my favourite places to get high and dance. It was a dark, dingy little hole but the music was amazing. There was a café area, a garage room and a drum 'n' bass room and they had an emcee walking around in the crowd, rapping as he went. You would be dancing away and the next thing you knew, he'd be right next to you, emceeing in your ear.

The nights at the Paradise Club went on until eleven o'clock in the morning and there was always a bustling market in full swing when we spilled out onto the streets. It was pretty daunting walking out of a gloomy, dimly-lit club into the daylight and seeing people who had been working all morning. That year, I had moved on from my part-time job at Tesco and had a full-time job as an income support officer. I couldn't imagine looking out of the office window during the day and seeing a load of ravers leaving a nightclub. It was quite surreal and we had to sit in KFC for a while to calm down before we made our way back home.

Whenever I got back from a rave, I was always still a little bit wired, but my parents never seemed to pick up on it. I didn't hide the fact that I was taking drugs from them; I just didn't bring it up. I don't think the possibility even entered their heads that I was taking Ecstasy and amphetamine during my nights out. It wasn't something that they would ever have suspected me of doing. My sister knew that I was getting high but didn't see it as particularly dangerous because lots of other people were doing the same thing at the time. She would sometimes go to raves with me and stay teetotal whilst I got off my head. I knew she wouldn't grass me up to Mum and Dad because we had a very close relationship and trusted one another.

I never worried about my speed and Ecstasy use; there is a hierarchy within the drug world and I always thought the things that I was taking were at the more acceptable end of the spectrum. I took recreational drugs, not hard drugs like crack or heroin. The people that used those kinds of substances didn't move in the same circles as us and we saw them as a level below. I think that this had something to do with the nature of these drugs. You can take Es and whiz recreationally, but most people who take crack or smack are addicts and take them because they have a habit.

Since then, I have worked as a substance abuse counsellor and discovered that a similar hierarchy exists amongst heroin users. There are three tiers of addicts; those within the top tier smoke their drugs on foil or sniff it, the users in the next tier down stick a needle in their arm; bottom-level users inject themselves in the main artery that runs through their groin. The top-tier users look down on the other two tiers and the middle tier look down on the groin-injectors, but in reality, it is all a matter of control. It doesn't matter what drug you are taking or how you are taking it; it's the level to which you grow to rely on it that dictates how much danger it poses. I was playing a dangerous game, which would eventually land me in a whole heap of trouble.

Crack and heroin were firmly imprinted on my mind as drugs I shouldn't take. I had seen what had happened to Zammo in

Grange Hill after he started using heroin and it had put me off for life. It's amazing how a kids' TV programme can have such a lasting effect on the way you think. Similarly, the crack-addicted character of Pookie in the cult 1990s gangster film, *New Jack City*, showed me that crack was another substance to avoid at all costs. TV taught me more about the dangers of substance abuse than teachers ever could. In fact I can't remember ever being warned about drugs at school.

Although it didn't rank alongside crack and heroin in terms of the level of danger that was associated with it, I was always wary of LSD. I didn't take it until a long time after I had started taking Es and speed, because it wasn't a drug to be taken lightly and I didn't want to end up having a bad trip. My first two acid trips were both a lot of fun. A myriad of patterns danced around in front of my eyes and the satellite dishes on the nearby houses started talking to me. It was a little intense, but nothing I couldn't handle. Then came trip number three, which I took whilst round at one of my raving buddies' flats in Milton Keynes. This time the effect of the tab was different from the times before. I was sitting waiting for it to kick in when the entire world suddenly folded up inside a box. I was terrified and genuinely thought that I was going to die.

'I can't believe she's dead,' sobbed a hallucinatory image of my mother, hanging over me and sobbing violently.

'She was far too young to die,' a mirage of my dad concurred.

By this stage, I was hysterical. I was writhing around on the bed, bawling my eyes out and shouting, 'I'm dying! I'm dying!'

I felt one of my friends stroking my head and heard her laughing at me.

'What the hell are you laughing at?' I screamed. 'I'm dying here!'

'You're not dying,' she assured me. 'You're just having a bad trip.'

The minute the words had left her mouth, my brain began to calm itself down a bit. The world edged tentatively out of its box and Mum and Dad disappeared from my side. I spent the next six hours crying my eyes out about what had happened and vowed never to take acid again. It's a good thing I was with my friends because we were in a high-rise block of flats and I would have probably jumped over the balcony if they hadn't been there. It was a harrowing experience and one I never want to repeat.

The 'world in a box' incident wasn't the only time that taking drugs ruined my night. Dealers were starting to cut their ecstasy pills with LSD because it is a particularly strong drug and made it seem as if their produce was more potent than it was. A couple of weeks earlier, I had hallucinated that the deejay at the Paradise Club had transformed into a monstrous, demonic clown. I was scared out of my wits and immediately left the club. My entire body literally shook with fright and no amount of persuasion from my friends could get me back inside.

Over the past year, the drugs had started getting more and more impure and I was becoming increasingly worried about taking them. Getting off my head had changed from being a pleasurable experience into something that had the potential to leave me scarred for life. It was time for me to call it quits. What's the point of carrying on doing something that has grown to be a constant source of stress?

Even though I no longer enjoyed the drug-taking side of things, I still liked the atmosphere at the raves so I decided to get a job behind the bar at The Sanctuary. That way I could watch everybody dancing and having fun without being tempted to get high with them. My sister Kelly worked there with me and it was one of the most enjoyable jobs I've ever had. I loved the music and the vibe was just as good as it had been when I was getting off my face. It was the best job England had to offer, but still had nothing on my dream of working in Tenerife. Every time we went on holiday, I longed to move there. I couldn't wait until I had saved up enough cash to leave my tiny, country village behind and laze around in the sun all day, sipping exotic cocktails and living the life of Riley.

In an effort to spend as much time as possible in Playa de las Americas, I began to save up all my holidays and go there for a month at a time. I would spend two weeks with my family and two weeks with Kelly after my mum and dad had gone home. During the final fortnight, I would work as a PR girl whilst my sister lay around in the sun. She didn't like the PR thing and wanted to spend as much time as possible partying it up and having fun.

The club that I did PR work for was on Veronicas Strip and I got to know a couple of the other people who worked in the surrounding bars. One of the blokes that I got talking to was a sleazy-looking, overweight Majorcan by the name of Antonio, who looked like a stereotypical hairy-chested, medallion man and who owned a nightclub called Heaven a couple of doors down. He was so obese that he had to wear a tunic because there weren't many other clothes that fitted him. My sister always thought that he was wearing his pyjamas. He had an aura of untrustworthiness, but I gave him the benefit of the doubt and chatted with him whenever I passed his club.

Although I was completely oblivious to the fact that my newfound friend was involved in crime, I knew that some of the other residents of the island could be a little bit on the dodgy side. There were a lot of English ex-pats who were on the run from the law and drugs were absolutely rife. One of the clubs got raided whilst I was heading inside to visit a friend and the police uncovered a stash of Ecstasy pills concealed in the toilet ceiling. Everybody who worked there got arrested, which included quite a few of my mates. The Spanish police don't mess about. They will usually arrest anyone who may possibly have had something to do with whatever illegal activity had taken place. It's not like in Britain, where they only arrest the main suspect. They will take in whoever they deem responsible, regardless of whether there is anything to suggest that they were actually involved.

Some of my friends ended up in court over the drugs that were discovered, even though there was no proof that they belonged to any of them. If the raid had been carried out in England, the police would have resigned themselves to the fact that it was impossible to tell who had stashed the Es but the coppers in Spain don't work that way. I was lucky because I was on the steps leading into the club when they came running in and they charged straight past me to arrest everybody else. I could well have ended up being nicked, despite the fact that I had nothing to do with the pills and hadn't taken any drugs since I had had my dodgy acid trip.

The raid shook me up and left a nasty taste in my mouth but it was going to take a damn sight more than that to put me off my yearly island holiday. I knew that Tenerife had a dark side but as far as I was concerned, it was nothing to do with me. I was there to get drunk and have a laugh – nothing more, nothing less. Unfortunately, in a place like Veronicas, drink leads to drugs, drugs lead to dependency and dependency leads to trouble. A series of events was about to take place that would make my dream of island life a reality, although I would end up becoming part of the seething underbelly that I had always sought to avoid. Sometimes your dreams can quickly transform into nightmares and in my case, it was to be a nightmare that would haunt me for the next thirteen years of my life. I was about to gain my passport to hell.

Chapter 2

LIVING THE DREAM

Sometimes something drastic needs to happen in order for you to follow up on a promise that you have made to yourself. Although I constantly told myself that I was going to move to Tenerife, it wasn't until my life in England started going pear-shaped that I made concrete plans to move. It started with a bang. I was driving round a blind bend on the main road towards Aylesbury when I suddenly became aware of a trailer with a hayrick on it sitting in the middle of the road. It managed to take me completely by surprise because it wasn't visible until I got close-up. Panic set in as I realised that I was about to crash.

Bam! I went straight through the windscreen of the car. I was with my boyfriend Peter and he went flying through the air and dislocated and fractured his hip. I was out cold, but he managed to remain conscious and shouted, 'Quick! Get out, now!'

I later found out that he had had a recurring nightmare in which he was in a car that crashed and blew up. Luckily the vehicle remained exactly as it was, but it was nice of him to try and save me from the imaginary explosion.

My neighbour had been behind us on the road at the time and went rushing off to fetch my mum. I was lapsing in and out of consciousness and all I can remember is her taking me to the hospital and a doctor saying, 'I can't do anything with that!'

'Mum, give me a mirror,' I whimpered, wondering if my injuries were as bad as he was making out.

'No,' came her reply, 'it's probably best that you don't see.'

I have since been told that my face was in a right old state. There was skin and flesh peeling off left, right and centre and I looked like something from a horror film.

Although they weren't particularly pleasing to the eye, my injuries weren't actually as bad as they appeared and I was eventually stitched up and sent home. The doctors even gave me the all-clear for our yearly trip abroad, which had been scheduled for a couple of weeks down the line. However, the scars that the accident left were mental as well as physical. They made me even more determined to leave the country for good and confirmed the fact that I needed to move to Tenerife rather than just visit every year.

I put in for compensation from the National Farmers Union because they had left the hayrick in the middle of the road with no way of me knowing that it was there. They denied everything and wouldn't accept the blame, which meant that my insurance company had to get involved in a lengthy legal process to try and get them to pay up. It was a lot of stress and over the next two years, my life gradually went from bad to worse. Peter and I had a massive argument and my sister, who I had always done everything with, decided to move away to London with her boyfriend and leave me on my own.

'Right,' I thought. 'The time is definitely right for me to move.'

Nothing was working out for me. The crash had left my nerves jangled and I was working full-time as an income support officer again, which was beginning to really drag. I needed a change of scenery. It was time to make my island dream a reality.

It took me a month to sort out somewhere to stay in Tenerife. I had met a lad called Bruno on a previous holiday, who had a spare room in his apartment and told me that I could live there. My family weren't overly concerned about my move because they had met Bruno before, knew that he was a decent lad and knew that Tenerife was a relatively safe place to live. So as far as they were concerned, they had nothing to worry about.

Bruno was one of those English people who look and dress foreign. He had lived over there for so long that he had developed an air of Spanishness. This was partly due to the fact that he could speak the language without a hint of an English accent, and partly because he bought all his clothes in Spain, which meant he dressed like a local. He was a loveable character and a lot of fun to be around.

My initial intention was for Tenerife to be the first of several places that I visited. I had always wanted to go to Thailand and figured that if my time abroad worked out, I could eventually hop from one country to the next. I had big dreams. I wanted to see the world.

Although my head was filled with visions of moving around from one exotic location to another, I still remained pragmatic. I made a contingency plan and scheduled a flight back to England for two weeks after I had arrived, just in case I struggled to find a means to support myself. I managed to get a job as a PR girl almost straightaway so my return flight was not needed. There are two types of PR: high-end, where all the girls look like models, and low-end, which is usually done by girls who like to party and have fun. I was definitely the latter rather than the former. I worked for a bar called The Coliseum on Veronicas Strip and it was a means to an end rather than something particularly glamorous or exciting. The money wasn't great and I still ideally wanted to work behind the bar.

When I wasn't busy dragging people into The Coliseum, I would either sit about in the sun or spend my time having a few too many drinks with friends before retiring back to the apartment. Our flat was in the Copacabana Complex, which was filled with people who worked at other nearby resorts. It was small but comfy and housed a mixture of Spanish and English residents.

I loved my new life on the island. Being away from my parents for the first time gave me such a tremendous sense of freedom. The fact that most of the other people there were on their holidays meant that there was a permanent atmosphere of excitement to the place as well. The holidaymakers had to go home after a couple of weeks, but I was smug in the knowledge that I could enjoy the sun, sea and sangria all year long.

The only thing that didn't live up to my expectations was my job. As the weeks went by, I grew more and more disillusioned with it. I had always known that PR work didn't pay particularly well but had assumed that I would be able to work my way up the ladder. Other girls that I had seen whilst I was on holiday as a teenager had managed to do this by sticking at it until somebody noticed how much experience they had and offered them a better position. I had underestimated how difficult it was to advance and it seemed as if I was permanently stuck at the bottom of the pile which made me increasingly frustrated.

I've always loved money. I like designer clothes as most girls do, and there's nothing like walking into a room dressed in an expensive designer label to make you feel on top of the world. Back in those days I was into Naf Naf and Chipie, the clothes the ravers wore. Until I moved to Spain, my dad had always bought me things. He didn't spoil me rotten but if I told him I needed something, he would usually dip into his wallet. Now that I was on the island, I could no longer rely upon his help in times of need. I had some cash at home but I had made a conscious decision to leave it where it was. My mind was made up that I was only going to spend the money that I earned in Tenerife. The problem was, that I was barely getting by. I was drinking and going out almost every night of the week so I had very little left to spend on clothing and accessories.

Although I was disappointed that I wasn't able to earn more cash, I never lost sight of the reasons I had moved to Tenerife, which were to take advantage of the nightlife, sit in the sun all day and meet good-looking boys. The PR girls were like a family and we always made the most of what little cash we had. We started work at eight or nine o'clock in the evening and by half ten, we were usually drunk. Every time I took somebody into a club, I was allowed to knock back a drink on the house to give me the confidence to approach my next target. Drinking comes hand in hand with doing PR work. If you don't like getting trolleyed then it's not the job for you.

As well as consuming excessive amounts of alcohol, a lot of the other girls also took cocaine. The island was awash with it and the PR workers seemed to love the stuff. I remember the first time it was offered to me. I had just walked into the office at The Coliseum and there were two, long, white lines laid out on the table.

''Ere Terry, have a bit of this.'

'Nah, I'm alright, I think I'll pass.'

I still associated taking drugs with the 'world inside a box' night and the demonic clown incident. I should have stuck to my guns and walked away but the little devil on my shoulder started coaxing me into trying some.

'What's the harm?' it whispered. 'It isn't going to hurt you. Take some. You never know, you might enjoy yourself.'

'Actually what the hell,' I caved in. 'Pass it over here.'

Coke is quite a socially acceptable drug. Although it is highly addictive, it doesn't possess the same level of stigma as crack or heroin so I assumed that it was safe for me to take. Think heroin and you think tattered clothes and track marks; think cocaine and you think Paris Hilton and Lindsay Lohan. It has an air of glamour to it and people who indulge in charlie are often seen as having expensive tastes rather than being addicted.

'Whoa,' I exclaimed, as the back of my throat went numb and I was hit by a sudden wave of energy. I felt wide-awake, on top of my game and ultra-confident. This was a drug and a half.

They say your first hit of cocaine is something that you can never reproduce and that was definitely the case for me. I tried, night after night, to replicate the effect of the line I had taken at The Coliseum but nothing could come close. I've never done anything in half measures and it didn't even occur to me that I would eventually end up with a habit if I continuously chased an unattainable high. After all, this was coke, not crack. It was nothing I couldn't handle.

As far as I was concerned, cocaine was the perfect drug. It made me lively, talkative and enthusiastic, which were essential qualities for my role as a PR girl. The only downside was that it cost the equivalent of £40 a gram and prevented me from getting any sleep. It soon reached the stage where I was up for all but three hours of the night, every night of the week.

Meanwhile, Bruno had got a new girlfriend and she was always round at our flat, which I didn't like. The flat seemed very crowded with three people in it. I was still very grateful to Bruno for letting me move in with him and didn't have anything against the girl; I just like my space. I wanted to move out, but how could I afford to pay the rent anywhere else? I was snorting and drinking away my earnings quicker than they were coming in.

Fortunately there was a nearby set of apartments called the Bungamar where the flats cost next to nothing. They were the equivalent of £40 a week and you got exactly what you paid for. The rooms were cockroach-infested and dirty, but beggars can't be choosers and I didn't care where I ended up, just so long as I could carry on getting off my face.

I moved in with a pretty blonde PR girl called Jackie from the north of England and we both slept in the same room. The fact that we were forced to live together in such a confined space meant that we got to know each other inside out within no time at all. She spent all night clicking her tongue piercing back and forth, which irritated the hell out of me, but apart from that we always got on well.

The Bungamar really was the pits. It was the place where people ended up when they were at their wits' end. I had travelled to the island full of hope and expectation but by this stage, my dream was beginning to fall apart. I barely had any money, I'd got a raging drug and alcohol problem and I was sick and tired of my job. It was my own fault for having unrealistic expectations of what life on the island would be like. I had assumed that everybody in Tenerife had a happy, carefree existence but the reality was that it was similar to England in a lot of ways. It had just as much petty crime and just as many drugs.

As the months passed by, I started feeling more and more alone. I spent my first Christmas away from home, by myself, because the other girls had all flown back to England. God knows why I chose to do this. I think I wanted to know what it would be like to celebrate the occasion in another country. I was used to waking up on Christmas morning to a pile of presents and the smell of turkey wafting through from the kitchen but this time I was still awake from the previous night's charlie session and had never felt more isolated. No presents were exchanged and I didn't even have a tree. Life was shit.

Rather than sitting about and wallowing in self-pity, I decided to go for Christmas dinner with some of the staff from The Coliseum. I knew for a fact it wouldn't be a patch on Mum's roast turkey but then again, very little would. To make matters worse, I was finally coming down off the coke and feeling fragile and exhausted. There was no doubt in my mind that this was going to be the worst Christmas ever.

Part way through my meal, I fell asleep on the table and somebody had to take me home. I could no longer hide the extent of my drug abuse from my colleagues. It was obvious that I had a problem and it was getting progressively worse and worse. Coke and alcohol were rapidly taking over my life and I would soon be under their complete control.

Within a matter of weeks, I had started spending £100 a night on drugs and drink and experienced extreme anxiety whenever I was forced to go without. I knew that I had a habit but kept trying to kid myself that it wasn't all that serious, which prevented me from seeking help. Even though I was shovelling all of my wages up my nose, I was still unwilling to dip into the savings I had left at home in England. I had promised myself that I would only spend the cash I earned in Tenerife and wasn't going to go back on my word.

Antonio always had a bucketload of coke on him so I figured I could save a lot of money by knocking about with him. He was generous with his drugs and regularly gave away free lines, which meant that all of the other PR girls acted as if they were his best friends in the world. Most of the addicts who hung around with older blokes were also having sex with them. They were known as 'drug sluts' and would do whatever it took to get their daily fix. A couple of them genuinely fancied the men who gave them drugs, but the majority were attracted solely to their wallets. A good proportion of these guys were in their mid-to-late forties and looked exactly like Antonio. They weren't what you would call good-looking by anyone's standards.

Antonio never tried it on with me, which I always thought was weird. He would let me snort his coke without expecting anything in return. This made me suspicious. I knew he must have had an ulterior motive but was unable to put my finger on exactly what it was. The other thing that worried me was the fact that he regularly smoked crack, which was strange considering how fat he managed to remain. I first became aware that he was a crackhead when he whipped out a homemade pipe at his club during an after-hours cocaine session.

'You want some?' he asked, casually offering it to me as if it was a cup of tea.

I immediately recoiled.

'No,' I told him. 'Not for me.'

Antonio shrugged his shoulders and took a long, hard drag, breathing the thick, white smoke deep down into his lungs.

'Suit yourself,' he muttered. 'More for us then.'

Although I still associated taking crack with the stick-thin, zombie-like character of Pookie in *New Jack City*, I was too strung-out on coke to care. Antonio could smoke whatever the hell he wanted, just so long as he continued to give me access to his mountains of cocaine. If I cut him off and refused to have anything to do with him, I would soon run out of money from having to pay for my own drugs. He was my ticket to free Charlie, which made him an invaluable asset. I carried on milking Antonio for his drugs, ignoring all the signs that I should give him a wide berth. I would sit around in his club after the customers had gone home, dipping into his coke whilst he smoked his crack. Drugs had now become my only motivation for getting up in the morning and he appeared to have an almost limitless supply.

Despite the scale of my addiction, I was still firmly in denial and thought that I had everything under control. During a trip across to England to spend time with my family, I realised this simply wasn't the case.

'We can go to Cinderella's while you're back,' my sister told me. 'Come on, it'll be fun.'

Cinderella's was a big, cheesy nightclub in the middle of a shopping centre in Dunstable. The owners organised a monthly bus from Aylesbury and it was always a good night out. 'Why not?' I thought. Maybe it would help to take my mind off coke.

But every minute without drugs seemed like an eternity. Going cold turkey was a lot more difficult than I had expected it to be and part way through the night, I realised that I was going to have to get a fix before I went insane.

'Excuse me,' I asked a boy I knew from Aylesbury. 'Do you know anybody who can get me any coke?'

'Nah, sorry,' he told me.

I felt a sudden wave of anger rushing through my body. What did he mean, 'no'? My hand balled into a fist and the next thing I knew, I was laying into the poor lad for not being able to sort me out. How dare he deny me the substance that I required in order to live my life without feeling like shit? I was absolutely furious. I'm not normally a violent person and hadn't had a fight since I was a teenager, but one of the symptoms of cocaine withdrawal is that it gives you uncontrollable fits of rage. Looking back, it was a very extreme thing to do and I can't apologise to the boy enough.

The rest of the night remains a blur but I can remember crying and telling Kelly how unhappy I was in Tenerife.

'I don't want to go back,' I blubbed. 'I want to stay in England; I don't want to go back.'

I somehow eventually managed to get hold of an eighth of an ounce of coke and two of my friends and I polished off the entire lot in a single sitting. It was originally intended to last us all weekend and had cost £160. I couldn't go on like this; the cycle that I had got into in Tenerife was destroying me. Drugs were a lot more readily available over there due to the presence of Antonio and I would end up losing my health, my money and possibly my life if I didn't move home. It was time to call it quits. I would return for a couple of weeks to put it all to bed and then that would be that. I needed to wake up from my dream before it was too late.

Chapter 3

BACK TO TENERIFE

As I boarded the plane back to the island, I felt tired, disillusioned and depressed. Part of me was distraught at the prospect of relinquishing my sobriety but part of me couldn't help looking forward to getting back on the coke. I felt full of conflict. I wanted to get my life back to normal and leave the drugs behind but Veronicas was calling out to me.

'Stay a little longer,' it cooed. 'Get a little higher. What's the worst thing that can happen?'

I started back at work almost as soon as I touched down in Tenerife and the moment I had my first line of cocaine, I began to feel myself again. I was still homesick and knew that I was taking far too many drugs but neither of those things seemed to matter any more. Maybe I would carry on living on the island after all. Back home in England, I had to pay for every gram of coke I took. On Veronicas, Antonio could hook me up whenever I needed a fix.

'Perhaps I should stay a little while longer,' I reasoned to myself, 'just to see how things pan out.'

I soon fell straight back into my old routine of spending all day off my nut. I still had days when I considered packing it all in but it was now only a possibility rather than a certainty. When you're either drunk or high, twenty-four hours a day, any semblance of rationality goes out of the window. The drugs had quickly re-established themselves as my number one priority. Besides, a couple of the local marijuana dealers had put me onto an opportunity to earn myself a bit of extra cash.

The dealers knew that the PR girls were the obvious people for clubbers to ask where they could get hold of cannabis so they offered me a commission-based wage for each new customer I brought to them, which provided me with a bit of extra income and ensured that they had a constant stream of buyers. I wasn't handling the wares myself. Fair enough, I was doing something illegal, but I didn't see myself as selling drugs. My boss at The Coliseum didn't see things the same as I did though. After a couple of weeks of making cash this way, he took me to one side and broke the news to me that he didn't want me working for him any more.

'I've been informed that you are selling cannabis on Veronicas,' he told me. 'I've got to let you go because we don't want that kind of thing associated with our club.'

I hadn't physically handed over a single bag of weed, so I don't know who he got his information from. Mind you, I hadn't applied for a foreigner's identification number , which meant that my PR job wasn't exactly legit in the first place. These numbers are a legal requirement if you want to work over there, which was convenient for the owners because it meant they could get rid of me without a valid reason. That was the way things worked; staff were usually taken on illegally so that they could be dismissed at the drop of a hat.

What was I going to do for money now? Half of me was panicking that I would end up as a stripper or a prostitute, but the other half felt relieved. I had been working as a PR for far too long and wanted to either do a job that I enjoyed or move back home to live with Mum. I was gutted that I had been sacked but pleased that I no longer had to traipse along the strip, harassing passers-by and being paid a pittance for my work.

Fortunately Antonio was still on hand to give me free cocaine. He seemed uncharacteristically sympathetic when I turned up at his bar to get my daily fix and promised to help me out.

'Don't worry,' he told me. 'It's not the end of world. You can manage my club. That way, you will get to stay in Tenerife and you will always have plenty of money to party with.'

'Do you really mean it?' I asked, taken aback that he was offering me such a high-paid job completely out of the blue.

'Sure,' he told me. 'I need to spend more time with you to know that I can trust you, but once I know the trust is there, you can have the job.'

This was it; the break I had been looking for. After months of working as a lowly PR girl, I was finally moving up the ladder. Pound signs flashed in front of my eyes, only instead of representing expensive designer clothing they now represented gram after gram of coke. I was over the moon. Once I became the manager of Heaven, I would be able to live the glamorous existence that I had originally associated with life in Tenerife. There would be no more standing out on the streets all night, persuading people to go to a club. It was time for me to call the shots. My dream was coming true.

'Rack me up a line,' I grinned, 'this is cause for celebration.'

My natural excitement was soon replaced by the type of short-lived, artificial happiness that only coke can bring. Half an hour later, I would be desperately craving more. By that stage, I would no longer care that I had been offered a new job. The only thing that mattered would be whether or not I could get hold of another bag. I didn't stop to question Antonio's motive for giving a managerial position to a cocaine-addicted foreigner who wasn't legally permitted to work in the country. All I cared about was the fact that I would have more money to spend on Charlie. Unbeknown to me, I was about to pay the price for putting my addiction above the need for simple common sense. Antonio had no intention whatsoever of letting me run his club. As far as he was concerned, I was just another silly English girl for him to take advantage of.

Chapter 4

THE HOLIDAY FROM HELL

That fat, sleazy, medallion man couldn't have been any less trustworthy if he'd had scales and slithered across the floor, but when you're in the grip of a powerful addiction, you are incapable of thinking straight. Anybody who can get you drugs becomes a person that you would follow to the ends of the earth. I knew that Antonio was a slime-ball and I knew that he was a crackhead, but this slime-ball crackhead was offering me what seemed the career opportunity of a lifetime. I would have been an idiot not to take him up on it.

I decided not to tell my mum about the good news until I was one hundred per cent certain that it was going to come to fruition. If it all fell through then I would feel ten times worse if I had to explain to everyone that I had been led up the garden path. Instead I rang her up as if it was just another day on the island and was greeted by the news that my compensation had come through.

'That's absolutely brilliant,' I beamed, my face looking like it did the first time I took Ecstasy.

The payout couldn't have come at a better time. It was just what I needed to tide me over until I started at the club. Now I could spend the short period before I became a manageress getting off my trolley and I would still have cash left over to eat and pay the rent.

I filled the next few days with stupid amounts of drugs and alcohol, the most excessive night being my twenty-third birthday, which saw my friends and I getting through enough coke to keep a snowplough busy for at least a week. The occasion marked the first year of my dream career, one of the few times I had money and the fact that I could now stay in Tenerife, which meant it was the perfect excuse to have an epic bender.

My housemate and I started my birthday evening off fairly tamely at a restaurant called Harley's, an American-style diner that did tortillas and fajitas. I loved eating there because they gave you such ridiculously big portions. If you didn't feel sick at the end of your meal then there was something wrong with you.

Much as I enjoyed stuffing my face, I spent the entire time I was at Harley's thinking about how much coke we were going to take when we hit Veronicas. By the time I got to my dessert, I was itching to get out the door so that we could start our drug and drink session. The last thing I remember is leaving the restaurant happy in the knowledge that I could afford to buy bag after bag of Colombian marching powder. Everything after that is just a cocaine-induced blur.

The next day, I woke up with a banging headache and a funny feeling that something wasn't right.

'What the hell happened last night?' I asked Jackie.

'I don't know, which means we probably had a good time,' she half laughed, half grimaced, sounding as if she was attempting to appear cheerful whilst in the grip of the comedown to end all comedowns.

As the room came into focus through my fuzzy, screwed-up eyes, I noticed that my passport was missing from my bedside table. I had very few belongings at the time so it was immediately obvious. There is nothing like waking up after a bender and realising that something as important as that has gone walkabout to make your heart skip a beat.

'Where the hell is my passport?' I gasped, feeling as if the air had just been sucked out of my lungs.

This was the last thing I needed. Had someone stolen it or had I just misplaced it whilst I was out snorting? I needed to know as soon as possible so that I could give my tired mind a break from panicking.

'Don't ask me, I haven't taken it,' my half-comatose flatmate replied. 'All I can remember is that you were talking to Antonio in his office for ages after we finished clubbing. Maybe he knows where it's gone.'

Without my passport, I would be stuck on the island and couldn't go running home to Wingrave if my dream job came to nothing, so I flew out of the door to see if my boss-to-be had convinced me to hand it over to him for some unknown reason. I had no time for niceties; the minute I set foot in his office, I shouted, 'Where is my passport?'

'I am keeping it safe for you. You're coming to Brazil with me, remember?'

Brazil? What was this crazy crackhead on about?

'When did I agree to this?' I asked, although I had an inkling that it was probably during the twelve hours that were missing from my memory.

'Last night. You agreed to come away with me on a trip because my wife can't make it.'

At this point I thought, 'You dirty devil.' It seemed to me as if he was attempting to get me alone with him in a foreign country so that he could make a move.

'I've got a spare ticket. I need you to come with me so that I can see whether you can be trusted to manage my club. I want to be sure that you won't run off with my money if I leave you in charge.'

His story seemed plausible enough. Looking after a club was a huge responsibility and there was a lot of cash involved. Maybe this trip to Brazil was a test to see how much I wanted the position. The more Antonio talked, the more convincing he seemed. I still thought that he probably wanted to have his way with me but figured I could always give him the cold shoulder if he tried it on. Putting up with an amorous, hairy-chested Spaniard for a week was a small price to pay for being given such a glamorous, well-paid job.

'You can't tell anybody else you're going though,' Antonio told me, his face wrinkling up and suddenly looking super-serious.

The sleazy bugger didn't want his wife to find out that he was taking a girl with him.

'Right OK,' I smirked. 'Your secret's safe with me.'

'And don't tell your mum either.'

Eh? This one didn't make much sense. Did he think my dear old mum was going to somehow find his missus's number and get on the blower to her from England to tell her what was going on? Of all the things Antonio had said to me, this was the only one that left me feeling slightly suspicious. Why the need for all the secrecy? He must have really set his sights on getting into my knickers. He was taking every possible precaution to avoid people getting on to his plan.

Part of me thought, 'Maybe you should give this one a miss,' but the other ninety-nine per cent of my brain thought, 'Tropical paradise. Lovely, long, golden beaches covered in palm trees. Holiday of a lifetime.' Not only was it the final obstacle before I could become a manageress but I was also getting a free vacation to an exotic Latin American country full of bronzed Latino men and beautiful, sun-drenched scenery. Once again, I felt as if I would be a fool to say no.

'OK, I'll keep it between us. Don't worry about that,' I told him. 'When do we set off?'

'We're going next week. I'm glad you have decided to take me up on my offer. You will love Brazil.'

I was excited about the trip but slightly disappointed that I couldn't tell my friends the news. There would be plenty of time for celebrating with them later on when I was raking it in at my new club though. I could almost smell the money – and I knew what money meant. It meant piles of high-quality cocaine. Now that I knew my dream career was just around the corner, I could afford to take things up a notch. The week before my holiday was spent hammering as much charlie as I could fit up my schnozzle. If it's possible to get higher than I did during that period, then it must be incredibly difficult, that's all I can say. I felt as if I was floating on a white, powdery cloud of drug-induced euphoria.

On the day of the trip, I was tired from the previous night's excess but at the same time eager to get on the plane. I didn't even tell Jackie I was leaving; I just packed my bags and went. To be honest, my life in Tenerife was such a mess that she probably assumed I'd finally had enough and returned home to England.

As I boarded the plane with my fat, greasy travel companion, I envisioned chilling out on a gorgeous, sunny beach, surrounded by happy, smiling locals, who had possibly just arrived back from some sort of carnival. Brazil was a party country; everyone knew that. It was a place where people danced the samba 24/7 and lived *la vida loca*. This was going to be some holiday.

We had to travel via Gran Canaria because there were no direct flights from Tenerife to Brazil, which was a bit of a pain in the arse. Gran Canaria was only twenty minutes away but the fact we couldn't fly straight to our destination added a lot of faffing about to the journey. When the plane finally touched down in Brazil, I felt a mixture of emotions. On the one hand I was buzzing at the prospect of exploring somewhere new, but on the other, I couldn't help but feel as if I was at Antonio's mercy. I hadn't brought any money with me, which meant I was totally reliant upon him. This made me slightly uneasy but then again, he had paid for the trip so it was only fair that he was in control.

We got a taxi from the airport to our hotel, which was in the coastal city of Salvador in the north-east of the country. The further we drove, the poorer the people on the streets began to look. The housing seemed to deteriorate as well. Every building we passed was more rundown than the last and we appeared to be heading into the centre of a slum.

'Are our digs on the other side of this little ghetto here then?' I asked Antonio.

'No, it's there,' he told me, pointing to the only fairly pleasant looking building in what could have passed for a shanty town. It was as if somebody had built a luxury hotel in the middle of Moss Side. I had known that bits of Brazil were impoverished but didn't expect them to be the parts the tourists stayed in. There were feral children everywhere, roaming the streets in packs. I felt like telling the taxi driver to turn around and take us back to the airport but gritted my teeth and thought of managing my own club.

As we dragged our luggage into the hotel, a mob of dirty, stick-thin street kids held out their hands in unison for change. It was very, very frightening. I made a mental note to never leave the hotel unless I had Antonio with me.

We checked our things into our room and then headed out for a bite to eat. I was now starving. The last of the cocaine was finally out of my system and I felt as if I had to make up for all the food that I had missed out on whilst too high to feel hungry.

'Do you want to go to a *rodízio*?' Antonio asked me. 'I will buy you a meal to celebrate the first night of our holiday.'

A *rodízio* is a traditional Brazilian buffet where waiters walk around the room at regular intervals with big plates of food and you have a card that says 'yes' on one side and 'no' on the other. You use the card to show whether or not you want each course and pay a fixed price regardless of how much you eat. I had been to one of these places before in Tenerife and liked the idea of having lots of different dishes. I'm the type of person who is always eyeing up other people's food in restaurants and wishing I could have a bite, which means that buffets are my ideal type of meal.

'Sounds good to me,' I said. 'I'm so hungry I could eat a horse.'

The food at the *rodízio* couldn't have been nicer. Waiters came round every ten minutes with big skewers of meat, which I devoured in two seconds flat. It took a hell of a long time for me to turn my card over. I think the owners must have been worried that I was going to eat them out of house and home.

That first evening, however, was the only time Antonio ever took me out for food. He hadn't brought much cash with him and barely had enough to get by. Splashing out for the meal at the *rodízio* was obviously a front to try and convince me that he was loaded. In reality his pockets were full of dust, lint and cobwebs.

As if the fact that we didn't have a bean to spend between us wasn't bad enough, it chucked it down with rain the whole time we were there. I had expected Brazil to be bone dry all year round.

Even if the weather had been nice and Antonio had had money, I still wouldn't have spent much time outside of the hotel because the whole of Salvador reeked of poverty. The locals were all dressed in filthy, tattered clothes and didn't seem very friendly, although in fairness this was probably a result of living in dire poverty whilst rich, Western tourists flaunted their wealth in front of them. I really felt for the kids on the street but hadn't had any coke since I left Tenerife and was growing increasingly more paranoid as the days went by. Being mugged was the last thing I needed, so I holed up in my room and spent a good part of the week in bed.

The more I lay there, the more anxious I felt. The lack of cocaine was sending me insane. I kept see-sawing between being mentally exhausted and uncontrollably angry. Every little thing annoyed me and I couldn't focus on anything. The one benefit to my withdrawal was that I no longer cared if Antonio made any advances on me. The only thing that I was capable of worrying about was the fact that I was desperately craving drugs and couldn't get my hands on any. He wasn't usually in the room for very long anyway. Most days he was out doing God knows what, whilst I tried in vain to sleep off my cravings.

One of the few times I did leave the hotel was when Antonio roped me into going on a drug-finding mission with him. He was in an even worse state than I was and seemed intent on getting a fix.

'We'll ask a taxi driver if he knows anybody who can help us,' he told me. 'If he can't tell us where to get drugs then I don't know what we're going to do. I really need *cocaína*, Terry. I need it right now.'

The cabbie told us that our best bet was to go to a street party and try to score some off the people there.

'Where there is music and dancing, somebody might have what you need,' he advised us. 'I can take you to one if you want?'

'Go for it,' said Antonio. 'It's always worth a try.'

The next thing I knew, we were surrounded by crowds of samba-dancing locals, who had turned their grim favela into the site of a makeshift carnival. It would have been exactly how I pictured Brazil to be if it wasn't for the fact that all the partygoers looked like murderers. Their body language and facial expressions had an undercurrent of menace to them, as if they were waiting for an opportunity to kick off.

'*¿Dónde puedo comprar cocaína?*' Antonio asked a grizzled local.

'*Não estou entendendo. Eu não falo espanhol,*' the puzzled man replied. Nobody at the party could understand Spanish, only Portuguese. We didn't have a cat in hell's chance of getting any coke. Even if somebody did manage to pick up what we were saying, they would be unlikely to point out who the dealers were to the only gringos at the party. For all they knew, we could have been the world's worst undercover cops.

We eventually went home empty-handed, which forced me to raid the minibar to blot out my craving out with drink. I downed everything that they had before curling up under the covers and wishing I was back in Tenerife. Some holiday in the sun this was turning out to be. I would have been better off going to Skegness or Bognor. Salvador was the grimmest place that I had been to in my life and I couldn't wait until I got to leave.

Midway through the week, Antonio had a large sum of money wired across to him, which I assumed was from his wife to tide him over until our return flight. The bill for the minibar alone was now enormous so it was a godsend. The first things that he bought with his newfound wealth were two large suitcases. He had taken an old battered one across with him so I figured he wanted something a little smarter to travel back to Tenerife with... but why did he need more than one? This left me scratching my head for a while until I eventually decided that it was nothing to do with me. If he wanted to spend his cash on random suitcases then that was up to him.

By the end of the holiday, Antonio was broke again and had no money left for fags. Budgeting clearly wasn't his strong point. I wondered where the hell it had all gone because he hadn't spent a single penny on me. He didn't seem to have blown it on drugs either so it was a total mystery.

'Oh well,' I thought to myself. 'We'll be back home soon enough, where I can relax with a nice, big, bag of charlie and forget all about this idiot throwing his cash away.'

The fact that he was so bad with money should have made me question how sound his business sense was. Most people would have been wary of managing a club for somebody who seemed to spend everything that he earned within a matter of days, but I was in too much of a state to properly consider what I was getting myself into.

On the day of our return flight, I was anxious to get home so that I could resume my addiction. Going cold turkey for a week had been no fun at all. It was just a pity we had to travel via Gran Canaria.

I spent the first leg of our journey fast asleep. My dreams were the only place where I could escape the mental anguish that the lack of drugs was putting me through. I was woken up by the plane touching down on the runway and thought, 'Only one more flight to go then I can finally get high.'

As I dragged myself out of the cabin and set off to pick up my luggage, I felt as if I was going to collapse from exhaustion. Without cocaine, I had zero energy. The level to which I needed it was frightening. Drugs were my master and I was at their mercy. Seven days without bowing down to them had left me feeling mentally broken.

Travelling from Brazil to Spain isn't like travelling within Europe. Brazil shares its borders with Colombia and Bolivia, which means that every item of luggage needs to be thoroughly checked. This was no problem for me because if I had any drugs on me, I would have hoovered them up within the first two minutes of the flight. I handed over my bag without giving it a second thought.

Antonio's first suitcase got the all clear straightaway but his second had the customs officers in a right tizzy. From what I could make out, they seemed to think that one side of the case was heavier than the other. The next thing I knew, he had been frogmarched out of the room, leaving me standing there like a lemon. I was a bit taken aback but it still didn't even cross my mind that I was in any kind of trouble because whatever the officers suspected might be in the suitcase, had nothing to do with me. I was as surprised as anyone that they were kicking up such a stink.

A couple of minutes later, a burly Spanish policeman came bowling back into the room, grabbed hold of my arm and dragged me into a side room. In Spain, you have three tiers of police; there are the *policía*, who deal with the piddling little crimes; the Guardia Civil, who deal with drugs and organised crime; and the Centro Nacional de Inteligencia, who are the Spanish equivalent of MI5. This guy was a member of the Guardia Civil. The girls on Veronicas were always talking about how untrustworthy they were and how they were to be avoided at all costs. They had a reputation for police brutality so I thought it best not to complain about the fact he was so rough with me. The look in his eyes told me that I was in enough trouble as it was.

By this stage it seemed unlikely that I was going to be able to distance myself from whatever it was Antonio had done. The coppers must have known that I was totally oblivious to the coke; the minute they ripped the suitcase open, my jaw fell to the floor and I couldn't have looked more gobsmacked if I had tried. They really didn't give a monkey's, though. As far as they were concerned, I was with a drug smuggler so I was as good as a smuggler myself. The holiday from hell had ended in the worst possible way. Antonio had rowed us both into the middle of shit creek, thrown away the paddles and drilled holes in the boat. He had destroyed our futures for the sake of a couple of grand to blow on crack.

'Antonio, what were you thinking?' I asked as white powder flew around the room and the Guardia Civil shouted manically in Spanish. 'Does this mean I'm not going to be managing your club?'

Chapter 5

SALTO DEL NEGRO

'*Tu amigo tiene una gran cantidad de cocaína. ¿Dónde lo conseguiste?*'

There was that word again: '*cocaína*'. By this stage I was getting sick of hearing it. Not only did it remind me what a mess I was in, but it also made my withdrawal symptoms ten times worse. I had no drugs in my suitcase and Antonio had already told the police that I knew nothing, so why on earth were they still bellowing? The entire situation was surreal. I was half expecting Jeremy Beadle to jump out from behind the Guardia Civil to tell me I'd been framed.

'Come,' said one of the officers. 'You follow me now.'

The heavy-set Spanish copper marched me over to a broom cupboard, shoved me inside and locked the door. The crazy thing was that I was still carrying my hand luggage. If I was such a big-time drug smuggler then why hadn't they torn it apart like they had done with Antonio's suitcase? It didn't make any sense.

By this stage, I was almost passing out from exhaustion so I opened up my bag to see if there was anything soft inside that I could use as a pillow. My teddy bear was fairly near the top so I got him out and curled up with my head on him. I take him everywhere with me; it's just something that I have always done. To be honest I don't think my brain had fully registered how much trouble I was in or I would have remained wide-awake, withdrawal or no withdrawal. I was still under the illusion that I was going to be released as soon as the police had finished their investigation.

As I drifted off, I remember thinking, 'This is all just a matter of routine. They're going to grill Antonio until they're sure I played no part in this and then I'm going home.'

Three hours later, I was rudely awoken by another Guardia Civil officer bellowing instructions at me. He was motioning towards the door so I forced my tired eyes open and stumbled to my feet. I was then walked through the airport to a small office, where I was greeted by a short, official-looking, Spanish lady.

'I am your translator,' she told me. 'You need tell police which suitcase yours is.'

Was this woman having a laugh? Translators are supposed to speak flawless English but she spoke with an almost incomprehensibly thick Spanish accent and didn't seem to have a strong grasp of our grammar.

'The green one without the drugs in it,' I said.

'Why you travel with owner of suitcase with drugs?'

'He's my boss. I was going to manage a nightclub for him,' I explained.

The words left a lump in my throat. My week of purgatory in Brazil was meant to lead to a step up the career ladder, not a stretch inside. Fair enough, the main aim of trying to get the managerial role was to be able to afford to snort even more coke than before, but I still couldn't help but feel as if my hopes and dreams had just been shattered into a million, tiny pieces.

'You are going to be strip-searched by two female officers,' the translator told me.

Ordinarily I would have found the idea of a woman I had never met before, looking at my naked body utterly repulsive, but by this stage, I was so shell-shocked that it didn't even faze me. I felt nothing whatsoever as I was searched internally. The woman who was poking about down there could have been anyone for all I knew because she wasn't wearing a uniform and didn't show me any form of ID. It was very degrading but luckily my brain was in a state of total confusion and couldn't process it. Nothing but tiredness and craving would register.

Once the police were satisfied that I hadn't got packages of cocaine strapped all over my body, the translator told me that I was entitled to a phone call and advised me to ring home.

'I'm not ringing anyone,' I said. 'I don't want anyone to know.'

Mum would be absolutely devastated if she found out that her daughter had been arrested for smuggling cocaine. It didn't even bear thinking about.

'You at least need to notify British Consulate...'

The message didn't seem to be getting through to her. I wasn't going to talk to anybody who could possibly pass the message on to my family. Even picturing their reactions in my mind made me feel physically sick.

'I'm not ringing anyone,' I repeated. 'Nobody at all, not even the Consulate.'

'OK then, you have made your choice,' said the translator. 'We can't force you to do it.'

As I breathed a sigh of relief and tried to get the image of my weeping mother out of my head, a pair of handcuffs snapped shut around my wrists and a Guardia Civil officer draped a coat over my hands.

'Come. We go,' he told me.

The coat was intended to protect my dignity whilst he walked me through the main part of the airport but it might as well have not been there because it was blindingly obvious that I was cuffed up. My hands were clasped together and I had two coppers escorting me; it didn't take a rocket scientist to figure out what was going on.

I was escorted through the front entrance and ushered into a Guardia Civil bus. The bus looked like your regular, run-of-the-mill coach, but had a load of miniature cells in it. I was flung into one of the compartments and locked up whilst the police drove to the cop shop. It was a relatively short journey and I was soon transferred to a holding cell in the police station, which had no toilet and was full of everything that could possibly come out of a human body. Rats the size of cats ran around on the floor, which was covered in traces of urine and faeces. The second I entered the room, I started shaking uncontrollably and couldn't stop crying. Was this the type of place that I was going to be stuck in for God knows how long if I was found guilty of smuggling? I sincerely hoped not.

I eventually managed to calm myself down a bit and sprawled out on the hard, concrete bench in the corner of the cell to get some sleep. It was difficult to nod off in such a filthy, stinking dive but my exhaustion eventually got the better of me. A couple of hours later, I woke up desperately needing the toilet, which was a bit of a nightmare considering the fact that there wasn't one.

'Hello?' I shouted out, hoping that somebody would come to my aid before I was forced to make the cell even dirtier. 'Can somebody please help me?'

A short, seedy-looking bloke appeared at the window and asked me what I wanted.

'I need to go to the toilet,' I told him. 'Can you let me out of the cell?'

The door opened with a clank and he beckoned me towards him.

'Can't I have a female officer take me?' I asked.

The copper pretended not to understand, which was to be a regular occurrence whenever I was in the company of the Spanish Old Bill. There was definitely something unsavoury about this guy. He had a nasty look in his eyes and seemed as if he shouldn't be left alone with a cat, let alone a vulnerable, young girl. He led me to a room that had a filthy hole in the middle of the floor and pointed a bony figure at it as if to say, 'That's the best you're going to get'.

'I can't go in that,' I gasped. 'Isn't there anything else?'

'You no like?' he asked me. 'Come with me instead.'

He took me to the toilet used by the police, which saved me from peeing myself because there was no chance in hell that I would have ever done my business in the hole. The man then handed me a cigarette and shut me back up in the holding cell.

I was beginning to think that I had been too quick to judge my pint-sized Spanish friend when I heard the door creak open and saw him standing there with his flies undone. A wave of terror hit me like a ton of bricks and I started screaming at the top of my lungs. He advanced towards me with his manhood flopping about in front of him so I pushed him away whilst bawling my eyes out.

This must have put the frighteners up him because he zipped his trousers up and started backing off. God knows what he would have done to me if I hadn't kicked up such a fuss. The thought of it still chills me to the bone.

I was kept in the cell until the following morning and spent the whole night worrying that the sleazebag cop would let himself in again. I didn't say a word to the officers who finally unlocked my cell because I didn't think that they would believe me. At the end of the day, it would have been the word of an alleged smuggler against a member of the Guardia Civil and I guessed whose side the coppers would have taken.

The officers escorted me out of the entrance and back into the transport bus. I was then driven to the local court to find out whether or not I was going to be remanded into custody. The courtroom was tiny and there was only me, Antonio, the judge and two duty solicitors in there. The duty solicitors both looked as if they were only present because they had to be and didn't even make eye contact with us. I had the feeling that they weren't going to be fighting our corner particularly vigorously.

The set-up wasn't how I expected a court case to be. For one thing, the judge didn't have a wig on and although she was quite smartly dressed, there was still nothing to distinguish her from the average office worker. She addressed the court in Spanish but luckily I managed to grasp the fact that she was giving me bail and denying it to Antonio. I was to be held at Salto del Negro prison in Las Palmas until the two-grand bail money was handed over to the authorities.

The entire hearing must have taken a maximum of ten minutes. The second it finished, Antonio and I were taken away and locked up in another holding cell. It was the first time I had been alone with him since our arrest at the airport so I took the opportunity to ask him what the hell was going on.

'I thought it would be easy money,' he told me, looking at the floor as he spoke. 'You seemed more respectable than the other girls and it's easier to get past customs if you're with a girl.'

'I'm not being funny with you Antonio but you're miles older than me and we look stupid together,' I set him straight. 'Who the bloody hell put you up to this and how much did they pay you?'

'You wouldn't believe me if I told you,' he mumbled.

'Try me,' I implored him. 'After everything that's happened today, I'm ready for anything.'

'OK it was two Guardia Civil officers and a judge. They were waiting just outside the airport to collect the drugs and I was meant to get 2,400,000 pesetas. I don't know what went wrong...'

I couldn't believe what I was hearing. Two million four-hundred thousand pesetas is only about twelve grand in sterling. The Guardia Civil are rumoured to control the majority of the drug trade in Tenerife and nick anybody who sells on their patch or poaches their customers. It was no surprise that they were involved, but the fact that a judge was in on it was another matter altogether. I had heard that Spanish society was corrupt but this was taking it to a whole new level.

Antonio told me that he had picked up the coke at a bus stop whilst I was in the hotel room asleep and that it had been smuggled across the border from Colombia. So we had risked our lives attempting to score drugs at a Brazilian slum party when all the while that idiot had a shipment coming in? I was so angry that I could hardly speak.

'Of all the people that you could have chosen to take with you, why did it have to be me?' I shouted, tears welling up in my eyes as I thought of everything that he had put me through for the sake of a measly twelve grand. It wasn't as if he would have invested the money in anything worthwhile either; the whole lot would have gone on crack the minute he got home.

'I am so sorry,' Antonio snivelled. 'I have told them that you have nothing to do with this and I will say the same in court. I would never implicate you in anything so there's no need to worry because you will be free soon.'

This made me feel a little bit better. At least I could be sure he wouldn't try and claim the coke belonged to me the minute he was in front of a judge. I was contemplating whether to have another go at him when the door of the cell banged open and two Guardia Civil officers came marching in.

'You go prison now,' they told us. 'The bus is outside.'

The coppers cuffed us up and shoved us back into the transport bus, which set off on the twenty-minute journey to Salto del Negro. Salto is the largest prison in Gran Canaria and has come under scrutiny from Amnesty International after reports of guards handcuffing inmates to prison beds and beating them with truncheons. It sits at the top of a hill and is fairly isolated from the rest of Las Palmas.

As I sat in a little, filthy, cramped compartment on the bus, it dawned on me that I was going to have to ring my mum to get money for bail sent over. This was the one thing worse than ending up in prison. I tried to put it out of my mind but couldn't help imagining the look on her face when she heard what had gone on. I just hoped that she would realise I was innocent.

The windows on the bus were too high to see out of so I didn't get to look at the jail from the outside. My first glimpse of it came from within its forbidding concrete walls. It looked like a grey block of flats with small, dust-filled prison yards at regular intervals. There were male and female wings, which is the norm in Spain because most Spanish jails are mixed. This seemed a little bit odd to me, as I had always thought that part of the punishment was being deprived of male company. It didn't make much difference though because the men and women were hardly ever allowed in the same sections of the prison as one another.

Antonio and I were split up and taken to separate reception areas, which suited me fine because I couldn't have cared less if it was the last time I saw him.

'Go to desk,' a short but stocky Guardia Civil officer told me as I entered the main building.

I did as he commanded and was asked a series of questions at the counter by a plain clothed prison guard.

'*¿Cuál es tu nombre? ¿Y cuál es tu fecha de nacimiento?*'

She would have had a better chance of getting through to a brick.

'I'm sorry I don't understand,' I told her, trying to remain strong and hold back the tears. 'I don't speak a word of Spanish. I'm from England, you see.'

I was just about to burst out crying for the umpteenth time that day when I felt a tap on my shoulder and turned around to see a pretty-looking girl with a head of bright blonde hair standing behind me. I figured she must have been passing through the reception area on the way to her cell. She was clearly an inmate but didn't look at all mean or predatory like I had expected a convicted criminal to be.

'You seem upset. Are you OK?' she asked.

'Not really,' I told her. 'I can't speak Spanish and don't know what's going on. Nobody speaks English. It's going to be a nightmare in here.'

'Don't worry,' Blondie comforted me. 'I'll ask the guards if you can share a cell with me. That way I can look after you and translate anything you are unsure of.'

The reception staff didn't seem to have any problem with this, presumably because it worked out easier for them.

'OK, off we go,' said the girl. 'I'll show you to your room. There will be five of us altogether now. Two of the other girls are OK but one of them is a pain in the ass. She is called June and she has horrible temper tantrums. Whenever it happens, the guards have to inject her with Valium, so try and avoid doing anything that could set her off.'

In ordinary circumstances I would have been scared out of my wits but I was so exhausted, that my emotions were now a fraction of their former selves. I felt fear but it was nothing compared to the overwhelming sense of tiredness that gripped my mind, body and soul. As long as my cell had a bed in it, it was OK by me.

'What did you do to end up in here then?' I asked Blondie as she escorted me down a noisy corridor towards the women's wing.

'Credit card fraud,' she told me. 'I'm originally from Holland, but I was arrested whilst I travelling round the Canaries doing scams. The crazy thing is that they traced crimes back to me that happened on five different islands so I have to spend time in prisons on every island. I've already done three so I've got one left after this and then I get set free.'

When we got to the cell, the other three girls were out on exercise, which was a bit of a relief because it meant that I could put off meeting the dreaded June.

'I'm going to leave you on your own for a while,' Blondie told me. 'I'm off to see my friends on the yard, but you should stay here and get yourself settled in.'

I nodded in agreement and Blondie motioned to a nearby guard to lock the cell door. The cell was empty apart from three sets of bunk beds and a toilet. There was no TV or radio. This was *real* prison.

Now that I was finally alone, I had some time to reflect upon everything that had gone on, which left me shaking with fright again. I was locked up in a foreign country with no idea how long it was going to take for my bail to come through and I had no way of finding out. My bottom lip began to tremble as I envisioned spending weeks surrounded by the same four concrete walls. I tried to stop myself from crying but eventually gave in and let the tears flow.

Fortunately by the time my cellmates got back from exercise, I had finished weeping and managed to dry my eyes. I knew it wasn't a good idea to show weakness in jail and didn't want them thinking I was a soft touch.

'This is June, Mariah and Paula,' Blondie told me, pointing to each of my new roomies in turn, who were all Spanish. Mariah and Paula were dainty little girls but June was absolutely huge. She was one of those people whose obesity eclipses all their other physical attributes. I shuddered to think of what she was capable of during her outbursts because one of her gigantic fingers probably weighed as much as an average person's hand.

Once she had got the introductions out of the way, Blondie told me it was dinner time and offered to lend me her phone card so that I could ring my mum.

'After our meal, we will be locked up all night,' she said. 'You need a card to make calls in here. If you have no money, you can't get minutes on your card so it's a good thing I am here for you.'

I was grateful for her help but crapping myself at the prospect of having to explain to Mum how I'd ended up in prison. As I ventured out onto the wing, criminals of all different nationalities milled about the place. There seemed to be a lot of South Americans, which figured because Spain is home to large populations of Ecuadorian, Colombian, Bolivian and Argentinean immigrants. Some of the inmates looked as if they were on drugs but others showed no visible signs of living their lives on the wrong side of the law. They were quite an eclectic bunch, which I hoped meant that my Englishness wouldn't make me stand out from the crowd too much.

The minute I caught sight of the prison phone, my stomach turned to jelly. I contemplated bottling it but forced myself to make the call because I knew that it was a necessity if I wanted to get out. Mum would no doubt be upset but there was nothing I could do about it.

Ring, ring...

Part of me was hoping no one would pick up but my more pragmatic side was eager to get it over with.

'Hello?'

This was it, the moment of reckoning...

'Mum,' I said, crossing my fingers and praying that she would be able to cope with what she was about to hear. 'It's Terry. I don't want you to panic but I've been arrested...'

'You've been what?' gasped Mum.

'I'm in Salto del Negro prison in Las Palmas. I haven't got long on the phone so I need you to listen. You've got to send some money over to me 'cause I need bailing out.'

'How do I do that?' she asked, sounding on the verge of tears.

'You can wire it over using Western Union,' I told her. 'I love you Mum. Please get me out of here. I just want to go home.'

'I love you too Terry. I'll go and send the money now. Are you all right in there?'

'Yeah, I'm holding up OK,' I lied. 'I've got to go now Mum. I'm using somebody else's phone card.'

I wished I had had more time so that I could explain to her that I hadn't done anything wrong. The idea of her sitting at home wondering why I was locked up was too upsetting for words. Although I was extremely grateful for her help, I now felt lower than I'd ever felt before. Even when I was on the worst comedowns imaginable, I was still never this depressed. Antonio had a lot to answer for. Not only had he put me through hell but he had also done the same to my dear old mother, who had never broken a law in her life. The more I thought about how selfish he had been, the more I hated him. But he wasn't the only one who was to blame. If I hadn't been so strung out on coke that I agreed to accompany him on the trip to Brazil then none of this would have happened. There is a big difference between being an addict and being a drug smuggler though, and I didn't deserve to be locked up for being hooked on coke.

'Are you OK?' asked Blondie, who had been waiting by the phone to show me where to get my food from after I finished my call.

'I'll survive,' I told her. 'I'll be a damn sight better when I get out of this hellhole.'

Dinner was the last thing on my mind but I figured that I should at least try to peck at something. I followed Blondie to the queue and waited in line, all the while replaying the conversation with my mum in my head. She had attempted to stay calm but sounded absolutely devastated. I just hoped she knew me better than to think that I had committed a crime that was worthy of being sent to prison for. Fair enough I was an addict, but I wasn't a drug smuggler. If I had been transporting millions of pounds worth of cocaine across from Brazil, I certainly wouldn't have carried on living in the Bungamar. My lifestyle couldn't have been further from that of a professional smuggler if I'd tried.

A stick-thin, track-marked inmate slopped a pile of mushy chickpeas onto my tray and I followed Blondie to a table. The food looked disgusting, which was exactly how I had expected it to be. As I sat and contemplated whether or not I could actually bring myself to eat it, I noticed a little South American lady walking across to the table next to us. She looked quite sweet and innocent, which made me wonder how she had ended up inside.

'That's Carina,' said Blondie, following my gaze and guessing what I was thinking. 'Her and her husband got caught smuggling coke. They were X-rayed at the airport and a load of condoms filled with drugs came up. Their kids were with them at the time as well. It must have been terrible for them.'

'Why did she do that?' I asked. 'She doesn't look like a criminal.'

'She's from Venezuela, which is a very poor country,' Blondie explained. 'She was probably trying to earn enough to move her children somewhere better. The sad thing is that everybody knows the swallowers are decoys. The people at the top rat them out to the cops and in return, their workers are allowed to pass through customs without being properly checked. Poor Carina is looking at fifteen years inside. My heart goes out to her.'

I glanced over at the lady again and tried to picture her swallowing condoms full of Class A drugs. She really didn't seem the type. I had heard about drug mules smuggling cocaine over from developing countries before but had never come face to face with one. She had a sad look in her eyes, as if she no longer had anything to live for now that her family had been taken from her. Her face still haunts me to this day and I often find myself wondering if she was ever reunited with her kids. I would like to think she was because she didn't look like a bad person, just someone who was willing to do whatever it took to get out of the slums. She reminded me of the people that I had seen at the Brazilian street party and hearing about her circumstances changed the way I looked at them. I now appreciated just how tough they had it over there.

After dinner, we returned to our cell where we were locked up for the night. It was strange sharing my living quarters with four convicted criminals, especially as I knew that one of them could go nuts at any time. They all seemed fairly ordinary and well rounded but then again, most people do when you first meet them.

My cellmates passed the time by bombarding me with every single English phrase they knew. It was extremely irritating because I just wanted to be left alone. I kept thinking about Carina and how bad her life in Venezuela must have been. It made me feel grateful that I had been born in a country where I didn't have to do risky things like she had done to guarantee my family a future. But then again I was now living in the same conditions as her. She might have had a worse start in life but we were now on equal ground.

I went to sleep that night hoping that my bail would come as quickly as possible. At least when I was released I would be able to get myself a lawyer and find out how much of a chance I had of keeping my freedom. I was even starting to miss the Bungamar. Jackie would no doubt be wondering where I was. Her tongue-ring clicking was nothing compared to the noise of sharing a cell with four people. I was so tired that I eventually dozed off regardless and dreamed of being somewhere else.

The following morning, Blondie started the day off by issuing me with a warning.

'There are some lesbians in this jail who prey on young girls,' she told me. 'Being locked up has bent them and now they try and bend others. You're best staying with me when you go out on the wing. They aren't the only danger in this prison; Salto is a very dangerous place.'

This was another worry to add to my extensive collection. I had heard of people turning gay in male-only prisons but wasn't aware that it happened to female prisoners as well. I made a mental note never to go in the showers without Blondie there to make sure that I was OK.

It didn't take a rocket scientist to figure out which women had been 'bent'. There was one couple in particular who couldn't have been more obvious. One, a butch, rugby-player type, the other a pretty, feminine little thing, they were all over each other twenty-four hours a day. The strange thing was that the feminine one had been straight before being locked up and had regular visits from her husband. I guess she couldn't cope with being single for the six days a week that he was unable to come and see her.

I tried to spend as much time as I could in my cell because the exercise yard was no bigger than my living room back in Wingrave and the wing was quite a scary place to venture onto. Whenever I needed to go outside, I always made sure that Blondie had my back. Unfortunately spending so much time in my room meant that I was forced to bear witness to several of June's hissy fits. She acted like a big, fat, spoilt brat and threw our things around the cell whenever she had a bad day. It took several guards to sedate her and stop her from rampaging about the place.

June couldn't handle being in prison. Her only way of dealing with being locked up was to get uncontrollably angry and take it out on everybody else. She was like a baby spitting its dummy out, although I had an equally destructive method for coping with being inside. I passed the time by fantasising about all the drugs that I was going to take after I had been released. It helped to take my mind off things and gave me something to look forward to. I was no longer suffering from physical withdrawal symptoms but my brain was still craving cocaine – and I would soon be able to cram my nose with it because four days through my time inside, I was told my bail had arrived. Blondie was sad to see me go but at the same time happy that I didn't have to spend another day in Salto. I can never repay her for everything that she did for me because without her, the prison would have swallowed me whole. I said a teary-eyed goodbye then went to tell the guards that I was ready to leave.

Chapter 6

COCAINE ON THE BRAIN

Being escorted out of the prison was just as intimidating as going in had been because I had no idea how I was going to get back to the centre of Las Palmas. The Spanish authorities don't give you any money to get home when they release you. The minute you leave the jail, you are on your own and Salto is in the middle of nowhere. It's surrounded by wasteland and there is no sign of civilisation for miles around. I was just starting to panic when a white BMW pulled up and a dodgy-looking Spanish guy poked his head out of the window. This fella looked as if he was some kind of big-time villain. He had the same air of criminality about him that the wide-boy club owners on Veronicas had, and his face was cold and expressionless. I just hoped he hadn't come to polish me off at the request of the coppers who had paid Antonio for the drug run.

'Are you Terry?'

'Yeah that's me.'

'I'm Antonio's brother. I've got some money for you from your solicitor. Open the door and get in.'

He bore no resemblance whatsoever to Antonio, mostly because he wasn't enormously fat, but I was forced to trust him because I would have been stranded if I didn't. I think if Fred West had turned up and offered me a lift I would have probably taken it.

Antonio's brother owned a bar that catered mainly for British tourists, which meant that he spoke perfect English.

'I didn't even know that you were getting out today until I got here,' he told me. 'I was coming back from a visit with Antonio when your solicitor came over to me. He said that there was some money left over from the cash your mum sent to bail you out and asked if I would give it to you.'

It was nice of my lawyer to trust my co-accused's brother with my money. For all I knew, the original sum might have been twice the amount I actually received.

'I'll give you a lift back to Las Palmas. Then you can book yourself into a hotel. You need to go to court tomorrow to have your bail conditions set. I will pick you up in the morning and take you there.'

It was a good thing he was there to tell me this, as nobody at the prison had explained a thing to me. I would have missed the hearing and had a warrant out for my arrest if he hadn't happened to be at Salto on the day of my release. My solicitor shouldn't have even told him I was there because for all he knew, Antonio could have been plotting to take me out of the picture so that he could make sure I didn't grass him up for anything else he might have done. I felt the Spanish authorities didn't seem to place too much importance upon the safety of foreign nationals. Safety seemed even more disposable than freedom, and that was saying something.

As we drove down the side of a steep hill towards the city centre, it dawned on me that I was going to have to spend the night alone on an unfamiliar island. The thought of it scared me, which was strange considering the fact that I had been in prison for the last four days. A night in a hotel should have been a walk in the park but for some unknown reason I felt really on edge.

'OK I'll drop you off here,' Antonio's brother told me, pulling up outside a building that resembled a YMCA hostel. 'It's the cheapest place going so it shouldn't set you back too much. I'll see you early tomorrow morning. Make sure you've got your stuff ready for court when I come to pick you up.'

Even if he was the brother of the person who had got me into all this trouble in the first place, it was still good of him to help me out. I nodded nervously and headed into the hotel to check myself in. God knows what the lady on reception must have thought of me because I was half asleep, wearing dirty clothes and too spaced out for words. I handed over enough cash for a one-night stay and then went up to inspect my room.

My digs were fairly basic but beat the hell out of a prison cell. I didn't have to share with a grown woman who had temper tantrums for a start, which is always a plus point. Now that I had somewhere to stay, it was time to ring my mum and explain why I had been in prison. Talking to her would no doubt make me feel a little bit better. I was still completely shell-shocked and couldn't wait to hear a familiar voice. There's nothing like a conversation with your mum to help calm you down. It was going to be a damn sight less stressful ringing Mum from the hotel phone than ringing her from a prison phone had been. At least this time I wouldn't have to worry about running out of minutes on my card. I just hoped that she would believe my story.

'Hello?'

'Mum, it's Terry. I'm in a hotel in Las Palmas...'

'Thank goodness you're OK. What on earth is going on? I rang your work to ask them what had happened and they said that you'd been sacked for selling drugs.'

Ah. I should have told her that I'd lost my job and explained the reason why. This wasn't exactly going to help my case.

'I wasn't selling drugs Mum, you've got to believe me. I went on holiday to Brazil with Antonio and customs found drugs in his bag and I had no idea at all and then I got sent to prison...'

I was talking so fast that she probably didn't understand a word I said.

'This is all too much to take,' said Mum. 'First Ricky and now this...'

Ricky was our beloved family cat. We had found him abandoned as a kitten and nursed him back to health.

'What's happened to Ricky?' I asked her, hoping to God that he was still all right.

'I'm so sorry Terry. Ricky died the other day.'

I was absolutely gutted. He was eleven, which is quite old for a cat, but I still hadn't been expecting it and couldn't believe that he was gone. He had apparently drifted off whilst purring away in my dad's arms. It sent me even further into the depth of despair and left me feeling as if the world was conspiring against me.

Mum and I had a good old cry together. Some people might think that the death of a pet cat would be the least of my worries but I've always been an animal person and couldn't get the image of his little face out of my head.

Once I had finally managed to calm down, I took a series of deep breaths and tried to focus on the task at hand.

'I've got to go to court again tomorrow. I'll ring you as soon as it's over,' I told Mum between tearful sniffles. 'I had nothing to do with the drugs and Antonio's going to tell them that. Hopefully that should be the end of things and I'll be able to see you soon.'

'Let me know me as soon as it's over,' she told me. 'I'll be waiting to hear from you.'

The phone call left me emotionally drained. As I headed back up to my room, I thought about everything that I had put Mum through and felt a sudden pang of guilt. Although I wasn't guilty of smuggling the coke, my hedonistic lifestyle had still helped to land me in trouble. If I hadn't got involved with cocaine, I wouldn't have hung about with Antonio and none of this would have happened.

Although I knew I needed a good night's sleep before my hearing, nodding off that night was easier said than done. So many crazy things had happened that I was now extremely paranoid. Whenever I heard a noise, I thought somebody was breaking into my room and almost had a heart attack. The few hours of shut-eye that I did get were riddled with nightmares and dreams about Ricky.

By the time the morning came, I was in a terrible state. I was tired, distraught and panic-stricken but knew I needed to hold it together. At nine o'clock I spotted my lift out of the window and checked out of the hotel. I was grateful for the ride but didn't really fancy talking to Antonio's brother because I had nothing to say to him. Instead I chose to sit in silence until we got to court.

It was just me and the judge in the courtroom this time round and I was sitting inches from her face. There was no security and I could have jumped over the desk and punched her if I wanted to. Fortunately for her, I wasn't a proper criminal and didn't have a violent bone in my body. I was just a confused, scared, young girl who had become unknowingly embroiled in Antonio's stupid scheme.

'You are to remain in Spain until the day of your trial,' the judge told me.

I was happy that she spoke English but gutted they were dragging things out even longer. Why were the Spaniards so intent on making me hang around? They were treating me as if I was the one who was caught with all the cocaine and Antonio was my innocent travel partner. As the reality dawned on me that it was all far from over, I began to cry again for the millionth time that week. I was surprised that I had any tears left to part with.

'You will have to hand over your passport, but you can still travel to the mainland or any of the Spanish islands without it,' the judge went on, as if this was supposed to somehow make me feel better. I wasn't bothered where I could or couldn't go to; I just wanted to clear my name so that I could carry on with my life.

'You also need to report once a month to the authorities but you can do this in Tenerife. We will be in contact with the date of your trial, which will be held at the Provincial Criminal Court of Las Palmas. You are now free to go.'

I placed my passport on the desk and left the building feeling angry and let down. How could I ever hope to relax with something like this hanging over me? I had been sentenced to another period of extreme uncertainty and anxiety.

The only positive result of the hearing was the fact that I could now go home to Tenerife. I still had some of the cash left over that Mum had sent, so I headed to the airport to book myself a flight. Whilst I was there, I took the opportunity to ring her from a payphone and tell her the bad news.

'Mum,' I said. 'It's still all going on. They won't let me leave Spain and I've got to go back to court. I don't know if I can take much more of this.'

'I'll book a flight to Tenerife and come and see you this Friday,' Mum told me. 'You'll get through this, Terry. You just have to remain strong.'

If only it was that easy. I didn't feel as if I was going to get through it at all. The tension was destroying me. As I boarded the plane, I remember thinking, 'Oh well, at least I'll be able to blot out the pain with coke soon.' I should have learnt my lesson but Veronicas was calling me. The fact that I still wanted to take a substance that had caused me so much trouble is testament to its power. Cocaine plays mind games with you and at this precise moment, it was saying, 'The damage is already done now. You might as well sniff more of me. After all, it can't get any worse.'

The plan was to call in at my flat, let my roomie know that I was OK and then head off to the strip to get plastered. Jackie was over the moon to see me because Mum had told her that I'd been arrested and she'd been worried sick.

'So you're a free girl now then?' she asked me. 'You got a 'not guilty'?'

'Not exactly,' I told her. 'I've got to go back to court for my trial. I'm free for now though so let's get mashed to celebrate. I've missed our wild nights out together.'

The sad thing was that I was telling the truth as well. Addiction had me in its grip to such an extent that even in the light of everything that had happened, partying was still my main priority. Drug habits are funny things. You can be teetotal for weeks if you know that there's no way that you can get hold of any but then, the minute you are in a position where they are readily available, your cravings resume as if they never went away. The fact that I had years in prison hanging over my head made me want them even more. I needed something to take my mind off everything that was going on.

'OK, well, there's something I've got to tell you,' Jackie told me. 'Everybody on the strip thinks you're a grass. They heard that Antonio's still in prison but you got released and think you must have given evidence against him. I know you're not a rat but they're convinced of it. You need to be careful, Terry. Antonio has a lot of friends and they are all pissed off.'

Being a grass in a place like Playa de las Americas means being a social pariah. It's a very vice-filled place and informers are treated like the lowest of the low.

'That's ridiculous,' I told her. 'It's not as if they've let me off scot-free. I'm still likely to get sent down. Why would I grass him up when I'd pleaded innocent anyway? It'd give the game away a bit!'

The only reason that anybody ever provides information to the police is to get time off their sentence. Innocent people have no need to take that route because if the wheels of justice run smoothly then they won't be locked up at all.

'You try telling them that,' Jackie said. 'They think you've stuck him in it to get yourself off the hook so don't expect a warm welcome from anyone on the strip.'

This was brilliant; Antonio had landed me in the shit and now his mates were accusing *me* of getting *him* in trouble. They were probably paranoid because they were all involved in crime themselves and didn't want anyone around them who could possibly rat them out.

'Well thanks for the warning,' I told her. 'I still want to go there and get trolleyed though. Are you coming or what?'

Jackie laughed and motioned towards the door.

'Come on then, let's get going. We've got a lot of time to make up for. I hope you haven't forgotten how to have fun.'

I followed her out of the flat and through the crowded, humid streets of Playa de las Americas. The minute I caught sight of Veronicas, my mouth began to water. I would soon be snorting coke and drinking Malibu until the world became a blur.

I walked up to the entrance of the nearest bar only for the bouncer to hold his hand out and tell me I was barred.

'We don't want your type in here,' he growled. 'You've got some nerve coming back.'

'She's done nothing wrong,' Jackie defended me. 'She didn't even know about the drugs so what could she have told anyone? You need to stop listening to gossiping idiots.'

'It's OK Jackie, leave it,' I told her. 'Come on, let's find somewhere that actually wants our money.'

We tried a couple of different places and eventually found a club where the door staff hadn't heard of me. Luckily the dealers weren't as picky about who they did their business with and sorted us out with coke without a word of complaint. They didn't care if I was a grass or not, just as long as I wasn't planning on grassing them up for selling to me.

The moment I snorted my first gram, it was as if I'd never stopped. All of the anxiety immediately left my body and replaced itself with the type of artificial confidence that only cocaine brings. It didn't matter that I was facing a long stint behind bars; all I cared about was getting high and having a good time. The next three nights were spent getting off my nut in the few clubs that would let me in. I was now Veronicas' most hated woman but couldn't have cared less. Cocaine liked me and I liked it back. In fact you could go as far as to say that the two of us were in love.

On the morning of Mum's visit, I woke up feeling nervous in case she was angry with me. She had been supportive on the phone but I still didn't know whether or not she was a hundred per cent convinced that I was innocent. Maybe she was bottling it all up ready to have a go at me when she saw me in person. The fact that I was on a comedown didn't make things any easier. My nerves would have been jangled walking down the street, let alone having my first in-depth conversation with my mother about being arrested for drug smuggling.

As I waited at the airport, I felt a mixture of emotions. On the one hand I was looking forward to being able to pour my heart out to my mum about what I had been through, but on the other, I was on pins in case she didn't believe me. I wanted to run and hug her the minute I saw her, but knew that I would have to wait to see what her take on the situation was before doing anything like that.

The first thing that Mum said to me was, 'Terry, did you do it?'

'No,' I told her. 'Antonio took me for a sucker, Mum. I had no idea what was going on until it was too late.'

'OK I just needed to be sure,' she said. 'That's the only time I'm ever going to ask you that. I'm your mother so I know when you're telling the truth. Now let's concentrate on fighting this.'

I was so relieved to hear those words come out of her mouth that tears of joy cascaded down my face. This set Mum off and we were soon hugging each other and bawling our eyes out in the middle of the airport.

'We need to get you a solicitor,' Mum sobbed. 'We're going to beat this, Terry. I know you're innocent and there's no way I'm going to let them lock you up.'

Now that I knew I had her full backing, I felt a little bit more positive. Perhaps a few months down the line, I would be able to look back at this and think, 'Wow that was a crazy period of my life. Thank God it's all in the past.'

Over the course of the next few days, we lounged in the sun, ate ice cream and discussed my case. Mum told me that there was no point in doing a runner and assured me that everything was going to be OK. We were walking back from the beach a week later, my mind feeling a little more at rest, when I felt a sudden pain in my head and dropped to the floor in agony. Blood started pouring from my nose and ears and I collapsed in a heap.

'Somebody help!' yelled Mum. 'My daughter's bleeding on the ground. She needs to go to hospital!'

I have no recollection of anything that happened after this. I've been told that paramedics were on the scene within minutes, but by that point I was unconscious so anything could have gone on. When I came round again, I was lying in a hospital bed with my dad standing over me.

'How did you get here?' I asked Dad.

My mind was in a pickle and the fact that he had travelled across from England seemed to be the most perplexing thing on earth.

'I've come to stay with you whilst you're poorly,' Dad told me. 'You've had an aneurysm. Try to relax, you're going to be all right.'

I had no idea what an aneurysm was at this point and all I could think to say was, 'Where are your suitcases? Where are you staying?'

'I'm staying in a hotel and all my things are there.'

'How'd you get here? Where are all your bags?'

He must have had the patience of a saint. Looking back I think my brain was struggling to process the conversation and I had to hear everything a million times before the information finally sunk in. My cerebellum had been bleeding quite profusely so I was lucky it still worked. Fifty per cent of people who have the type of brain haemorrhage that I had, die on the spot and twenty-five per cent don't make it to the hospital. With that in mind, I think that I did well to remember anything at all.

The doctors were unable to operate on me straightaway because my brain needed time to recover from the trauma before they could go to work. This meant that I would have to remain in the ward for another couple of weeks. Dad only stayed in Tenerife for two days but Mum made arrangements to live with a Colombian family that we had met on holiday so that she could stay for longer. The family were called the Silvas and I had grown very close to them on our trips to the island during my teenage years.

The Silvas lived in a city called La Laguna in the northern part of the island, which meant that Mum could visit me almost every day because it was only an hour's drive away. I wasn't allowed to move from the hospital bed in case I jarred my head so I was glad to have somebody to talk to. My only other form of entertainment was Spanish TV, which was bizarre to say the least. They don't have a watershed over there, so you can turn the telly on during the day and be confronted by the types of things that are only shown after midnight in the UK.

COCAINE ON THE BRAIN

As the day of my operation drew near, I became incredibly nervous. The doctors were planning on using a new, experimental surgery, which had me absolutely terrified. They were going to thrust coils up through the artery in my groin, push them all the way into my brain and pack the aneurysm with them. It was quite a controversial method of stemming the bleeding and if they accidentally punctured the vein then it was 'bye bye Terry'.

Fortunately I was put to sleep whilst they did the surgery. Their first attempt didn't work, which added a week to my stay in hospital because they had to wait until my artery recovered before trying again. Attempt number two was a success. I couldn't leave straightaway because they still needed to keep me in until my brain had fully recovered, but I could get out of bed without fear of dying. This meant that I was finally free to move about the room after weeks of lying in the same position.

Up until this point I had been unable to get up and shave my legs so one of my first ventures out of bed was a trip to the bathroom to give them a going-over with a razor. Once I had got them looking nice and smooth again, I had a sudden urge to get some fresh air so I headed out onto the hospital balcony. This proved to be a big mistake. There was some building work going on nearby and the smell of the site reminded me of cocaine because a lot of dealers cut their drugs with brick dust. It brought my addiction back to the forefront of my mind and made me want to go out looking for a dealer.

Although the doctors never specifically told me that my haemorrhage was drug-related, it didn't take a rocket scientist to figure out that coke was definitely a factor. My nose was itching for a bag but I knew full well that it would mess me up and decided there and then that I was never going to give in to it again.

Shovelling that stuff up my nose was far too risky now. I would just have to be strong and learn to say no.

I have since found out that being under the influence of alcohol and cocaine at the same time is particularly bad for you. The chemicals contained in the drugs combine to form a third even more dangerous substance known as cocaethylene, which heightens both the positive and the negative effects. In hindsight it was probably all the times that I had snorted a line, then downed a shot of Malibu that brought on the haemorrhage. Stress could have also played a part but there is no point trying to pretend that drugs weren't at least partially to blame.

My alcohol intake was also going to have to come right down. I didn't have the willpower to cut it out altogether but promised myself that I would at least stop getting blotto. Ending up in hospital again wasn't an option. My poor mum had suffered enough the first time round without me knackering my brain again.

On the day of my discharge, I took a moment to reflect upon how close to death I had been and thanked God I had managed to pull through. I couldn't waste my second chance at life; I'd obviously been given it for a reason. It was time to take things easier and put the partying to one side. Some of the Silvas' relatives had agreed to let me stay at their place until I found my feet again, which was good because they lived in the sticks, where there was no cocaine. Their house was on a *finca*, an area in the middle of the countryside where people lived in shacks. I can't thank them enough for putting me up because it was the ideal place to unwind and detox.

The downside to living on a *finca* was that we had no roof, electricity or running water. The house looked like a barn and left us exposed to the weather. It was strange because most of our neighbours worked on the nearby farms, but the family I was staying with owned their own bar in the centre of Los Christianos. I guess they liked the simple life.

Grateful as I was that that my hosts had agreed to let me stay with them, I soon grew tired of their rather humble accommodation and started looking for a place of my own. The Bungamar had suited my purposes whilst I was in party mode but I didn't fancy going back there now that I was off the drink and drugs. If I had seen it in the sober light of day I probably wouldn't have touched it with a bargepole.

I eventually got word that a girl in one of the town centre complexes was looking for a housemate and decided to move in with her. This was to be a true test of my resolve. It was easy enough to remain clean-living whilst I was tucked away in the back of beyond but I wondered whether I would give in to temptation in a place with bars around the corner. I hoped my aneurysm had changed me for the better and given me more respect for my body. Maybe it was the wake-up call I needed. Only time would tell.

Chapter 7

MY DAY IN COURT

My new place was a huge improvement. It was in a pleasant location, I got on with my housemate and I even managed to find myself a job at one of the local bars. Things were really starting to look up. I had the occasional alcoholic tipple but no longer felt the urge to drink myself under the table. Perhaps I had finally got things under control. It was just a pity the threat of jail still hung over me. I felt as if my perfect life could come toppling down at any given moment.

The bar that I worked at was owned by a family from Leeds called the Fitzgeralds, who were old friends of mine. A lot of people would have hesitated to take on a girl with an outstanding court case but they didn't seem to have a problem with it, which shows how kind-hearted and non-judgemental they are. The only downside to working at their bar was the fact that I was constantly surrounded by drink.

Although I no longer consumed half as much alcohol as I used to, I still had boozy nights out every now and then. Oestrogen can cause blood clots if you've had an aneurysm so I had to stop taking the pill after my haemorrhage. This should have made me more cautious but when you're under the influence, you rarely stop to consider the consequences of your actions. Tenerife is all about drinking and cavorting with men and I did plenty of both. I tended to move on from one bloke to another fairly quickly and it was only when I took a pregnancy test and got a positive result that I realised just how foolish I had been. Alcohol had clouded my judgement and I had failed to take the necessary precautions.

The baby's father seemed nice enough at first. He was short with cropped hair and had a very cute look to him. The problem was that he was also a cokehead and after a week of knocking about with him, I realised that the drugs had had a major effect upon his personality. One minute he would be laid-back and friendly, the next thing he would act like a nutter. Even if he would have made the number one daddy, I still don't think I would have kept the baby because I didn't know if I was going to get sent down or not and it would have been unfair on the child.

After a lot of soul-searching, I eventually came to the conclusion that there was no other option but to have an abortion. It was a difficult decision but I couldn't face leaving my little one wondering where its mother was whilst I was trapped behind bars. Having a baby was completely out of the question. Going to the clinic was a necessity rather than a choice.

Even though I knew that I was doing the right thing, the abortion still left me feeling like shit. Drink had contributed yet again to my misery. I found myself cursing the day that I first picked up a glass of Malibu and wished I had spat it out.

The next piece of bad news came in the form of a phone call from my mum. She told me that she had received a letter from the court saying that I was due for trial on the 24 March. This didn't give me much time to prepare. My boss at the bar had given me the details of the solicitor that he used, so I scheduled an appointment with him as soon as possible.

The solicitor was called Pedro and reminded me of a thinner version of Antonio. He absolutely reeked of corruption but I reasoned that this was probably nothing out of the ordinary where members of the legal profession were concerned. Something wasn't quite right about this guy though; he seemed even less trustworthy than your average legal professional. There was nothing about his physical appearance that made me feel this way. It was something intangible that I couldn't put my finger on.

'I'm not a criminal lawyer but your case is quite clear cut so I'll take it on,' he told me. 'I need three million pesetas up front before I can start though.'

This was the equivalent of fifteen grand in sterling and should have rung alarm bells but I'd never been in trouble with the law before so I had no way of telling whether or not it was the norm. I wasn't too happy about it but felt I didn't really have a choice. If that was the price of securing my freedom then I would just have to cough up – or should I say my long-suffering mother would, because the abortion had already set me back a fair bit and I was almost broke. Without my mum I wouldn't have been able to afford any legal representation whatsoever so I am eternally grateful to her.

Once the cash had been wired over, Pedro advised me to plead 'not guilty' and told me that it should be quite an easy case to win.

'They've got nothing on you,' he assured me. 'I can't believe they're even going ahead with this. You would have got off scot-free if you had left the country earlier. The court was going to hit you with a deportation order in place of a prison sentence but you were in hospital.'

This was just my bloody luck. Trust my aneurysm to strike at the time it did. It seemed as if everything that could possibly go wrong had done. At least now I could set about taking positive steps to clear my name. Pedro and I spent the next few weeks going through what little evidence the prosecution had of my supposed involvement in the crime. I was determined to prove to the world that I was no crook.

'They are trying to use an entry from your diary against you,' Pedro told me. 'They say you wrote that "the parcel has arrived" and said that you were dreaming about what you would do with the money.'

I did write both of these things but neither of them had anything to do with transporting drugs. The first sentence related to the money that Antonio's wife had sent over and the second was about my payout for the car crash. I had only spent a fraction of my compensation and couldn't wait to blow the rest on coke. If I had been smuggling large amounts of blow do they really think that I would have been stupid enough to write about it in a diary? I felt insulted that their case hinged around the assumption that I was a complete idiot.

'They will have a hard job securing a conviction using this,' Pedro carried on. 'It's circumstantial evidence at best and they have no other proof that you were anything other than a naïve innocent. We're going to win this one hands down.'

He was telling me exactly what I wanted to hear. In hindsight this was probably an attempt to make me feel better about the fact that I had spent fifteen grand on him. It's difficult to be critical of somebody who offers hope in a desperate situation. He probably could have told me anything with a vaguely positive slant to it and I would have believed it.

By the day of the hearing, I no longer felt nervous. Pedro had spent so long convincing me that I was going to get off that I was confident I had nothing to worry about. It was just a matter of turning up at the trial, stating my case and going home. Our flight to Gran Canaria left at six in the morning and I boarded it with a sense of eager anticipation. I was about to put the lid on this whole horrible episode.

All the way through the flight, Pedro went on about what an open-and-shut case it was. The more he talked, the more I trusted him. For somebody who wasn't even a criminal lawyer, he sure seemed to know his stuff. The prosecution wouldn't know what had hit them. We were going to wipe the floor with them.

As I approached the Provincial Criminal Court of Las Palmas, a small, dumpy Spanish woman came running up to Pedro and asked him what I was doing there. Pedro said something to her in Spanish and she stormed off into the building.

'What was that about?' I asked him, wondering what the lady's problem was.

'That was your co-defendant's solicitor,' he told me. 'She seems surprised that you've turned up.'

I think that everybody had been expecting me to do a runner. This was clearly the done thing for Brits on the island but I was determined to clear my name.

The court proceedings in Spain are very different to England. You don't swear in or take any kind of oath; you just walk in and sit down. The judges looked like random people who had strolled in off the street. There wasn't a wig or robe in sight and one of them was chewing a sweet whilst waiting for the case to start. I almost didn't recognise Antonio when he first entered the court. He had dropped from 19 stone to 9 stone and looked pale and unhealthy. I later found out that he had got hooked on heroin whilst on remand. I guess smack must be a lot worse than crack because he never had any problem keeping his weight on when he was smoking rocks.

'Are you all right?' he asked me as he shuffled past to his seat.

What made this pathetic junkie think that I would want to talk to him after everything that he had put me through?

'No I'm not all right,' I told him. 'I'm not all right at all.'

Shortly after Antonio had sat down, the judges started jabbering away in Spanish. Once they had finished, the prosecution took the floor to ask me some questions.

'In the diary that you wrote during your trip to Brazil, you made references to receiving a sum of money. What was this money for and why were you receiving it?'

'It was compensation for an accident I had back home,' I told them. 'I'd just been paid it before my holiday and I was excited about spending it.'

'Can you prove that this was what the sum was for?'

'Yes I can. My mum can send the papers across.'

This brief conversation was to be the only time I spoke throughout the course of the trial. The judge thanked me for my answers then motioned for Pedro to stand up. He made some brief comparisons to a couple of past cases that were similar to mine and then sat down again. For all his bluster in the run up to the hearing, he didn't seem to have a lot to say. I wasn't sure if this was a good thing or a bad one. Maybe he didn't have to talk a lot because it was already so blindingly obvious that I was innocent.

Now it was Antonio's turn for a grilling. The prosecution interrogated him for a good twenty minutes and he gave lengthy monologues in answer to each question. Every now and again he waggled his finger in my direction, which made me feel a little bit on edge. Was he putting the blame on me or was he telling the court that I knew nothing? I had no way of knowing either way. He also got up out of his seat at one stage and handed the court usher a Filofax. This seemed to create a lot of commotion and had everybody murmuring.

The amount of time Antonio was questioned for made me wonder if I had been brought in as a witness rather than a defendant. The prosecution were obviously a damn sight more interested in him than they were in me. Maybe the police had only arrested me to make sure that I would turn up at court. Surely they would have picked my brains a lot more than they did if they thought that we were partners in crime.

'Is there anything else that you would like to add?' the head judge asked me after Antonio had finally shut up.

'Just that I thought I was going to Brazil purely for a one-week holiday,' I told her.

What else could I really say? The only bits of the hearing that I understood were the questions they had directed towards me in English. Everything else was complete gobbledegook.

'El juicio ha terminado.'

I guessed this meant that we could now leave the courtroom, judging by the fact that everybody was getting up out of their chairs. They don't announce the verdict straightaway in Spain, which meant that I was condemned to another period of uncertainty whilst I waited for it to be sent on to me in the post.

It was as if they wanted to prolong my torment for as long as possible.

'How do you think it went?' I asked Pedro on the way out of the building.

I needed reassuring and he was the perfect person to do it.

'Really well,' he smiled. 'I think you're definitely going to be found not guilty. I'll explain the details on the plane back home.'

As we made our way towards the airport, I replayed the court case in my head and couldn't help thinking there was something Pedro wasn't telling me. What was all the pointing and gesturing during Antonio's speech and why had the judges looked at me as if I was a big-time criminal? I had a feeling that the trial had gone a damn sight worse than he was letting on.

During the flight, Pedro summarised what each person had said.

'This is quite some case you've got here,' he told me. 'Your co-accused told the judges that two policemen and a judge had paid him to pick up the drugs on behalf of the mafia. He handed over a file containing the names and addresses of everybody who was involved and argued that he was just a link in the chain. He also said that he had been threatened into smuggling the cocaine.'

This was beyond belief. I had been given so much grief in Tenerife because Antonio's friends thought that I was a grass and now here he was informing on the Spanish mafia.

'I hope he didn't try and stick me in it,' I told Pedro.

'No, he kept saying how innocent you were,' Pedro assured me. 'He said that if you didn't agree to go to Brazil, he would have taken anyone. You were just somebody to make the trip across look more natural.'

At least Antonio had kept to his word then. It still didn't make up for the fact that he had used me as his cover though. He obviously hadn't given a second thought to what might happen to me if he got nicked at customs.

'The strange thing is that the court dismissed the file that he gave them as evidence,' Pedro went on. 'He clearly named one of the ringleaders as a man called Ernesto but the written record of the trial says that the police can't investigate his claims because he only gave the man's nickname. Ernesto doesn't sound like a nickname to me; it sounds like the man's first name.'

This wasn't the only suspicious thing about the case. Apparently the cocaine was only fifty per cent pure and there was 3.7 kilos of it. Antonio had told me that there should have been 4 kilos, which meant that 300 grams were missing. Also why would it have been so impure if it had come directly from Colombia? Somebody had clearly helped themselves to some of the seizure and cut the remaining coke to cover up the fact that a load had gone walkabout. It was looking likely that the police had set Antonio up so that they could get a free drug run. They had put part of the hoard through as evidence and kept the rest to sell.

The fact that the drugs were all packed in the same side of the suitcase also seemed dodgy. It was as if the person who had handed it over to Antonio wanted him to get caught, 3.7 kilos is quite a weight and the difference between the two sides would have been immediately obvious. To this day I still find myself wondering why on earth he chose to trust the Guardia Civil. According to Pedro, he had already been nicked twice for smuggling, which meant he should have learnt his lesson and called it quits rather than allowing himself to get caught in such an obvious trap.

'It's bad news for him but good news for you,' Pedro told me. 'He's pleaded guilty so he's definitely going down but you're still likely to get found innocent. They are charging you with possession and importation, which will never stick. You had no drugs on you and there's no evidence to show that you knew your co-accused had any in his bag.'

How they could even consider charging me with importation when I hadn't been caught with any drugs was beyond me. Clearly logic didn't even enter into the equation. Still, it was a good thing in a way because there was no way they could pin the crime on me unless they somehow proved that I knew what was going on. Pedro had put my mind at rest again. When the plane touched down in Tenerife, I thanked him for his help and told him I would keep my fingers crossed until the verdict was delivered.

'There's no need to do that,' he assured me. 'You will definitely be found innocent.'

The sad thing was that I actually genuinely believed him. The minute he had gone, I raced over to a public telephone to ring my mum and update her.

'It looks like nothing's going to happen,' I said. 'I have to wait to find out for sure but my solicitor says I'm likely to get off.'

Mum was relieved to hear my voice. She had been worrying in case they revoked my bail and I was sent to prison.

'That's brilliant,' she told me. 'You'll be home before you know it. As soon as you get your result, it'll all be over for good.'

I hadn't got a clue how long they were going to take to tell me if I was getting sent down or not. For all I knew it could be anything from a day to a year.

I spent the whole of the next day trying to get my head around what had happened at the hearing. Although I was ninety-nine per cent sure that I would be found innocent, there was still a tiny element of doubt in my mind. I didn't even know how long a sentence I was facing. It was a hell of a lot of coke so I figured it could land me with a fair whack behind bars.

The following morning, I was woken up by a frantic knocking at the door. I prised myself out of bed to answer it and was greeted by my boss's anxious face.

'You'd better come and use our phone,' he told me. 'Your mum's rung up with some bad news. She's very upset and needs to talk to you.'

It didn't take a genius to work out what her call was about. The court had been in touch about my verdict. Mobiles phones weren't about yet at this stage so I had given my solicitor her number because I didn't have a landline. As I walked the short distance to the bar, my legs felt weak and my heart beat ninety to the dozen. I was finally about to find out my fate and it didn't sound to me as if it was likely to be too positive.

The minute I heard Mum's voice, I could tell that I was in for some horrendous news.

'I'm so sorry Terry,' she sobbed into the phone. 'You've been found guilty. This is the worst day of my life.'

'How long have I got?' I asked her, still holding onto a glimmer of hope that they had given me a short sentence.

'Ten years.'

Her words felt like somebody kicking me in the face. The thought of spending a full decade in jail made me feel physically sick. My life was now officially over. I was the property of the Spanish prison system.

'We're going to launch an appeal,' Mum attempted to comfort me. 'We're going to fight this to the end. I won't let them take you.'

In Spain, they don't send you to prison until after the appeal process has finished, which meant that I still had a small slice of freedom left. I had no bail conditions either but the court still had my passport so I was unable to leave the country.

'I really hope you're right,' I said. 'Ten years is a lifetime. I don't know what I'd do if I got sent down for that long.'

'You need to keep thinking positive, as hard as that might be,' Mum told me. 'Just keep trooping on and we'll get there in the end.'

The phone call left me feeling numb from head to toe. My brain didn't even know what emotions to produce. I felt relieved that I wasn't being sent to prison straightaway. Every time my incarceration was put off, it gave me hope that I would somehow wriggle off the hook. I was running out of lifelines though. The next time the Spanish authorities got in touch it would be to order me to hand myself in. The final countdown had begun and once the timer had run out, there would be no chance of redemption. The three scruffy, sweet-chewing judges had made their decision. I just hoped that somebody with a little bit more sense would overturn it.

Chapter 8

THE FINAL COUNTDOWN

The minute I got off the phone to Mum, I headed off to see Pedro. Why had I been found guilty if there was supposedly such a miniscule chance of the verdict going against me? He had a lot of explaining to do.

Pedro was very blasé about the whole situation.

'I told you from the start that I wasn't a criminal lawyer,' he shrugged. 'The appeal is going to the High Court in Madrid so you're going to have to hire somebody else. I'm not qualified to pursue the matter any further. Good luck with your case.'

'Can I have your notes then?' I asked him.

We had spent hours going through the details of the case so the least that he could do was pass the paperwork on to me.

'You can,' he smiled. 'But it's going to cost you another 600,000 pesetas.'

This was the equivalent of three grand. I felt like punching him in the face. My poor old mum was going to have her savings eaten into even more by this human parasite. There are procedures in place to prevent dodgy solicitors from scamming you in England, but in Spain, anything seemed to go. Pedro had screwed me out of as much money as possible and now he was effectively holding my documents to ransom.

After a lot of cursing, I eventually agreed to pay for the paperwork and was shocked to see that Pedro's name wasn't on a single sheet. He had put down the names of the court usher and a solicitor who I had never met, as being my legal representatives. This was clearly to prevent people getting onto the fact that he wasn't qualified to deal with my case. It just goes to show the level of corruption there was. Part of the reason that I was found guilty I realised, was because I had a lawyer who was so bent that he didn't even want his name associated with the hearing.

I was determined to avoid being taken in by another conman so I picked my representative for the appeal from a list of British Consulate-approved solicitors. I went for a bloke called Fernando Gernstein and arranged for my documents to be sent over to Madrid, where he was based. Appeals are carried out in the defendant's absence in Spain, which is a little bit bizarre. I didn't even get to meet Fernando so for all I know, he might not have even been a real person.

The crazy thing was that nobody said anything about the fact that I was working illegally at a bar without an identification number or passport whilst awaiting the result of the case. If I was such a dangerous criminal, why was no one keeping tabs on me? I somehow doubt they would have allowed Reggie Kray to serve tourists with drinks down at the local boozer whilst he was waiting to be sent to jail.

Shortly after I hired Fernando and got the cogs in motion for my appeal, a reporter for *The Telegraph* rang to ask if she could interview me for an article that she was writing about foreign convicts in Spain.

'I'd love to do it,' I told her. 'When can we meet up?'

I felt as if I was finally being given a platform to let the world know how I was being treated.

The reporter, who was called Elisabeth, ended up staying on the island for four days and asked me all sorts of questions about what it was like to be arrested in the land of bullfights and paella. Drug mules had been in the news a lot in the UK and the public were interested in what happened to these people when they were caught in Spain. This woman seemed like somebody I could trust. I sensed that she was interested in getting to the truth rather than twisting my words around, which allowed me to build-up a good rapport with her. She came across as your average, down-to-earth, middle-aged woman, not one of the bloodthirsty media types that people always talk about.

Elisabeth wanted to know what the British Consulate had done to help me, which was an easy question to answer. The only assistance that they had offered since my initial arrest was the list of solicitors that I could use. Other than that, they had done nothing whatsoever.

'I'm a convicted drug smuggler so they want as little to do with me as possible,' I explained. 'They don't seem to care at all.'

'Would you be willing to travel to their office in Santa Cruz with me so that I can see the response they give you when you ask for help?' Elisabeth asked.

'Yeah, why not?' I told her. 'Then you'll be able to see what they're like for yourself.'

The staff at the Consulate were just as I expected them to be. Not only were they about as much use as a chocolate teapot, but they were also very rude and made it clear that they classed me as the lowest of the low. As far as they were concerned, I had been found guilty, so they wanted nothing more to do with me.

'Thanks anyway,' Elisabeth told them as we wrapped up the meeting.

Little did I know that as I was leaving the building, shaking my head at how pathetic the Consulate were, one of their employees was phoning up the Guardia Civil to tell them that I was trying to procure emergency documents in an attempt to leave the country. I returned home to a phone call from my mum warning me that the court was thinking of revoking my bail.

It was a good thing I had Elisabeth with me or I could have been hauled off back to Salto del Negro. As it was, I had a witness to the fact that I only went to find out what help I could receive. The British Consulate are meant to be on the side of British citizens, so why they were so intent on having me locked up, I will never know. They did a lot more harm than good and destroyed what little trust I had left in the establishment.

When the article finally went to print, it was nice to see that Elisabeth had portrayed me as a human being rather than the druggie scum the Consulate thought I was. The piece not only highlighted the plight of foreign nationals dealing with the Spanish legal system, but also created much-needed publicity for my case. It would have been easy for me to pass unnoticed because I was one of many Brits who had got themselves in trouble on the island. There are probably more British criminals in Tenerife than there are in some parts of Britain. The only thing that separated me from the masses was my innocence, which was something that I still had to convince the public of. The more they knew about my case, the more likely they would be to offer their support.

The problem was that some people's methods of helping made my life a lot more difficult. My boss was adamant that I should flee back to England and fired me from my job to try and hammer the point across. His logic was that I would run out of money without a regular income and have to go back home to live with Mum again. He was being cruel to be kind but it sure didn't seem that way at the time. I cut off all contact with him and immediately set about finding work elsewhere.

A couple of days later, I managed to get a job at a Celtic Football Club bar called the Irish Fiddler. Celtic are a traditionally Catholic football team who are popular with Catholics from all over Scotland and Ireland. The Fiddler showed all of the team's big games and had live bands on at night-time playing Irish music. It was a lively place to work in and had a smashing atmosphere.

All of the other workers at the bar were either Scottish or Irish but the clientele were a wide variety of different nationalities. Everybody got on really well with one another and there was never any hint of trouble – even though a Northern Irish lad turned up one day, dressed in full Rangers' kit. For those of you who aren't familiar with Scottish football, the rivalry between Rangers and Celtic goes much deeper than football because while Celtic's following is predominantly Catholic, Rangers are traditionally Protestant and sectarianism is still a major issue north of the border. You don't walk into a Celtic bar wearing a Rangers top unless you're trying to get a reaction.

'You've got some balls coming in here in that,' I told him.

'Yeah, and what of it?' he grinned back at me.

He had quite a rural accent that sounded a lot softer than the Belfast dialects I had heard on telly.

'Nothing,' I shrugged. 'You can wear what you like. If you want to wind people up then that's up to you. What brings you to these parts anyway? You over on holiday?'

'Yeah,' the lad told me. 'I've been working hard defending the country so I needed a week off in the sun.'

Now it all fell into place. This fella couldn't have come across as more of a stereotypical squaddie if he'd tried. He had that rough edge to him that most army boys have got and there was an anger behind his eyes that suggested that he had probably seen some things he wished he hadn't. Physically speaking he was unremarkable. He was tubby with a receding hairline and a very Irish-looking face.

'My name's Jamie. It's good to meet you.'

'Likewise,' I told him. 'I'm Terry. Welcome to the bar, I'm sure you'll fit right in.'

This fiery-looking customer was certainly a character. I've always had a thing for Irish boys, possibly because my father's family are from there. Jamie didn't exactly fit the bill of my perfect man but I admired his confidence and self-assurance so I decided to stay and have a drink with him after work. He drank like only the Irish know how to and we were soon both paralytic. I got the impression that he probably had a drink problem. He put the pints away like there was no tomorrow and didn't show any signs of slowing down.

'You're a good-looking girl, you know that?' he slurred as we staggered down Veronicas together, almost bumping into drunken holidaymakers as we went.

'Thanks,' I told him. 'You aren't too bad yourself.'

Before I knew it, we were passionately kissing one another, breathing beery vapours into each other's faces. Looking back, I don't know what I saw in him. He definitely wasn't my usual type but there was something about him that I was attracted to. Maybe it was the fact that he was a fellow drinker. I didn't go out boozing half as much as I used to, but still loved to get drunk every now and again. An alcoholic's passion for getting uncontrollably blotto never truly goes away. The best that you can hope for is to keep it at bay.

'I'm going back to Northern Ireland soon,' Jamie told me. 'I've got another holiday planned for a few months down the line so maybe I can see you then?'

'Sure,' I said. 'Why not?'

This was to be the start of a very unconventional relationship. Whenever Jamie visited the island, we would be like boyfriend and girlfriend, but then as soon as he went home, I lived the single life again. I was never faithful to him and I daresay he probably went with his fair share of women in Northern Ireland as well. When you're going out with somebody who lives hundreds of miles away, it's difficult to prevent your affections from wandering. It was a holiday romance that extended past its natural finish point and really should have ended when his flight left for Ireland.

Now that I had a man in my life I needed a place of my own so I moved into a posh new apartment in the Windsor Park complex. Windsor Park was at the opposite end of the spectrum to the Bungamar, filled with large, extravagant flats that you could really feel at home in. I had a spare bedroom and a balcony to sit out on when the heat got too much for me and I felt as if I was living in the lap of luxury. It was just a pity I would have to trade it all in for iron bars and bunk beds if I didn't win my case.

By this stage I was used to having what little hope I had left dashed, so it came as no surprise when my appeal failed. This time I didn't even feel upset; I just thought, 'Oh well, it was to be expected.' I was allowed to start a second appeal so I was still free for the time being, which meant that my perfect flat and job and not so perfect relationship could continue for a little bit longer.

As per the first appeal, I had no idea how long the second one was going to take or what it would entail. Once again, it was to be done in my absence, which I found a bit disconcerting because there would be no way of knowing how well my solicitor was fighting my corner. I hoped that the process would take a while so that I could put off going to prison for as long as possible.

The weeks went by and I eventually managed to put my case to the back of my mind. There was no point spending every waking moment thinking about it, so I tried to act as if it had gone away. The court kept me in the dark for what seemed like an eternity. The optimist in me thought, 'Maybe they've forgotten about me', but the realist knew that ten-year prison sentences don't just disappear into thin air. As more and more time elapsed, the optimist became louder and the realist grew quieter. Before long, the one remaining voice was telling me that the Spanish authorities had probably lost me in the system. They seemed so incompetent that it was perfectly plausible. Perhaps my luck had finally changed. It was about time something went my way for once.

My mum was convinced that the government had washed their hands of my case. Her logic was that they wouldn't have left me in the free world for so long without any restrictions if they truly believed that I was guilty.

'You should just apply for a passport,' she told me. 'If it comes through then they surely can't want you to stay there.'

'What have I got to lose?' I shrugged. 'I might as well give it a go.'

Whilst I was waiting to see whether or not my application was successful, Mum received a letter from our local MP John Bercow. She had been corresponding with him about the case and he had been giving her advice and support. Apparently he had got a letter from the Spanish ambassador saying that I was 'released on 17 June 1997 without further admission'. This could be taken in one of two ways: it either meant I hadn't returned to prison yet or that they had decided not to send me back at all.

'If her passport comes through then you could maybe try and see if she can come home,' John told my hopeful mother later that day on the phone. 'It's a little bit ambiguous but it seems as if the ambassador's saying that they've let her off the hook.'

Mum was absolutely ecstatic but I remained a little sceptical. The wording was so vague that it could have meant anything. They could still decline my application and tell me that the case was ongoing. I was just going to have to sit tight and see how it all panned out.

Sure enough, a couple of days later, Mum rang up to tell me that my passport had arrived. I had ordered it to my address back home and it had been delivered there without any problems. This time I was convinced that my ordeal was over. I knew that my case was at risk of being re-opened if I stayed in Tenerife but still felt gutted that I had to leave the island. I had finally got some stability in my life and was sad that I had to abandon it. My friends and family seemed to think that I should get the hell out of the country whilst I had the chance. Jamie kept going on and on about how I should come and live with him in Northern Ireland. Everybody was oblivious to my feelings and expected me to be as overjoyed as they were.

Mr Fitzgerald was particularly pleased when I told him the news. I wasn't planning on speaking to him again but one of my friends invited me to a birthday celebration at his bar and seeing him made me realise what a good mate I had lost.

'Look this is stupid,' I told him as the rest of the group tucked into their birthday meal. 'I know you only had my best interests at heart. I'm going to be leaving the island pretty soon so we might as well make up.'

'You know you would have never won your case, don't you?' he asked me. 'Your appeal would have failed and you would have had to do ten years. You've made the right decision Terry, and I'm glad we're friends again.'

'Keep it between me and you that I'm going,' I told him. 'I don't want it spreading round the place just in case the cops get wind of it and try to throw a spanner in the works.'

'You can count on me,' Mr Fitzgerald assured me. 'I wouldn't want to mess things up for you.'

I felt a lot better now that we were mates again. Looking back, I think the fact that he was so intent on forcing me to go home showed how much he cared about me. He was a kind, warm-hearted person and I couldn't have asked for a better friend to confide in.

Mum and I came to the decision that the easiest way for me to get back to England would be to get a train from mainland Spain to London. I had decided against flying because I didn't know if it was safe after my haemorrhage and didn't fancy having another aneurysm part way through the trip. The only piece of advice that I had been given at the hospital was 'don't travel anywhere by plane' and although they didn't specify how long this applied for, I felt it would be foolish to risk disobeying them. This meant that the journey would be a lot more nerve wracking because it would take longer to arrive safely on British soil. I was going to have to travel overnight and endure a full twenty-four hours of bracing myself in case the Guardia Civil got onto me.

The night before my flight to the mainland was spent absolutely bricking it. Even though I knew I had a legitimate passport, I still had a funny feeling that I was going to be arrested. If I got caught at customs, they might charge me with being a fugitive and add a couple of years onto my sentence. My voyage home could either end in triumph or tragedy. There was no way of knowing which one it would be until it was too late.

Mum was planning on flying over to Tenerife and getting the plane across to Spain with me. That would be the easy part of the journey because I wouldn't need a passport. After that I was going to find out once and for all if I could leave the country without my name being flagged up as awaiting jail. There were two possible outcomes to the trip: freedom or immediate imprisonment. Option number two would at least get it over with. If I was going to be locked up then I figured they might as well just do it.

Chapter 9

TERRY THE FUGITIVE

'Are you all set for your great escape then?' Mr Fitzgerald asked me the following morning as I exhaustedly plonked myself down in the passenger seat of his car.

It was nice of him to offer to take me to the airport but his kindness made me feel sad because I knew that I was probably never going to see him again after he had dropped me off. The only circumstances in which I would be likely to return to Tenerife were if I was dragged back kicking and screaming to face my punishment. My dream of living in a tropical paradise had amounted to nothing. Not only was I heading home with my tail between my legs, but it was also now impossible for me to ever give the island another go. I felt like a complete and utter failure.

'Yeah I guess so,' I told him. 'I owe you one for the lift.'

Mr Fitzgerald was the only person I had told that I was leaving. Nobody else could be trusted to keep their mouth shut. If the Guardia Civil had got wind of my plan they might have taken steps to keep me in the country. They could have even reminded the court that I still needed sending down and made sure I was jailed straightaway.

The journey to the airport was both heartbreaking and terrifying. I didn't know which emotion was worse: the sadness that I felt at having to leave behind the life that I had worked so hard to create or the mind-numbing fear of being busted.

'You take care of yourself,' Mr Fitzgerald told me as we pulled up at the airport entrance. 'If you ever do come back, you're more than welcome at the bar.'

I thanked him for his help and heaved my heavy suitcases out of the door and onto the scorching hot tarmac. It was time to put on my poker face. If I looked anxious and upset then people would be more likely to twig that something was up. I was going to have to act as if I was just your average British citizen coming back from a holiday.

Mum was pleased to see me but nervous in case our journey ended in disaster. She gave me a quick hug then ushered me over to our terminal. At least I would be able to relax during the flight to Spain. It was only when I crossed the border on the train that I needed to worry. We had to change at Paris, which added an extra leg to the trip. I couldn't wait until it was all over.

The flight to Madrid-Barajas Airport took no time at all. Before we knew it, we were at the train station, waiting impatiently to board our carriage.

'*Excusez-moi* ladies, I need to take your passports from you before you get on. I'll return them once you reach your final destination,' a French ticket collector instructed us as we made our way towards the edge of the platform.

I didn't understand why he couldn't give them back to us straightaway. This was going to add a whole new level of tension to our voyage. It meant that rather than being able to relax once we had been given the all clear, we would be on pins for the entire journey, wondering whether or not I was going to be flagged up as a fugitive.

We were forced to share a carriage with two French girls, which was a pain because it meant that we were unable to comfort one another for fear of them overhearing us. As the train pulled out of the station, all of the air felt as if it had been sucked out of my lungs and my heart pounded away like an Indian war drum. Was the train going to stop part way through the trip so that the police could come aboard and arrest me? The more I thought about it, the more paranoid I became, until I started seeing Guardia Civil officers hiding behind every tree we passed. Mum had brought a load of snacks to eat but I felt physically sick and couldn't manage anything. It was going to be a very long journey.

Luckily our fears turned out to be completely unfounded; we were able to travel all the way to London without any trouble whatsoever. The ticket collector handed back our passports as the train came into Waterloo and I breathed a heavy sigh of relief. Then a customs officer beckoned us towards him the minute we left the carriage.

'This is it,' I thought to myself. 'We've managed to make it all the way to England only to be busted at the last minute.'

My palms were sweaty and all of the spit in my mouth had suddenly dried up. Attempting to act casual was going to take every ounce of my energy. I prayed to God that it was just a routine check but knew deep down that we had probably been rumbled.

'Is there a problem?' I asked the officer, knowing full well that there was.

'No, no problem,' he lied through his teeth. 'I just need to check what's in your bags.'

This was when it all clicked into place. I was carrying the same hard-shelled Benetton suitcase that I had seen being smashed apart by customs officers on countless documentaries about smugglers. These bags were notorious for being used to conceal drugs. The officer hadn't got a clue about my conviction on the island. He was just convinced that Mum and I had something illegal stashed away in our cases.

'Go ahead and check,' I told him, wondering what it was about me that gave off such a criminal vibe. This time there would be no mountains of cocaine for him to find though, just the mountains of personal belongings I had amassed in Tenerife. I had nothing whatsoever to hide, so the fact that he had singled us out was more of an irritation than anything.

Once the officer had finally finished going through our things, he eyed us both suspiciously and then put everything back into the cases.

'What's the purpose of your trip?'

'We've been travelling round Europe,' Mum told him. 'We were planning on doing a couple more countries but my dad's been taken ill so we had to come back in a hurry.'

'OK you're going to have to follow me,' he said. 'I'm not one hundred per cent convinced by your story, so I'm afraid I'm going to have to get a female officer to carry out a strip-search.'

By this stage, having my dignity violated was something that I had become depressingly familiar with, but I was angry that my mum would have to go through it. She had never broken a law in her life so what right did this jumped-up idiot have to treat her like a criminal? I felt like telling him where to go but somehow managed to keep calm.

Even after they had poked and prodded us all over our bodies, the customs officers still seemed convinced that we had something to hide.

'I think we need to do a couple more checks here, just to be on the safe side,' the head honcho told me. 'Can you please show me your passports so that I can make sure that they're valid?'

Now I had good reason to be concerned. I did as he commanded and braced myself ready for a pair of handcuffs to snap shut around my wrists.

'OK that one seems to be in order. Now what about the other one?'

I felt like jumping up and punching the air with joy. This meant that my passage to England was one hundred per cent legit. Surely if it was illegal for me to leave Spain then there would have been a record of it on the system and customs would have got onto it. It looked as if my case really had disappeared into thin air. The officer scrutinised Mum's passport for at least a good five minutes before finally passing it back to her.

'Sorry for the inconvenience,' he conceded. 'We need to check these things through thoroughly; it's nothing personal. You can leave the station now.'

Mum looked at me and I looked back at Mum. We had done it; I could finally relax.

'Let's get the hell out of here before he changes his mind,' she told me.

My sister was waiting outside the station to pick us up. She had been going out of her mind with worry because we were so late.

'What on earth took you so long?' she shouted, tears welling up in her eyes.

'It's a long story,' I told her. 'Now put your foot down and drive because I really don't want to stick around much longer.'

We headed off back to Wingrave at a rapid rate of knots. As we approached the lush, green fields that surround the village, I thanked my lucky stars that I had finally managed to make it home. The Guardia Civil couldn't touch me now that I was no longer on Spanish soil. The British police could arrest me and send me back to Spain but it was highly doubtful that they would. It looked as if everybody had forgotten about Terry the international cocaine trafficker and I had now reverted back to being Terry the average citizen.

The car pulled up into our drive and I thought, 'This is it then. No more island life for me.' It was a cold, overcast day that couldn't have been in starker contrast to the constant scorching heat of Tenerife. I was relieved that I had managed to avoid a decade in the slammer, but gutted to be back in rainy old England.

My first few days at home were spent grieving for the life of sun, sea and sangria that I had left behind. Wingrave is a lovely little village but it isn't exactly what you would call the height of glamour. I longed to feel the heat of the sand against my back as I lay on the beach, or hear the excited chatter of English tourists on the first day of their holidays. Although I missed Tenerife like crazy, I was also terrified in case I ever got sent back. I was really mixed up.

Jamie came to visit me a week after my return to the UK, which only added to my misery. He was in England for an army training exercise and decided to pop in to see me whilst he was there. I should have been pleased that he wanted to spend time with me but felt as if it was partly his fault that I had left the island. If he hadn't gone on and on about how I should come and live with him in Northern Ireland, then the thought of going back to Britain probably wouldn't have been at the forefront of my mind. As it was, I had abandoned my friends, my job and my flat despite the fact that the Spanish government might not have even followed up my case if I had just stayed put.

To be honest I probably put a downer on Jamie's visit with my attitude. It's difficult to seem enthusiastic about anything when you feel as if your dreams have been put through a paper shredder. He still seemed made up to be in my company though.

'Now that you're not on the wanted list any more, you can move in with me and we can be a proper couple,' he crooned to me as I sat and sulked.

'Yeah maybe,' I shrugged. 'I'll see how I get on here before I decide either way.'

I probably would have remained just as noncommittal if I hadn't had some bad news a couple of weeks after his visit. My dad was diagnosed with oesophageal cancer. He had a tumour in his gullet and there was a danger that it could spread throughout his body. The doctor recommended chemotherapy but if that didn't work then he was going to die. I couldn't even imagine what my life would be like without him. We had always been extremely close and he had been there for me whenever I needed him.

The news sent me spiralling into another fit of depression. I was even more scared for Dad than I had been for myself when I had my haemorrhage. As well as being worried sick in case I lost him, the fact that he could be in perfect nick one minute and then get diagnosed with something as serious as cancer the next, made me worry about my own health. I hadn't had a check-up for a while so I booked myself an appointment just in case anything had gone wrong since my operation.

It was a good thing I went in because the doctor told me that blood was seeping back into my head.

'Your coil's slipped out and become ineffective,' he explained to me. 'I'm afraid we're going to have to operate straightaway. It's extremely dangerous for you at the moment. You could drop down dead any minute.'

I would have been absolutely bricking it if Dad's cancer hadn't eclipsed everything else in my mind. I had been successfully operated on once before and knew that my condition was curable, even if there was a lot of risk involved. Dad, on the other hand, was going to have a major struggle on his hands. I just hoped to God that he was going to pull through.

The recoiling operation ended up doing nothing because the neck of my aneurysm was too wide for it to work. The doctor told me that this was the reason the last coil was unable to permanently stem the bleeding. I couldn't help but wonder why the Spaniards hadn't deduced this when I first went into hospital. I could well have died if I hadn't gone in for the check-up.

Fortunately, coiling isn't the only way to fix a brain haemorrhage. There is another method known as 'clipping', which involves removing part of the skull and closing up the aneurysm using a clip. This technique succeeded in patching up the leak but left me with a shaven head and twenty-five stitches. I looked like Frankenstein's monster when the surgeon was done with me.

I've got a tendency to run away when things go wrong and after being discharged from hospital, I made up my mind that I was going to Northern Ireland as soon as I had made a full recovery. I figured that there was little point in living in a sleepy village in the sticks if my existence was still going to be characterised by one horrendous, unexpected incident after another, so I made plans to fly across. Dad was still awaiting his chemo and I couldn't face seeing him get sick as a result of the treatment. The idea of somebody that I loved suffering so much discomfort made me want to get as far away as possible. Kelly was still living in London so Mum might have benefited from me being at home to comfort her, but I just couldn't bring myself to stay.

Jamie was over the moon that I was going to live with him.

'I share a house with my mum and dad but they'll love having you here,' he told me. 'Northern Ireland is a lot different to England so I'll send you some books to read to let you know the crack.'

The books that he sent me were all about Protestantism and 'the troubles' but to be honest I didn't really think much of it at the time. My mum's a Protestant and my dad's a Catholic so sectarianism had never been an issue in my family. I was brought up as a Protestant and still practiced the faith but could have easily been a Catholic if Dad had got his way.

Jamie sent me a lot of political literature as well, which was equally uninteresting. I couldn't have cared less if Ulster was part of Britain or Ireland; it made no difference whatsoever. In hindsight, the nature of the things that he was posting should have given me an indication of what type of place I was heading into, but I failed to see the signs until it was too late. I was in for a major eye-opener; I was about to enter a world where being in the wrong place at the wrong time could cost you your kneecaps.

Chapter 10

ANOTHER ESCAPE

On the day before my flight, I felt excited but at the same time slightly sad because I knew that Ulster would never be able to compare to Tenerife. I was going to be living in a little town called Randalstown, which has a similar-sized population to Wingrave. It wasn't a place that I would have ever chosen to visit if I hadn't met Jamie, but I was still determined to make the best of things and find out what it had to offer. At least I would get a change of scenery and be able to get away from everything that was going on back home.

My first impression of Randalstown was that it was your average quaint, little village. Appearances can be deceptive though because it was a hotbed of religious prejudice and the Catholic and Protestant populations hated each other with a passion. It was about three-quarter Catholic and a quarter Protestant, which meant that Jamie and I were surrounded by people who cursed the ground we walked upon.

As well as being segregated in terms of religion, Northern Ireland was also split in terms of the paramilitary groups that each area was associated with. There were five main terrorist organisations in the country: the IRA and the Real IRA, who were separatist Catholics; and the Ulster Volunteer Force, Ulster Freedom Fighters and Ulster Defence Association, who were all loyalist Protestants. The Protestant part of Randalstown was controlled by the UVF, who were a little more peaceful than the other loyalist groups. The UDA and the UFF seemed more like gangsters than paramilitaries. They were involved in selling drugs and stolen property and had been nicknamed the Wombles because they were said to be able to get hold of anything, just as the Wombles on kids' TV could get their hands on whatever they needed by making it out of rubbish. The main difference is that the cartoon characters would make things to help people out but the UDA seemed more interested in getting hold of bombs, machine guns and the like.

So where did I fit into all this craziness? Well the Catholics classed anybody who was English as being a loyalist so I was forced to associate only with Protestants, even though I was technically half Proddy and half Catholic. I would be lying if I said it wasn't a major culture shock. You don't expect such hatred to exist in a tiny place like Randalstown. I found it difficult to take in the fact that people could despise each other just because they chose to practice a slightly different form of Christianity. It all seemed very bizarre to me.

You would think the Protestant paramilitaries would have all got on with one another seeing as they were fighting for the same cause, but there were even divisions within each denomination. The UDA and the UVF had had several bloody feuds over the years and definitely weren't the best of mates. The best way of looking at each faction was as a gang rather than a terrorist group. The country was basically divided up among violent criminals.

I first became aware of the level of support that the UVF had in the local area when I went for a drink at the pub near Jamie's house shortly after I arrived. People were chatting about what good work the group was doing and seemed to regard them as being heroes rather than terrorists. The fact that the drinkers were openly praising violent paramilitaries should have put me off staying, but I figured that nobody was giving me any hassle so it was nothing to do with me. The Protestants liked the English because they saw Northern Ireland as being part of the UK. It was the Catholics that I had to worry about, as I soon learnt when I tried to go in one of their boozers.

I rubbished the idea of only socialising in the areas that Jamie picked out for me and thought that surely nobody would be nasty enough to hate me just because I was born in a different country. I had been warned to avoid the Catholic districts like the plague but couldn't see the harm in trying out a pub on the edge of one, just to see how the drinkers would react to me. It looked to be a bit of a rough old place, but then again most pubs I'd seen so far in Northern Ireland were, so I thought nothing of it.

The second I opened my mouth to order a drink, everybody stopped what they were doing.

'Get out,' the barman told me. 'We don't want any trouble in here.'

'What are you kicking me out for?' I asked him. 'I haven't done anything.'

'Because you're English,' he told me. 'I'd keep well away from here if I were you.'

He didn't sound annoyed; he sounded as if he was getting rid of me for my own safety. I was still pissed off though because I didn't like the idea of people telling me where I could or couldn't drink.

'Fine I'll go,' I frowned. 'I know when I'm not wanted.'

The Catholics couldn't have cared less what I was like as a person; as far as they were concerned all Englishmen were their enemies and there were no exceptions. It was a reminder that I was living in a place where identity meant everything. Jamie had walked into a Celtic bar in Tenerife in a full Rangers kit and nobody had said a word to him. Had he done the same in Randalstown, he probably would have ended up getting a bullet in his head. If you didn't follow the same set of beliefs as somebody else in Northern Ireland then they viewed you as being against what they stood for. It was certainly going to be interesting living in this crazy mixed-up country.

Jamie was just as sectarian as the rest of his townsfolk. He would point out that he was a British citizen at every available opportunity and even painted the curb outside his house red, white and blue. I couldn't understand why he was so obsessed with being British. As long as I was treated equally to the rest of the population, I couldn't have cared less which nation's government laid claim to the land I lived in.

Although I wasn't too keen on the country's politics, there were still enough things about Northern Ireland that I liked to encourage me to stay there. The Protestants were all very friendly people and treated me as if I was one of their own. I soon got to know all of Jamie's friends and adjusted to life in Ulster fairly quickly. The problem was that the main pastime was drinking. It was the worst place on earth for a recovering alcoholic to move to because alcohol was treated as a religion by the locals rather than just something to drink. I got the impression that pubs were like Irishmen's temples and they worshipped at them morning, noon and night.

Jamie drank even more than I did and became aggressive when he had had a few. Every time we went out boozing together we ended up having a massive row, which put a strain on the relationship. He would argue at the drop of a hat and get very physical, shoving me around the place and grabbing hold of me so hard that it hurt. If I hadn't had so much on my mind I would have probably seen the signs and got out fairly early on, but as it was, I was so preoccupied by my dad's illness that I didn't even notice the direction things were heading in. I often sat alone in my room, worrying about how Dad was holding up. I was so anxious that I couldn't even bring myself to ring Mum up to ask how he was doing. One of the few times that I did phone her, she told me that Dad wanted me to stay in Northern Ireland so that I didn't get upset by how much he was suffering. Mum agreed that this would be a good idea. In my heart of hearts I knew that running away wasn't going to solve anything but I lacked the strength to face up to reality.

Meanwhile, Jamie's temper tantrums went from bad to worse. He would get in uncontrollable fits of rage, where he threw his things around the room and shouted at the top of his voice. One of the places where his anger manifested itself was at the football. He was a massive Rangers fan and used the Rangers/Celtic rivalry as a way of expressing his hatred of Catholics. I foolishly agreed to go to one of the games and couldn't believe the levels of animosity. The Rangers fans were shouting sectarian abuse for the entire ninety minutes. I left the city straight after the game because it felt as if there was going to be a full-on war between the fans. They say that we have problems with the football in England, but it's nothing compared to what I saw there.

Despite being so heavily into loyalist politics, Jamie still celebrated St Patrick's Day, which I could never understand. If he was so obsessed with Ulster being part of the UK, why did he want to commemorate a day in honour of the patron saint of Ireland? It seemed to me as if he just wanted an excuse to go out and get trolleyed. It would have been better for me if he had refused to acknowledge the occasion altogether, because it was on this day that he decided to propose to me.

Most people are over the moon to get engaged but I can't say I was too excited about the prospect of marrying someone whose anger was so out of control. The only reason I said 'yes' was because I knew that our relationship would be over if I said 'no' and didn't fancy heading home to England yet. The thought of making such a powerful commitment to somebody who was as volatile as Jamie made me feel sick, but still beat returning to Wingrave and seeing Dad get more and more poorly.

Jamie didn't seem particularly excited either. I think he popped the question because his family had been putting pressure on him to tie the knot. His mum and dad were all for it and set about building a house for us to live in at the bottom of their garden, which I thought was bizarre. Why any newly married couple would want to shack up with one another in their parents' backyard is totally beyond me. The Northern Irish did a lot of things that weren't the norm in England, but this definitely wasn't one of them. It was just as peculiar a thing to do over there as it would have been to do in England. The whole family seemed absolutely bonkers.

The only thing that Jamie and I had in common was our love of drink. I soon reached the stage where my hands would shake if I was unable to get any booze, which made me realise that I was once again in the grip of a serious addiction. This time though, I was drinking to forget. Every time I rang home, Mum would tell me how poorly my dad was and I would be desperate to cleanse the thought of his discomfort from my brain. Sometimes I drank so much that I blacked out and came round hours later. It was very disorientating. I found myself having to quiz my friends after I had regained consciousness to find out what had gone on earlier in the night. The dangerous thing about Northern Ireland was that there was nobody there to tell me to slow down. It was the norm to overdo it, which meant that no one ever put the brakes on my excessive boozing.

My drinking hit the roof when Dad started his chemo. He found it impossible to keep his food down and felt permanently exhausted, which had me beside myself with worry. The only thing that I could do to avoid going under, was constantly reassure myself that the therapy would eventually cure him. If it got rid of the cancer then his pain and suffering would all be worthwhile.

The staff at the hospital kept feeding us false hope. They let us think that Dad still had a fighting chance right up until I got the call to say the tumour was inoperable.

'It's spread to his liver,' the doctor told me. 'I'm really sorry, there's nothing more that we can do for him.'

So this was it then; Dad was going to die. I have since learnt that only a small percentage of people ever recover from oesophageal cancer. By the time it's diagnosed, it has usually spread too far to be effectively treated. Why did they constantly tell me that he was likely to pull through? They should have said, 'Your dad is probably not going to survive no matter how much chemo he has. You might as well say your goodbyes to him now.' At least then it wouldn't have come as such an awful shock to me when I got the news.

Jamie's mum and dad were standing behind me when the call came through. They were quick to throw their two pence in, which really got my back up.

'You should go home and be with him right away,' his mum advised me. 'There's no sense staying here. You need to be with your family.'

'I'm not going anywhere,' I told her. 'I'll cope with this in my own way, thank you very much.'

The thought of seeing Dad on his last legs sent shivers down my spine. I wasn't ready to face him so soon after hearing the bad news so I decided that I was going to stay in Ireland until I had managed to get my head round what I had just heard. Jamie's family would no doubt go on at me ad infinitum but at the end of the day, he was my father not theirs so it was up to me how I handled his illness. I know they probably had my welfare at heart but I was irritable, angry and just wanted to be left alone.

You would have thought that Jamie would have been especially nice to me after hearing that my Dad was going to die, but he was just as hot-headed and argumentative as ever. The more I got to know him, the more mixed up he seemed to be. When I looked him in the eyes, I saw such an intense hatred that I felt scared to be in the same room as him. He was definitely not someone that you could ever describe as being sympathetic. Maybe the fact that I chose to stay with him was a reflection of my self-destructive tendencies. I could have walked away at any time but didn't, which meant I was as much to blame for the dysfunctional state of our relationship as he was.

The other thing that bothered me about my loving fiancé was his tendency to randomly go missing. Sometimes he would disappear for days on end and I would be left alone with his family. At first I assumed that it was something to do with his job but then one day I was in the house on my own when I received a phone call from a girl who claimed that she was pregnant with his baby. I felt angry that he had lied to me but can't say that I was particularly sad because I had known that the relationship was doomed from the start. I think the only reason I didn't end things earlier was because being engaged to a Northern Irish lad gave me an excuse to stay in Randalstown and avoid facing up to Dad's cancer.

The minute Jamie arrived back home I unleashed a torrent of abuse in his direction and let him know exactly what I thought of him.

'I knew that there was something going on,' I shouted. 'I trusted you and you betrayed me. Why didn't you just tell me if you weren't happy? You didn't have to go and get somebody up the duff.'

Jamie gave as good as he got and called me every name under the sun. Looking back, I strongly suspect he engineered the situation so that he could cause an argument and use it as an excuse to get rid of me. There was usually at least one member of his family in the house at any given time, so why had I been left alone when the girl who was carrying his child had his landline number? It seemed as if he wanted me to find out about his cheating ways and finally end our turbulent relationship.

A couple of days later, Jamie ordered me to pack my bags and leave.

'You're not welcome here,' he told me. 'You need to book yourself a flight home. You can stay at Nanna's house until you get a ticket sorted out, but after that you're off.'

I usually feel sad when a relationship ends no matter how bad it is, but this time I just felt relieved. His gran was a hardened loyalist like the rest of his family but it was still nice of her to put me up, and living with her beat staying with him any day of the week. I wished his baby's mum the best of luck because she was certainly going to need it.

Luckily one of the friends that I had made during a stint working at a factory to earn a couple of extra quid was in need of a new housemate, so I was able to put off moving home and facing up to my dad's illness for a little bit longer. I should have gone back to comfort my mum but remembered Dad's advice that I should stay in Northern Ireland. My pal lived in the nearby town of Ballymena, a lot bigger than Randalstown and even more divided. It was around three quarters Protestant and the loyalist areas were split between the UVF, the UFF and the UDA.

The street I moved onto was called Patrick Place and could have passed for Coronation Street. It was a cobbled road lined with old-fashioned terraced houses that suited their inhabitants to a tee because a lot of the locals agreed with the politics of the UDA and had very backwards-thinking views on religion. As with Randalstown, nobody made any effort whatsoever to put the past behind them and get on with the Catholics. The two faiths hated one another with a passion and would rather have died than mixed.

The strong UDA presence in the area didn't bother me too much because they sold gold jewellery, which I have always been into. In hindsight it was almost certainly stolen but I was blissfully unaware of that at the time. I didn't ask where it had come from and they didn't tell me.

The girl that I was living with was a drinker, which was also fine by me. There was a pub five minutes from our house so we spent most of our time in there. It was a little more risky going into the local boozers now that I was single though, because the other drinkers were suspicious of a lone English girl drinking in a rough-and-ready Irish watering hole. A few of the regulars thought that I was an MI5 agent sent to infiltrate the paramilitaries. I found this hilarious at the time but in hindsight it could have got me into serious trouble.

Fortunately most of the locals were sensible enough to know that I was about as far from James Bond as you could get. One of them even invited me to a parade on Shankhill Road in Belfast in honour of a dead terrorist. I agreed to go out of morbid curiosity and spent the whole time feeling horribly on edge. Shankhill Road area was a notorious Protestant ghetto with murals commemorating fallen paramilitaries all over the place and bullet holes in the walls. It looked like a cross between a sink estate and a war zone. If I had known what it was like before I went then I would have definitely made my excuses and given it a miss.

The territorialism of the locals in Belfast was even more extreme than I'd seen elsewhere. Shankhill Road was divided up between the UDA and the UVF and the two groups hated one another. I found it unbelievable that you could walk down the road and suddenly enter an area where completely different rules applied. There was political graffiti everywhere so at least you knew who controlled which part of the street. It must have been terrible for the children who lived there because they had to walk past huge pictures of machine-gun-toting blokes in balaclavas every time they went to school. It was little wonder so many people from the area ended up as extremists. Sectarian propaganda was sprayed on every available surface.

At the parade, a local band played pipe music and people stood about and drank. It would have been quite cheerful if there weren't banners emblazoned with pictures of paramilitaries all over the place, and signs warning that anybody caught selling drugs would be tarred and feathered. This was the UVF's way of having a go at the UDA for peddling dope. The UVF didn't approve of criminal activity whether the proceeds were going to 'the cause' or not, which was the claim made by the UDA. How anybody could think that publicly tarring and feathering someone was somehow less immoral than selling drugs was really beyond me.

I left the event later that evening wondering how on earth people could live their lives with so much hatred in their hearts. The Shankhill Road locals thrived on bigotry and seemed to enjoy creating tension. Compared to Belfast, Ballymena and Randalstown were both relatively tame. If I had wandered into a Catholic pub in the capital then I would have no doubt got more than just a friendly warning that I was in the wrong neck of the woods. I might have ended up with at least one less kneecap.

It was funny because even though I was surrounded by sectarian nutters, the thing that really bothered me about my life in Northern Ireland was my housemate's whining. She was quite a bit younger than me and complained bitterly about every little thing. Don't get me wrong, she was a damn sight easier to live with than Jamie, but still drove me round the twist. One of her main whinges was the fact that she never had enough money to go out with. She barely earned enough to pay the rent, which caused me no end of earache. In the end she decided that it would be more practical to live with her parents and left me in peace.

I was never lonely in the house on my own because the pub was so close by. Whenever I got bored, I went and had a natter and a drink with the regulars, which helped to take my mind off what was going on with Dad. I would have liked to hide away forever but unfortunately reality always catches up with you. It was a Monday morning when I got the call to say that Dad was dying. It was the worst news I have ever had in my life.

'Terry you've got to come home right away,' Mum told me. 'Your dad's only got a week left to live. He's got pleurisy and his lungs are filling up with liquid. He's in hospital at the moment but we're bringing him home tomorrow so that he can spend his last days with the family.'

Even though the doctor had already told me that Dad wasn't going to get better, I still felt shocked that he was going to die so soon. Pleurisy is one of many secondary illnesses that can be brought about by cancer. It causes the lining of the lungs to swell and can also create a build-up of pleural fluid in them, which is what happened to Dad. It was bad enough that he was being sick all the time whilst he was having the chemo; thinking about him drowning in his own lung juice was unbearable. The difference was that this time, there was to be no more burying my head in the sand. It was time to face up to my fears.

I assured Mum that I would be there as soon as possible and rushed round to my friend's house to ask him if he could look after my place whilst I was away. The area around Patrick Place wasn't hugely upmarket and I didn't want to come back from my father's deathbed to find that somebody had broken in. My mate agreed to check up on it at regular intervals, which gave me one less thing to worry about.

The journey to England was spent on the edge of tears. I knew I had to be strong for Dad's sake but it was easier said than done.

At around four o'clock that evening I arrived at Stoke Mandeville Hospital in Aylesbury to see a pale, stick-thin version of my father struggling to stay alive. He had gone from 14 stone to 9 stone and looked as if he was in a lot of pain. It was heartbreaking to see someone who meant so much to me in such an awful state.

The following day, we arranged for an ambulance to take Dad home so that he could spend his final moments in a comfortable environment. There was no sense in leaving him to die in hospital. He was better off in the place where we had shared so many happy memories.

On Friday 15 June, Dad finally passed away. We were all there when it happened, which made it extra traumatic. The only small piece of comfort that I could take from it was the fact that he no longer had to endure his body being ravaged by disease. If he had died a painless death then we might have been able to cope with it, but as it was, he left this world in horrendous circumstances. I just pray he's in a better place and smiling down on us.

We had the funeral a week after Dad's death. Knowing that he was going to die a long time in advance gave him time to plan his own send-off. An old, Cockney-style horse-drawn cart carried his body from our house to the village church whilst his favourite Irish songs played in the background. The minute it was over, we all headed to the local pub to drown our sorrows. Mum and Kelly were both absolutely devastated. Kel has a funny way of dealing with death; she tends to remain quiet and withdrawn rather than letting it all out and having a good cry. It was a lovely, sunny day so I sat on a bench outside and drank myself into a stupor. I don't think I'll ever be able to fully get over my father's death. It's the worst thing that has ever happened to me and believe you me, I've got of a lot of tragedies to choose from.

I only stayed in Wingrave for just under a month after the funeral. It's difficult to come to terms with a death in the family when you're surrounded by memories of the person that you've lost. I would have stayed longer but everything in the house reminded me of him so in the end I thought, 'I've had enough. I need to get out of here.' The Orange Day Parade was on in Northern Ireland so I asked my mum if she wanted to go to it with me. I figured it would help to take her mind off things.

'Yes, why not?' said Mum. 'I need every distraction I can get right now. It sounds like it could be a good day out.'

The Orange Day Parade is a day of festivities to mark the anniversary of the Protestants' victory over the Catholics in the Battle of the Boyne. It is supposedly an occasion when tensions run high between Protestants and Catholics, but it was still quite fun and light-hearted compared to the parade that I had been to on the Shankhill Road. There was no trouble whatsoever in the Protestant areas. It was only when the procession went through Catholic estates that things began to turn a little bit ugly but we stayed well away from that part of the march.

The parade held a dual purpose for the Protestants. It allowed them to gloat about their victory over the Catholics and also gave them another excuse to get drunk. I couldn't have cared less about the Battle of the Boyne; it was the drinking that I liked. I just saw it as a day of music and boozing. Mum enjoyed the procession so we were both happy. When she finally left for England, I felt pleased that I had managed to put a smile on her face. Nothing could ever erase Dad's death from her memory but I had at least been able to momentarily divert her attention from that fateful day. It was just a shame that I was unable to stop thinking about it for even a single second.

The next few weeks were spent drinking myself into oblivion in a desperate attempt to forget. A lot of the clubs in Randalstown and Ballymena had a strict 'no soldier' policy, which meant I knew which places I could go to without having to worry about bumping into Jamie. One of my favourite spots to dance the night away was at a big club in Ballymena town centre that played garage and house music. This was where I first laid eyes on Billy. He was small with spiky hair and had a cheeky look to him that I was immediately attracted to. I spent half of the night eyeing him up before eventually making a move and kissing him.

Within a matter of days, Billy and I were girlfriend and boyfriend. He was a lot more cheerful than Jamie had been and I appreciated the warmth of his character. Our relationship developed very quickly and we soon became incredibly close to one another. He was a fanatical Protestant but that came with the territory. You would have been hard pushed to find anybody in Ballymena who wasn't extreme in their views.

I felt as if I fitted into Northern Irish life a lot better as part of a couple than I did on my own. Nobody accused me of being a secret agent any more and I was able to live a relatively hassle-free life. Up until this point, the country's sectarian issues hadn't caused me any serious problems; I had been able to ignore them and go about my business without getting involved. This was all about to change. In Northern Ireland, you don't always get to choose which side you're on. Sometimes one of the sides chooses you and the first you get to hear of it is when the cops are hammering on your door.

Chapter 11

TERRY THE TERRORIST

It was ten thirty on a Friday night when the boys in blue came knocking. I had been drinking and felt a little worse for wear but managed to stumble down the stairs to answer the door. The sight that greeted me when I undid the latch will stay imprinted on my brain until my dying day. Patrick Place was rammed from one end to the other with police and army men. The soldiers were in full uniform but the coppers were plain-clothed, although it didn't take a rocket scientist to figure out that they were Old Bill. I could have deduced that from their knock alone, which sounded as if they were attempting to cave the door in.

'We're here to execute a search warrant. We have reason to believe that you have firearms on the premises.'

My jaw dropped so low that I'm surprised it didn't leave a dent in the floor. By this stage I was used to being accused of things I hadn't done but this was something else. What on earth made them think I had a gun in my house? Was it something to do with my arrest in Spain? A million questions buzzed about in my head as I stood gobsmacked in the doorway. I had hung about with some unsavoury characters in the past but had never come into contact with a firearm, let alone decide to keep one in my home.

'Before we start the search, have you got anything in the house that you shouldn't have? We're going to tear the place apart so you might as well say now.'

'No, feel free to take a look,' I told them. 'I've got nothing to hide.'

'Has anybody else got access to your property?'

This was when it struck me. My friend still had the spare key that I had given him on the day I hurried back to say goodbye to Dad. Had he hidden something in my house without letting on to me?

'Yeah one other person does,' I said. 'What the hell is all of this about?'

'Wait here with me,' the copper told me, completely ignoring my question and carrying on with what he was saying as if he hadn't heard. 'The other officers are going to have a look around the house. If they find anything then you'll be arrested on suspicion of possessing illegal weaponry.'

As the police rifled through my belongings, I felt very foolish for giving somebody else the means to come and go as they pleased. In a place like Northern Ireland, this was an unspeakably bad move. I had met the lad I gave the keys to at the local pub and trusted him despite only being friends with him for a matter of months and not knowing a great deal about his life. It wasn't as if it had been essential for him to check up on the house either; it was just something that I thought would put my mind at rest. What if he was a member of the UDA? They were always looking for places to hide their arms, drugs and stolen property. I was frantically attempting to get this thought out of my head when a smug-looking copper came striding down the hallway to confirm my fears.

'We've got a sawn-off shotgun, some ammunition and what looks to be a pipe bomb, Sarge,' he told his superior. 'They were hidden in a box under the stairs. There's a load of balaclavas in there too so somebody was obviously planning on doing something nasty. It's a good thing we found them when we did or we could have had a major incident on our hands.'

At this point, I thought, 'Here we go again.' It was like an action replay of the airport in Gran Canaria only with a gun and a bomb instead of drugs. I didn't know whether to laugh or cry. If I wasn't in such a horrendous amount of trouble then it might have been funny. The fact that a single person could be in the wrong place at the wrong time so often was totally surreal.

'Cuff her up,' the sergeant ordered his lackey. 'We'll see what she has to say about this down at the station.'

As the handcuffs snapped shut round my wrists, I wondered how I was going to wriggle my way out of this one. I was completely innocent but had to admit that it looked very bad. Surely the coppers realised I was English, though. Most of the UDA are born and raised in Ulster so the Old Bill must have been aware of how unlikely it was that I was a terrorist. I was praying that they had connected the dots and figured out that someone had used me; otherwise I was going to be spending years of my life in a grim Irish slammer surrounded by Sectarian fruit loops.

The officers shoved me into the back of a van and drove me to the police station, where I was interrogated for a good half hour. By this stage I was shaking so much that it looked as if I had Parkinson's disease. My whole body was completely wracked with fear. Memories of Gran Canaria came flooding back as the coppers bombarded me with question after question. The only slight plus point was that I could actually understand what they were saying this time, although I almost wished I couldn't.

'I'm going to ask you one more time,' the interrogator told me. 'What were you planning on doing with the weapons?'

'I didn't even know that they were there,' I sobbed. 'You have to believe me. I only found out that they were in my house when the police searched it. Somebody must have put them there.'

The coppers didn't look convinced. As far as they were concerned, I was just another guilty criminal putting on an act.

'We found a message on your mobile phone saying, "That was a great result tonight." What exactly did you mean by that? It sounds to me like you were referring to an attack.'

I was talking about the result of a Liverpool game. Were they going to read sinister hidden meanings into all of my private conversations? I couldn't believe that they were genuinely convinced that I was some kind of terrorist hit woman. Did they really think that I looked cold and emotionless enough to be a UDA assassin?

'I meant that Stevie Gerrard and the boys had won a match,' I sniffled. 'I'm really not the person that you think I am. I'm not the only one who's got a key to the house. I'm telling you I didn't have a clue.'

'A local male let himself into the property shortly after your arrest,' the copper told me. 'We suspect that he's your accomplice. Both of you are being charged with terrorism. If we find any blood on the gun, the charges could be upped to murder so I hope for your sake that we don't.'

His words sent an icy chill down the base of my spine. Murder? They thought I might have killed somebody? I just prayed that the truth would come out now that they had taken the real owner of the weapons in for questioning. Otherwise it looked as if I had narrowly escaped imprisonment in Spain only to be jailed for another crime I hadn't committed back in the UK. Unlucky really wasn't the word. It seemed as if a black cloud followed me wherever I went.

I was kept in custody for the entire weekend and spent the whole time feeling on the verge of a major panic attack. The police had told me that I was looking at eight years if I was found guilty of terrorism or even longer if it came out that the gun had actually been used. I wondered how they would take to an English girl in a Northern Irish prison. Eight years is a long time to be banged up in a place where a good number of the inmates hate you solely based upon your nationality. If the jails were half as divided and territorial as Northern Irish society was in general, then I was in for a right time of it.

On Sunday morning, Billy turned up at the station to drop off a suit for me to wear in court. The police allowed him into the cell so that we could have a chat, which helped to calm me down a bit. He told me that he had been taken in for questioning as well because he was a regular visitor at my house but that he had eventually been released without charge. It was nice to see a familiar face but the fact that he had been set free and I still had to go to court didn't bode too well. It meant the police obviously thought that I was more likely to be a terrorist than him. As he left the cell, I wondered when I would next get to see him and more importantly, whether or not it would be in a prison visiting room.

'When am I due in court then?' I asked the cop who came to lock the door.

'I'll come and get you tomorrow morning,' he told me. 'Make sure you're ready when I come to the cell.'

This meant I had another twenty-four hours left to contemplate my fate. I still wasn't sure if I was going to get bail and didn't fancy being remanded. The prisons where they sent terrorists awaiting sentence were guaranteed to be hardcore. Salto del Negro was bad enough and that was on a peaceful little island in the sun so I didn't even want to think what life behind bars would be like in a country known for violence and extremism. It would no doubt be a place where the strong prospered and the weak became victims.

After a night of bad dreams that were actually less scary than reality, I woke up with a stomach full of butterflies and a head full of uncertainty. The copper came to my cell shortly after I had got up to tell me it was time to go, so I flung on my suit and followed him out of the door. I was taken to the court in the passenger seat of a minibus. The driver told me that the lad that I had given my spare key to was being held in a compartment in the back and warned me not to talk to him.

'If I hear a single whisper from either of you, you're going to be in even more trouble than you're already in,' he threatened us. 'Anything you want to say to each other can be said in your trial.'

As with my court appearances in Spain, I wasn't required to state my case straightaway. The only reason that I had been summoned was to enter my plea and to see if I was eligible for bail. After a short drive, the copper ushered us out of the vehicle and into the Crown Court building. We were made to sit in front of a judge and asked if we pleaded guilty or not guilty to the charge of terrorism.

'Not guilty, Your Honour,' I told him.

'Guilty,' said my co-accused.

I breathed a sigh of relief. The fact that he had confessed would surely get me off the hook. The judge told him that he was to be remanded without bail and then turned to address me.

'Teresa Daniels, I am setting your bail at two thousand pounds. Do you have the money with you now?'

'No, Your Honour,' I sheepishly replied.

Surely he was going to allow me to remain free until my mum could get there with the cash.

'In that case you are to remain in custody until you're able to pay. You are to be taken to Maghaberry Prison pending the receipt of your bail money.'

So they were still sending me straight to jail even though I hadn't been remanded? This was just my luck. I was going to be eaten alive the minute I arrived.

The same policeman who had escorted me into the court building walked me to the minibus and put me in the front again. The only slight silver lining was the fact that I knew I wouldn't be locked up for too long. No matter how horrific life in Maghaberry was, I was sure that I could stick it out until my bail arrived.

The prison was only a short drive from the court. It was very old-fashioned and looked as if it was a dungeon rather than a jail. As we passed through the huge, imposing metal gates that separated the free world from the world of terrorists and criminals, I swallowed hard and prepared myself for the worst.

The minibus came to a halt within the prison grounds and a hard-faced warder ordered me outside. He marched me through the doors of the reception building and took me to the front desk, where I was searched for drugs and weapons. The screws also did rigorous checks to see if I had anything with sectarian or political imagery on it. Items that contained paramilitary symbols or Rangers or Celtic logos were strictly forbidden. Once the staff were satisfied that I didn't have an IRA necklace on or an 'I love the UDA' bracelet hidden away somewhere, I was told to follow a big bruiser of a guard through a doorway into the bowels of the prison.

It was only when I reached the wing where I was to be housed that I appreciated just how dangerous the other inmates in Maghaberry were. There were only six cells in the unit with a single prisoner in each. This was because the prison held the worst of the worst and the residents were considered too much of a risk for there to be any more than this in each section of the jail.

To say that Maghaberry has had a colourful history would be a major understatement. It has housed the likes of UDA leader Johnny 'Mad Dog' Adair, UVF commander Billy 'King Rat' Wright and Real IRA bomber Marian Price, along with many equally notorious non-sectarian prisoners. It is Northern Ireland's highest-security jail, reserved for the maddest, baddest and craziest inmates going. Why on earth they ranked me alongside these people I will never know.

The wing was only a fraction of the size of the unit that I was kept on in Salto. It was literally just a small seating area, a servery and some cells. I got the impression that the inmates didn't spend a lot of time out of their rooms, which was all right by me because the less I had to mingle with the bombers, murderers and lunatics that I was forced to share the unit with, the safer I would be.

As I scanned the names above the cell doors to try and get an indication of what type of people I was in with, I noticed that they were all Catholic. It doesn't take long to learn which surnames are Catholic and which are Protestant when you live in Northern Ireland. If you value your kneecaps, you soon learn how to identify the people that would eagerly remove them if they got the chance.

Was I the only Protestant on the wing? Surely not. The guards wouldn't put a lone English girl in with five Catholic nutters, would they? Well, they might put an English girl with a Catholic surname in with them. My dad was an Irish Catholic and they probably decided which unit people were sent to based upon their names. This was just my bloody luck. I was locked up on a unit with a load of Northern Irish separatists who hated anything remotely British. It was looking increasingly unlikely that I was going to get out in one piece.

The guard who was escorting me unlocked one of the cells and motioned me inside. At least I would be safe whilst I was locked up in my digs. I shuffled through the entrance and heard the key turn in the lock behind me. If I was going to survive until Mum arrived with the cash then I would have to play upon the fact that I was half Irish. The offence that I had been charged with would no doubt get me killed if the other prisoners got onto it. Even the name of the street the bomb was found on would mark me out as a Protestant. Life in HMP Maghaberry was going to be like walking through a minefield.

After spending what seemed like an eternity with only my thoughts for company, the door finally clunked open and a guard poked his head through the gap.

'Come on, let's have you,' he told me. 'You've got half an hour's association.'

'Association' is the time in which prisoners are allowed out of their cells to socialise with one another. I would have rather remained banged up but didn't have that choice available to me so I held my breath and stepped out into the lion's den. As the other inmates hurried over to check out the new arrival, I prayed to God that I would be able to convince them that I was a Catholic because otherwise I would be beaten to a bloody pulp.

My fellow prisoners were an eclectic bunch. Some of them looked like drug users but others seemed as if butter wouldn't melt in their mouths. They were all female because although Maghaberry was a mixed prison, the men and women were never allowed to socialise with one another.

'Hey, how are you finding it in here?' asked the most typically Irish-looking girl that I have ever seen, with dark brown hair and a thick, Northern Irish accent.

'Yeah it's OK,' I mumbled, hoping that she wouldn't pick up on my accent and kick off straightaway.

'Whereabouts are you from then?' she asked, eyeing me suspiciously.

'I was born in England but I'm half Irish,' I told her, getting my mitigation in before she had a chance to throw a punch. Now it was just a matter of crossing my fingers.

'Well, so long as you're not a Protestant 'cause they reckon I was trying to blow them up. The coppers caught me with a bomb in my shed. They said that it was even bigger than the Omagh bomb, so they did.'

God almighty. She looked as innocent as they come. If I had met her on the street I wouldn't have thought she had a violent bone in her body, but here she was talking about an act of terrorism as if it was the most normal thing on earth.

'No my dad insisted on bringing me up Catholic,' I lied. 'I hate the Protestants just as much as you do.'

The next girl that I spoke to was even crazier than the bomb girl. She was the only inmate who wasn't in for terrorism, which would have made her less of a threat if she wasn't a complete nut-job. When I asked her what she had done to end up in Maghaberry, she laughed and told me that she had cut off her boyfriend's head. I thought that she was taking the mickey at first but then she started telling me how she did it and I realised she was being deadly serious.

'He was knocking me about so I taught him a lesson,' the sadistic loonie grinned at me. 'He got what was coming to him.'

Decapitating somebody is not something that any sane person could ever find amusing no matter what their motivation was for doing it. She came across as if she had gained some kind of perverse satisfaction from talking about her crime, so I marked her down as another inmate to avoid and edged away to talk to the other girls, who were all in for minor terrorist offences. Most of them had kept things for their boyfriends and ended up getting caught with them.

As soon as I had got all my introductions out of the way, I headed over to the phone to give my mum a call. I felt awful ringing up to spring another disaster on her but knew that there was no other way of getting out. She was absolutely dumbstruck when I told her the story of how I had ended up in prison and promised to get to Northern Ireland with my bail as soon as possible. Hearing the stress and fear in her voice made me feel terrible. All my poor old mother ever got from me was heartache and worry.

I was glad when association was finally over and I could return to my cell. The call to Mum had stressed me out no end and the other prisoners oozed menace from every pore of their bodies. Even the girls who were in for the least serious offences looked liable to snap at any given moment. Some of them seemed OK until you talked to them and got a measure of what their personalities were like. The hatred behind their eyes burnt like the fires of hell, especially when they talked about the Protestants. I was lucky nobody had a problem with me being half English. If they were willing to blow up people that they had never met just because of their religion then what would they be likely to do to somebody who had willingly deceived them? The head-chopper girl would probably wear my liver as a hat if she ever got onto the fact that I had lied to her about my faith.

Luckily I was only in Maghaberry for a total of four days so none of the other prisoners had time to grill me too heavily about my crime. Whenever anybody asked what I was in for, I babbled on about various different made-up offences. My stories weren't in the least bit believable but I still somehow managed to convince my fellow inmates that I was fiercely pro-Catholic. I kept up the pretence until a guard came to my cell to tell me that it was time for my court appearance and then breathed a heavy sigh of relief and thanked my lucky stars that I would soon be home.

The prisoners in Maghaberry were considered far too dangerous to attend court sessions in person so I was forced to watch my bail hearing on a TV screen. One of the screws escorted me to a phone booth with a flat-screen telly in it that displayed an image of Mum sat in front of a judge.

'Do you have Teresa's bail money with you?' the judge asked my nervous-looking mother.

'Yes I do,' Mum told her.

'OK I'm granting your daughter bail on condition that she stays out of Northern Ireland until the day of her trial.'

I didn't know how to feel about this. I was made up that I was heading home but gutted that I would have to leave Billy behind.

Our relationship was just beginning to get serious and would be difficult to carry on from across the Irish Sea.

'You are now free to leave the court,' the judge proclaimed.

Everybody got up off of their seats and walked out so I opened the door of the booth and signalled to a nearby guard that I was ready to be returned to the wing.

Looking back, I think the judge probably ordered me to keep out of the country for my own protection. The UDA would no doubt have been fuming that the lad that I had given my key to ended up in prison. I had been sent back to England to ensure that their foot soldiers didn't blame me for it and come after me, but the expulsion still upset me and put a downer on my release. By the time Mum had arrived to pick me up, I was in the mood to end all moods. I was going to have to start my life from scratch again and wasn't pleased about it.

A guard walked me over to the entrance to the prison and opened the gates for me. I had survived being on remand but there was still a chance that I would be sent back to Maghaberry if I got found guilty. In the meantime I was an outcast, forced to leave my house and all my friends behind for a second time. Mum greeted me outside the prison with open arms and a smile but I was unable to reciprocate.

'I'm so glad that you're OK,' she told me. 'I was worried sick about you.'

'Let's just get out of here,' I sulkily replied.

I should have been gushing with gratitude but only thought about myself. When I look back at it now, I feel ashamed of how I acted. Mum had travelled overseas to bail me out and I was going on like a stroppy little madam.

'Don't worry,' Mum reassured me, assuming I was upset because I still had a court case pending. 'I'll get you a lawyer and we'll sort all this out. I'm sure the court will realise that you had nothing to do with bombs or terrorism or anything like that.'

'But Mum, they're making me go back to England,' I complained. 'My life is in Northern Ireland now. Whenever I get settled anywhere, I have to go back home.'

Mum was rightfully annoyed by this.

'You selfish cow,' she scolded me. 'Is that all that you can think about? You could wind up dead if you stay there. They found a bomb, you know? This isn't a game, Terry.'

My mum was clearly in the right. She deserved a medal for getting me out of so many sticky situations, not an earful of bad attitude. I should have spent the journey back home thanking her but I was too stressed and depressed to express anything other than moodiness and frustration.

Arriving back in Wingrave made me feel even worse because the village brought back memories of Dad's death. It was also strange being at home again because Dad had told his best friend Mickey to look after our family once he had passed away and Mickey was now getting very close to Mum. She liked him a lot and he was kind and supportive so I had no problem with it, but it was still a lot to take in.

One of the first things that I did when I got home was ring Billy and tell him what had happened. He was a hard little lad and didn't show too much emotion but I could still tell he was gutted.

'I'll be able to come and see you again once this is all over,' I assured him, although we both knew deep down that we were finished as a couple. Over the next few weeks, we spoke to each other less and less until the relationship gradually fizzled out.

It was a shame because I really liked him but it's impossible to carry on going out with somebody when they're living in a country that you're banned from visiting. He didn't fancy abandoning his life in Northern Ireland to move to England, so there was nothing that we could do.

I spent the build-up to my court case moping around the house and feeling very sorry for myself. Stress was eating away at me and I could hardly even drag myself out of bed each morning. The thought of going back to Maghaberry scared the living daylights out of me. It had been bad enough spending four days there so God knows what eight years would be like.

My trial took place a few months after my release. I got the plane across to Northern Ireland and met my QC in the Crown Court waiting area. It was the first time I had seen him and he reminded me of a crazy old professor. His wig was ruffled, his cloak was tattered and he looked as if he belonged in a museum. Appearances can be deceptive though because he seemed to know his stuff. He told me that I had a good chance of getting a 'not guilty' but added that the prosecution was aware of my conviction in Tenerife, which meant I couldn't claim that I had previous good character to help convince the jury of my innocence.

'I thought that was all over,' I told him.

This was yet another source of worry. Even if I won the case in Northern Ireland, the smuggling charge clearly hadn't completely gone away. In ordinary circumstances, the resurgence of this case would have scared me half to death, but as it was, I only had enough energy left to worry about one thing at a time so I decided to put it to the back of my mind until my trial was over.

After a brief chat with the mad professor, I was escorted into the courtroom by two well-built security guards and placed inside a bulletproof glass box. This was presumably to prevent the UDA from doing a hit on me part way through the hearing. Three very stern, official-looking judges sat at the opposite end of the room and pierced me with deep analytical stares. The entire set-up seemed as if it was designed to scare the wits out of me before the case started.

Luckily I didn't have to say too much during the trial because my QC was on hand to fight my corner for me. He did a brilliant job of defending me, despite the police's various attempts to fit me up. The bomb had been recovered from a cupboard under the stairs that was so crowded with junk that anything could have been hidden there without me being aware of it. This wasn't the picture that the Old Bill painted though. They had taken photos of the interior at a funny angle to try and make out that the cupboard was brimming with space.

'So you believe that my client regularly checked the bag the weapons were kept in?' the professor grilled the arresting officer.

'I do,' the copper nodded.

'OK then, can you please explain how this is possible, given the fact that the bag was recovered from behind a picture and a disused fireplace, both of which were covered from head to toe in dust? This dust would have been displaced if the bag had been opened in the weeks leading up to its recovery. I put it to the court that my client was completely unaware of its contents until the day of her arrest. None of her fingerprints were found on the explosive device, the ammunition or the gun, which goes even further to support my theory. The real terrorist has already pleaded guilty, so why make poor Teresa pay for fact that she was trusting enough to give somebody a spare key to her house?'

His defence was good enough to secure a unanimous 'not guilty'. This should have been a cause for celebration but something didn't seem right. The arresting officer cracked a toothy smile whilst the verdict was read out, which made me wonder whether he was planning on pinning another crime on me. It was as if he knew something I didn't. I was relieved that I had got off but felt as if more trouble was definitely looming on the horizon.

I went straight back to Wingrave after the verdict was delivered and decided that I was going to stay there for the immediate future. Living in Northern Ireland had been interesting but I didn't fancy getting either stitched up for something else by the police or tarred and feathered by the UDA. I had seen the bitterness in the local people's faces when it came to matters of politics and knew they didn't mess about. It was probably for the best that I stayed as far away as I possibly could.

I had got used to living in Wingrave whilst awaiting trial so I no longer found it strange being back. If anything, I enjoyed being closer to my family. My mum had done a lot for me and I really appreciated it even if I sometimes had a funny way of showing it. If it wasn't for her, I would have languished in Maghaberry for weeks on end and the other inmates would have eventually seen through my cover story and started terrorising me.

Mickey had now become like a member of the family as well. He had moved into the house, and he and Mum were a couple. This was quite hard for me to adjust to but I was still happy that she had found someone. The only thing I didn't like about being home was the fact that it could be a little bit boring. I seemed to be lumbered with far too much spare time so I decided to apply for a job to keep me occupied.

I have always been a caring person so I went for an interview for a job as a care assistant, working with women with cerebral palsy. The interviewer seemed impressed with the answers that I gave him and promised me the job on the condition that I had no criminal record.

'You can start work straightaway but I'm afraid we'll have to strike you off if your CRB check comes back with anything we don't like on it,' he warned me.

I had no convictions in the UK so I assumed it would be clean. My second appeal in Tenerife had never been followed up so I wasn't even really a convicted criminal. The Spanish authorities only jailed people after their appeals had failed so by that logic there was nothing to indicate that I had done anything worthy of imprisonment.

Unfortunately CRB checks also list convictions that are pending, which meant that I was called into the boss's office after a couple of weeks at the job.

'Your record says you're part way through being prosecuted in Spain for drug smuggling,' he said as he confronted me. 'Now would you care to tell me what this is all about?'

I explained what had happened and the boss told me that I could carry on with my job, but that I should have let him know about my conviction earlier.

'It was a long time in the past though, so hopefully you can put all that behind you now,' he added, as if to try and lessen the sting a bit.

I loved caring for people so I was made up not to get the sack but also gutted that the allegations were still hanging over me. This meant that Interpol could drag me off and shove me on a plane to Spain at any given moment, although I seriously doubted that anybody was still after me. If I was a wanted criminal then the coppers would have surely caught up with me by now. Leaving a convicted drug smuggler free to commit more crimes for so long didn't make any sense at all.

Even though there was only a tiny chance that I would ever be rearrested, I still wanted to be one hundred per cent certain that I was off the hook so I got in touch with Fair Trials International, a charity offering free advice and legal aid to anybody facing prison overseas. I needed to know where I stood and it seemed as if they were the perfect people to help me find the answers I was looking for. The lady that I spoke to told me that she would make enquiries as to whether or not my case was still ongoing and start the procedure for a royal pardon if it was. This put my mind at rest and made me think that there was finally an end to this nightmare in sight. The fact that she thought I stood a chance of getting a pardon hammered home how unfair my trial had been, because the King of Spain has only ever been known to pardon convicts in exceptional circumstances.

Now that I had a regular source of income and Fair Trials had helped to stop me from worrying so much about being packed off back to Spain, I decided to let my hair down a bit and go out clubbing at the weekends. Up until this point, I had been spending a lot of time indoors because I was paranoid about getting into more trouble. It was nice to be able to let off steam and mingle with other people on a Saturday night. After a few weeks, I eventually got talking to a local lad called Jack and hit it off with him. We had a laugh together and before I knew it, we were going out.

Jack was ten years younger than me but had the kind of cheeky personality that I like in men. We got on well with one another and things were going great until I got another positive result on a pregnancy test. I should have been more careful but had been drinking. The fact that I had repeated the same mistake twice made me feel distraught. Although there was less chance of me going to prison than there had been the first time I got pregnant, the charges still hadn't fully disappeared so there was no way that I was going to have the baby. If I got sent down, Mum would be left looking after it and I had caused her enough trouble as it was.

Abortion number two was just as difficult as the first but I knew that it was the only sensible option. I travelled down to a clinic in London with Jack's sister and never once questioned my choice. My life was far too unpredictable for motherhood and I could barely look after myself, let alone a child.

Jack was supportive of my decision and promised to keep it between the two of us. It made me feel a little bit depressed but didn't do me any serious harm. Before I knew it, I was carrying on with my life as if nothing had happened. The only difference was that I was now a lot more wary about getting pregnant again.

I had to admire the way Jack handled the situation. Blokes have a tendency to run a mile when the little strip changes colour but he was really kind and caring. If our relationship was going to progress then I would have to get a place of my own though. I enjoyed living with Mum but felt as if it was time that I moved out.

As luck would have it, one of my friends from Aylesbury was looking for a housemate so I went to have a nosey at her place to see if it was somewhere that I could see myself living. Her house was in Watermead, which isn't a bad area, and it looked really nice so I told her that I would move in. I should have been excited about my new digs but as you have probably noticed by now, whenever I get my own place, disaster always strikes.

I wondered how long it would be before my life plunged back into chaos. Hopefully I would at least get to settle into my new accommodation this time.

Life in Watermead was fairly uneventful to begin with. I enjoyed the feeling of independence that I got from being away from my family but as the months went by, I couldn't help but think that I was teetering on the edge of a precipice, just waiting to fall. Something told me that Gran Canaria was about to finally catch up with me. Trouble never seemed to go away for me. It just lay dormant until my existence seemed as if it was finally hassle free, before coming back with a vengeance.

Chapter 12

OUT OF THE FRYING PAN AND INTO THE FIRE

It was a Monday morning when I got the call.

'Terry, I think you'd better come home.'

Mum didn't even need to tell me what the matter was, because I knew straightaway from her tone that it was about Brazil. I felt nauseous and the blood rushed to my head. I had being given a brief respite from going mad with worry; now it was back to living on my nerves again.

'Why, what's up?' I asked.

I was hoping she was going to tell me that she just wanted me to come round for a chat or that she missed my company.

'Just come over here and we'll deal with it.'

I wanted to run away but knew I couldn't put my mum through any more stress than she was already going through. She sounded worried enough as it was without me pulling a disappearing act. I had been out all weekend so it took a while for everything to sink in. Waking up to a call like that is enough to send you loopy. Luckily I was thinking straight enough to ring Fair Trials. There was no point waiting for my mum to confirm what had happened because I already knew the score.

After briefing Fair Trials on the situation, I flung on a tracksuit over my pink Disney pyjamas and raced off to Mum's. The more I thought about the prospect of going to court again, the more anxious I felt. Was this all my life consisted of? It was one wrongful arrest after another. I seemed to spend more time in the dock than I did at home.

Three burly Scotland Yard officers were waiting for me at the house, which made me feel like public enemy number one.

'Why are there three of you?' I asked them. 'I'm only little.'

'You don't look good on paper,' the officer-in-charge told me.

My criminal record might have made me out to be some kind of major drug smuggler but I was actually a frightened girl in her PJs. They were treating me like Pablo Escobar.

The coppers told me that I needed to go to court to see if I would be extradited. The officer in the court in Northern Ireland had been smiling because he knew that I was facing imprisonment in Spain. He had seen it on my record and wasn't fussed what country I ended up in jail in, just so long as I got locked up.

'You will probably have to put up a lot of cash to get bail,' the Old Bill advised me. 'It's best somebody follows you to court with their bankbook to prove they've got the funds. Otherwise you'll end up being remanded.'

So much for my 'release without further admission'. It was all very predictable. The Spanish authorities had effectively added five years onto my sentence by leaving me in uncertainty for so long. At least I would know it was all over if the courts ruled against sending me back. As the police bundled me into the back of an unmarked car, I resigned myself to my fate. There would be no more quietly getting on with my life; from this moment onwards I would never have a stress-free day. Every waking minute would be spent wondering what the future held.

The officers took me to my house to pick up my passport and we then drove to Bow Street Magistrates in London. They didn't seem to know anything about my case and picked my brains for the entire hour-and-a-half journey. Bow Street was a really horrible, uninviting place; an old, ugly, imposing building with a slightly daunting quality. The ambience of the court gave the impression that anybody who passed through the front entrance must be in serious trouble – and in my case it was very accurate.

The coppers led me into a dirty little holding cell beneath the court. This was where I was to remain until my hearing started. I was pacing the room, wondering if I was going to spend the next ten years somewhere very similar, when the door clanged open and the lady from Fair Trials International came in. She had a barrister in tow, which was a godsend. At least now I had somebody to fight my case for me. I didn't fancy the prospect of going into the courtroom on my own; I would be like a lamb to the slaughter.

There is an easy way of determining whether a barrister is any good or not; it's all in how battered their cloaks are. If it looks brand spanking new then it means that they are inexperienced and probably aren't that great. The fella that I was assigned to had a particularly moth-eaten rag draped over him so he was obviously a pro. Even with my ragged-cloaked lawyer on board, I was still extremely nervous when I entered the courtroom. The judge was older than the ones that had dealt with me in the past and looked very stern and intimidating.

'Are you Teresa Daniels of Wingrave, Buckinghamshire?'

'Yes,' I told him, praying that he wasn't going to tell me I was being shipped straight back to Spain.

'The court is still yet to determine whether you will be extradited. Since you have a record of absconding, I am going to have to set your bail at £10,000. Can you afford this amount?'

Mickey had taken the police's advice and followed me to court on the train. Had he stayed at home, I might have had to spend the night in the clink. He showed the judge his bankbook, which served as proof that he had ten grand available. He didn't have to hand the money over there and then; it was just so that the authorities knew the cash was there in case I did a runner.

'The conditions of your bail are as follows; you are to remain at your current place of abode, you will surrender your passport and remain in the UK and you will report to your local police station at regular intervals. Do you agree with these conditions?'

What choice did I really have? It was a case of either nodding my head and saying 'yes' or saying 'no' and being locked up, so I went for option number one.

'You are now free to leave the court.'

I was mentally exhausted. As Mickey and I made our way to the station, I felt relieved that I still had my freedom but at the same time overawed by the struggle that now lay before me. The Spanish authorities seemed intent on ruining my life. It was just a matter of whether or not the English government would allow somebody who was clearly innocent to be imprisoned over there. I prayed the answer would be no but suspected it might be yes. With all of the things that had gone wrong over the last few years, I felt it would be a miracle if I avoided extradition.

I spent the whole journey back home talking to Mum on my mobile. She had been waiting with baited breath to hear the outcome of the hearing and seemed happy to hear my voice. I explained the situation and she told me we would fight my case together. She sounded so panic-stricken. The constant drama seemed to be really taking its toll on her. It can't be easy seeing your daughter being carted off by Interpol. I just hoped that it would all work out for the best and her stress would come to an end soon.

Mum picked us up from the station, spent a while consoling me and then dropped me off at my house. By this stage I was tired out so I ran upstairs, buried my face in my pillow and attempted to blot out the whole horrible scenario. Even if I did manage to avoid jail, I was never going to be able to relax again. The moment one crisis came to an end, another seemed to rear its ugly head. My brain was absolutely fried so I closed my eyes and willed myself to sleep in order to forget.

Over the next few weeks, the situation went from bad to worse. My boss at work retired and a new bloke took over who claimed that I had hidden my conviction from the company. He was annoyed that I had been in the local paper and promptly fired me. This meant that I was forced to spend my days at home doing nothing, which drove me further into depression. I just prayed that my pardon would eventually come through so that I could prove my innocence.

As well as campaigning to clear my name, Fair Trials were also doing everything in their power to keep me in Britain. They wrote to the court highlighting my haemorrhage and my father's death and suggested that I should see a psychiatrist to ascertain whether I was mentally fit to be flown overseas. The judge agreed and put my case back ten months until May 2004 so that I had time to be assessed.

I had a lot to tell the psychiatrist because the minute I found out that I was facing extradition, I had stopped sleeping properly and lost my appetite. My concentration dropped to zero and I had regular attacks of extreme anxiety. He also asked me questions about my history of drug and alcohol abuse so I confided in him about how bad I had been when I was at my worst. The results of the consultation were sent on to the court so that they could get a clearer picture of how unwell I was.

To my dismay, the word came back that I was still considered healthy enough to be imprisoned. I wasn't getting out of my fate that easily; the Spaniards were determined to punish me no matter what. They didn't give a monkey's whether I would be able to cope with life behind bars or not; all they were concerned about was making sure I didn't get away with my imaginary crime.

Jack was upset that I was facing extradition but tried his best to keep my spirits up. He kept reassuring me that I was going to win my case, which made me feel a tad more optimistic and calmed me down a bit. His friends were also very nice to me. I would often hang about with them and they spent a lot of time consoling me and offering me advice.

'You need to do something to take your mind off things,' his mate Tony told me one day as we sat about drinking and discussing my uncertain future. 'We're off to a rave at the weekend. You should come along with us.'

'I didn't know that they still had those things,' I replied. 'Are they still the same as they were?'

'Yeah,' he grinned. 'Still just as crazy as ever. Seriously, you should come. It'll make you forget all about your court case.'

'I'll think about it,' I told him.

I had assumed the raves had died out. On the one hand I wanted to see if they were still as good as they were during my teenage years; but on the other, I still remembered my scary experiences on Ecstasy and acid and felt a little apprehensive. Part of me wanted to give them a wide berth but a more persuasive part of my subconscious was saying, 'What have you got to lose? Enjoy yourself whilst you've got the chance.' I was facing ten years in a hellish Spanish nick; I needed something to take my mind off things. Maybe dancing the night away would help to lessen the depression and anxiety that was taking over my life. The devil on my shoulder was right: what did I have to lose?

By the time the weekend arrived, I had made up my mind that I was going to go along with Jack and his friends. It was years since I had been to a party and I was curious to see how raving had progressed. Had the music changed? Was the vibe still just as loved-up or had the mood turned sour? And were the majority of the crowd still off their heads on drugs? It was time for me to find out.

As I clambered into the back seat of Jack's car, I felt as if I was doing the right thing. I needed something so intense that it would erase all traces of worry from my psyche. The risk involved in entering an environment like that so soon after I had recovered from a drug problem didn't even register. But then again the thought of a decade inside does funny things to a girl. Activities that would have previously rung alarm bells failed to merit a second thought. The enormity of the problems surrounding what had happened in Brazil dwarfed all other concerns. My freedom was now the only thing that mattered. Everything else had become inconsequential.

The rave was in a dusty old quarry in Bedfordshire. It wasn't exactly the most glamorous location but then again you would hardly expect an illegal party to be held at The Ritz. The friendly vibe was definitely still there. The good thing about events where everybody is taking Es is that they all act like you've been their friend since birth. It didn't matter that I was new to the scene; I was now part of the family.

Although most of the ravers were having a good time, I noticed a fair few people lying on the ground, seemingly paralysed. I wondered what the deal was with them. Everybody had been so full of energy at the parties I had gone to as a teenager.

'Don't worry about them, they're just on ketamine,' one of Jack's friends explained.

Ketamine is a horse tranquilliser that makes people hallucinate so badly that they can hardly move. It seemed a bit of a strange drug. None of the ravers who were on it appeared to be enjoying the experience. I remember thinking, 'Each to their own but I'm definitely never taking that.' It didn't appeal to me at all. The crazy thing about ketamine is that it's perfectly legal to possess unless it has been prepared for use. This is mad considering it's capable of sedating a horse. Even the most hardened drug takers know to treat it with respect. One of my friends once took it and told me that he spent the whole night pinned against the wall. He said he felt as if he was a character in a pop-up book and everything had taken on another dimension. This was somebody who had got mashed on everything from weed to heroin so he was no stranger to narcotics and wasn't fazed by much.

The other thing that had changed about the raves was that there was now a slight undercurrent of menace. The parties still felt safe, but the atmosphere was somehow different to how it had been back in the day. It was nothing I couldn't handle though because there were enough loved-up people there to outweigh the moody ones. A little bit of shadiness certainly wasn't going to stop me turning out to the next event.

I managed to remain sober for the first three raves. I was wary of LSD and Ecstasy and didn't fancy getting hooked on coke again. The problem was that the parties sometimes went on until eleven in the morning and I found it hard to stay awake. Amphetamine seemed the perfect drug to stave off tiredness. It wasn't trippy like acid or Es and I didn't have to snort it, which was a risky business after my brain haemorrhage. I didn't give a monkey's how addictive it was as I was facing a ten-year prison sentence and no longer gave a shit. I should have learnt my lesson from the coke. I was about to plunge myself back into a world of dizzying highs and earth-shattering lows and it would only be a matter of time before drugs ruled my life again.

Rather than sticking to the regular powdered amphetamine, I took a particularly strong form of speed called base whenever I went to a rave. It was a yellowy white paste and gave me the energy that I needed to dance enthusiastically all night. I started off taking it every weekend but my addictive personality soon got the better of me. As I've said before, I've never been one for taking things in moderation. The minute I discover something that I enjoy, I tend to go completely overboard with it.

I quickly went from taking speed on Friday and Saturday nights to taking it throughout the week as well. I kidded myself that I just needed a couple of grains to wake me up after a night of partying. I would like to be able to describe a long, drawn-out process in which I gradually took more and more, but this simply wasn't the case. One minute I was taking a little dab here and there, the next I was an addict.

Within the space of a few weeks my drug intake had rocketed. It was frightening how quickly I switched from recreational use to needing base to function. I would get off my head for six days in a row then spend my one day of sobriety feeling angry and frustrated. This was probably due to lack of sleep because I found it impossible to get shut-eye whilst high. I still didn't make the connection that I had got to the stage with whiz that I had been at with coke. It's funny how drugs play tricks on you. They lull you into a false sense of security and assure you that there's nothing wrong. If only that was the case. I had no job, I was facing extradition and now I was a whiz addict. The situation wasn't looking good.

One thing led to another and I ended up back on booze as well. Other drugs don't mix well with alcohol but speed is perfectly compatible. The raves were filled with drink and I was soon getting through six bottles of Malibu every weekend. Looking back it was probably a means of self-harming. I didn't have the balls to cut my wrists but I was fully capable of slowly draining my health with drink and drugs. I was a total mess. The only thing that I had to look forward to in life was the parties. It's funny how enjoyable it can be to pollute your body with crap. Getting wasted was the highlight of my week.

Most of the raves were held in Bedfordshire, Oxfordshire or Norfolk. These were illegal, underground events and weren't in venues like The Sanctuary, where you had to pay to get in. They usually took place in fields and forests, although they would occasionally be held in barns when the weather was too cold to rave outside. Some of the parties only lasted a single night, others would go on for days. I remember a rave in Wales that started on Friday night and was still going strong on Tuesday. I stayed up for the full four nights and had the time of my life. The advantage of sticking to amphetamine was that I had more stamina than a lot of the other ravers. The ketamine-heads fell over part way through the night and the Ecstasy-heads became paranoid, but I stayed lively and alert.

It wasn't just the opportunity to get high that attracted me to the raves; I liked the idea of heading to a secret location at a moment's notice and transforming a field into a dance floor. Every weekend was different; we never knew which area of Britain we would travel to or what the party would be like. Some of the characters that I met were unbelievable. There was a guy who always turned up in an ice-cream van and sold cornets and iced lollies to the ravers. He must have made a packet because everyone was usually hot and sweaty from taking drugs and needed something to cool them down.

Whilst I was busy ruining my life with amphetamine, the other partygoers were getting more and more into ketamine. They wrecked the raves a bit by spending half the time on the floor, but it was funny to watch them keeling over. When people are off their faces on that stuff, they go into a state known as the 'K hole', which is where they lose all sense of spatial awareness. Watching them stumbling about the place was like a comedy show. Some of them would try to fight the K hole and struggle to their feet whenever they took a fall. They were the most entertaining ones to watch because no sooner had they managed to stand up than they were on the ground again.

As the months went by, other more harmful substances began to take hold. People started smoking crack at the raves, which used to be unheard of. When I first went to the parties, hard drugs like that were a completely different scene. The ravers would stick to things that made them happy and carefree. Crack had the opposite effect. It created a dark and angry vibe. The minute the two cultures crossed over, the moodiness of the parties went through the roof. Addicts went round robbing everyone and love and peace were soon replaced by a drug-fuelled aggression. The happy, smiley raves that I once knew were soon a thing of the past.

My relationship with Jack also began to suffer during this period. He started hanging around with a girl of his own age, which rang alarm bells. Whenever I questioned him, he assured me there was nothing going on, but I suspected that he was cheating. His sly ways created a lot of tension and made me realise that our time together was limited.

Now that the parties weren't particularly safe anymore and I could no longer trust my boyfriend, the speed put me on edge and I started to feel desperately scared and anxious whenever I got high. Reality blurred with paranoia and I thought that all of the other ravers were undercover Old Bill. It was no longer a case of happily dancing the night away; my sanity was gradually eroding.

When you're awake for six full days and nights, your mind becomes a haunted house. Your sleep-deprived brain can't interpret what is going on and drums up all the worst-case scenarios. I thought that harmless passers-by were following me and attached a sinister agenda to everyday events. The stress of my extradition mingled with drug-induced fatigue and sent me spiralling into a state of permanent fear and tension.

As if I wasn't paranoid enough, somebody spiked my drink with rohypnol at one of the parties. I lost twelve hours of my life that night. The only thing I can remember is coming to and being violently sick. It's terrifying when I think of all the things that could have gone on during the time that I was under. I hadn't taken anything that I wasn't accustomed to, so why would I have passed out if somebody hadn't put something in my drink? It was a horrendous experience that destroyed what little trust I had left. From that day onwards I vowed never to let anybody near my Malibu. I was suspicious of anyone who came within a hundred yards and found it impossible to relax.

I wasn't the only victim of the new breed of ill-intentioned raver. The ketamine users were the perfect targets for robberies because they spent most of their time completely incapacitated. Crackheads don't care what they do to get a fix. They probably would have amputated the fallen ravers' legs if they thought that they could get a couple of quid for them. When I first started going to the parties you could leave your car door open with the keys in the ignition and nobody would touch it. The raves were the polar opposite of how they used to be. Love and positivity had transformed into hate and dodginess.

I could no longer unwind at the parties so I started developing new ways to take my mind off the extradition. I had always been artistic and enjoyed creating things so I got into sewing cushions. I started off sewing one or two to pass the time and soon got to the stage where I was sitting up all night, making mountains of them. That shows what an addictive personality I've got. I must have completed a couple of thousand cushions altogether. Looking back I probably had some kind of OCD. Drugs can often make you want to do repetitive activities. The monotonous nature of the tasks that you are performing somehow feels rewarding. I'm not sure if amphetamine brought on my condition but it definitely made it worse.

The other thing that I became obsessed with was my niece Emma. I knew that she would be a teenager by the time I got out of prison, which caused me no end of upset. I wanted to spend as much time as I could with her and ended up going overboard. I spent every waking moment in her company and couldn't bear to be away for too long. Saying goodbye to go to prison was going to tear my heart apart. It was going to be horrendous.

My family made allowances for my moodiness and obsessiveness but not everybody was as sympathetic to my plight. In late 2003 I got a phone call from my landlady telling me to meet her at the office. I knew exactly what it was about; she had heard about my status as public enemy number one and wanted to evict me.

'I'm afraid I'm going to have to terminate your tenancy,' she told me. 'I can't have somebody who's been involved in criminal activity living in my property.'

It was just another humiliating experience to add to the collection. I wasn't angry with her because it was her house, which meant she had the right to kick me out. I didn't have the energy to plead my innocence either so I just said 'OK' and left.

Some of my raving buddies were looking for a housemate at the time so I moved in with them in Aylesbury. They lived in an area called Haydon Hill on the less upmarket side of the town. Haydon Hill itself was quite a quiet place, but it was near a rough estate called Quarrendon. This might have unnerved some people but I couldn't have cared less that I was going to live on the doorstep of the area known locally as Beirut. Home was now wherever there was amphetamine. My house was just a place for me to crash out during my one night a week of sleep.

OUT OF THE FRYING PAN AND INTO THE FIRE

I would have got on well with my new housemates if it wasn't for the fact that one of them was a little bit on the messy side. I'm a very tidy person; I like everything in its place. Not everybody can be as clean as me, so I should have just put up with it, but instead I screamed my head off at them whenever they left their things about the place. I guess a week of sleepless nights can turn a nice girl into a monster. Looking back I must have been a nightmare to live with.

My obsession with tidiness had pros as well as cons because I managed to get a job working for my landlord's cleaning company. I was running low on cash so it was a godsend. I also gained a lot of satisfaction because I loved the challenge of sprucing up a filthy home. I liked comparing the dirtiness of the rooms at the start to the spotless end result. The only thing I didn't like about my job was the unpredictability. I worked whenever there was work available rather than following a set timetable. I would have preferred to have had a weekly routine but beggars can't be choosers. Some of my friends from the rave scene made their money in less reputable ways.

When you're hanging about in an environment that is centred around drugs, it becomes impossible not to mix with shady people. Dodginess comes with the territory. I would have liked to have kept my world separate from theirs, but unfortunately life always seemed to find a way of dragging me into other people's mess. I didn't like the shadiness but the shadiness liked me – and one day it came knocking at my door... or rather booting it off the hinges.

Chapter 13

A SENSE OF DÉJÀ VU

'Don't move! Keep your hands where we can see them. Stay exactly where you are.'

It was eleven in the morning and I was still in bed. I had spent the last few days immersed in an amphetamine-induced haze and had no idea what was going on. Who were these rude, aggressive people and what were they doing in my room? I hoped it wasn't the UDA. What if they had spent the last few years tracking me down? The intruders were all in police uniform so I should have known straightaway that they were coppers, but your brain doesn't always work the way it should do when you're on a comedown. I wished that I had stayed out partying another day. Sobriety was scary.

'We're here to conduct a thorough search of your property. We have reason to believe you're in possession of a large amount of cocaine.'

It was the Old Bill. They weren't exactly my favourite people but at least they were unlikely to take me out the back and blow my kneecaps off. I remember feeling relieved but at the same time wondering what was going on. It was like the airport in Tenerife all over again.

'If you do find any coke it's nothing to do with me,' I said. 'I'm out on High Court bail and my mum's boyfriend's put up ten grand. Filling my house with drugs is the last thing I'd do.'

'If you're in so much trouble anyway then why would you even give a shit?' the officer-in-charge sneered back at me. 'You're up to your neck in it as it is and you're still breaking the law. Sad really, ain't it?'

Who did this bloke think he was? I honestly didn't have a single gram of cocaine in the house. He was going to be extremely disappointed when he did the search.

The coppers carried out the most half-arsed drug bust that you could possibly imagine. Some of my dodgier friends from the rave scene had been raided before and told me that the Old Bill tore the place apart. Something definitely wasn't right. The officers didn't even use sniffer dogs and hardly moved a thing. Stranger still, they made me stay upstairs the whole time they were there, which is against police procedure. The drug squad are supposed to let you keep an eye on them so that they can't set you up.

When I was finally allowed downstairs, I saw a strange man with a briefcase furtively leaving the house. Where did he fit into all of this? And what on earth was in the case? He had either brought something in or smuggled something out. Was the raid a ruse to plant some kind of listening device? When I thought about everything that had gone on, it actually seemed quite plausible.

The Old Bill found a pair of weighing scales in my room and tried to make out it was proof that I was selling drugs. The scales weren't used for portioning out mountains of cocaine though; they were for weighing jewellery. I just wanted to know whether I was being ripped off or not when I was buying gold. When I told them this, the coppers looked dejected. I think that they were hoping I was Aylesbury's answer to Pablo Escobar.

'You got lucky this time,' snarled a disgruntled officer.

The drug squad had demolished my front door and broken part of the wall whilst forcing their way in so I asked them if they were going to pay for the damage.

'We don't have to pay a thing,' came the predictable reply. 'We had intelligence from a reliable source that you were stashing drugs.'

This meant that an informant had given them my address. For somebody as paranoid as me, it was an absolute nightmare. I found it hard enough to trust my mates as it was and now I had good reason to be suspicious because it looked as if one of them was trying hard to get me nicked.

It was unlikely that I was the target of the raid because the police had sent an all-male drug squad and they normally send a policewoman to bust female suspects. I had an inkling that they might have been after one of my dodgy raving friends who occasionally visited. The mysterious man with the briefcase had been doing something in the front hall. Maybe he had hidden a bug in there in the hope of finding out who came and went.

I removed everything that was in contact with the hallway wall and sure enough, there was a tiny hole behind one of the pictures. It looked as if it had been made with a drill. I began to panic. I had somehow become embroiled in another epic piece of dodginess. How did this keep happening?

Word travels fast in Aylesbury. It's the type of town where everybody likes to gossip. My mates were no exception and by four o'clock that afternoon, a group of ravers had arrived at my house, looking to find out what the deal was.

'I've been bugged,' I told them, still visibly shaken up. 'Somebody's put something in my wall.'

Most people would have passed this off as paranoia but my friends were a little more clued-up. They knew full well that the Old Bill would go to any lengths to catch somebody who they thought was dealing large amounts of coke. Having my hallway bugged seemed a bit far-fetched but when you're hanging about with addicts, anything is possible. Rather than telling me that I was going mad, my mates were quick to offer advice. They said they knew somebody who had a bug detector and asked me if I wanted to borrow it.

This was living proof that you can get hold of anything at a moment's notice if you know the right people. To your average, law-abiding citizen, a bug detector might sound like something out of a James Bond film, but it didn't come as much of a surprise to me that to me that somebody had one of these devices – there were a lot of dealers in Aylesbury at the time. I wouldn't say that it had any more of a drug problem than your average town; everywhere has its users and its dealers. If you're part of that scene, you could probably get your hands on a similar thing anywhere in the country.

'Yeah that sounds like just what I'm after,' I said. 'I want to get to the bottom of all this. Drill marks don't just appear in walls. Something is definitely going on.'

'Leave it with me,' my friend told me. 'I'll bring it round in a couple of days and we can find your bug.'

By the time my mates came back with the machine, I couldn't wait to use it. It was a small, black, square box that resembled a

Scalextric controller and was designed to beep when it passed over an electrical device that could potentially be a bug. I didn't know how to use it so I got my friend to do the honours and no sooner had she turned it on than it started going off. It was beeping right next to the drill hole, which meant the Old Bill really had been messing about with my wall. I felt a little panic-stricken but also strangely reassured. I could now take steps to remove the bug and make sure that my private conversations weren't the talk of the police station. I guess being paranoid isn't all that bad when people are actually listening in on you.

I carried on hovering the detector over anything and everything and soon uncovered another bug, this time in my mobile. This was great; I wasn't even safe to speak to people over the phone. The police clearly didn't want to miss a single word I said. I wondered how many more devices I was going to find. My life had now transformed from an episode of *Banged Up Abroad* into a scene from *Mission Impossible*. I just wanted it to go back to the way it was before I ever got involved with drugs.

I discovered the third and final bug in Mickey's car, which was parked outside the house. The police had obviously thought that it was mine and wanted to listen in on me whilst I was driving. They would be disappointed when they realised they had bugged a car belonging to someone who had never broken a law in his life. Maybe it would teach them to do their homework a bit better the next time they decided to play at being spies.

I knew the bugs weren't aimed at exposing any criminality on my part because I hadn't done anything wrong apart from taking drugs. They couldn't have been targeted at my housemates either; they weren't even overly concerned by what had happened because they had nothing to hide. I wasn't about to let the coppers eavesdrop on my friends though, so I immediately rang up everybody that I knew and told them to stay away. The bug in the hall was easy enough to remedy. I just turned the TV up to full volume so that the coppers couldn't hear a thing. Now all I had to do was get rid of my phone and the Old Bill's attempt to intrude on my life would be a wasted effort.

Even after I had rendered the bugs useless, I couldn't help but feel as if the police were somehow monitoring my every move, and also wondered whether they would up the stakes and do something else when they discovered that I was onto them. I propped a clothes horse and a coat stand up against the front door and curled up on the couch that night because I was paranoid that they were going to burst into my room to do another raid. This became my nightly routine. Sanity was slowly slipping through my fingertips. I found it impossible to relax and didn't trust a soul. All of the sunshine gradually ebbed out of my life until my world became pitch black.

My fragile mental state grew even more delicate when I realised that an unmarked police car was posted outside my house. It was blindingly obvious that it was full of Old Bill because it was there twenty-four hours a day, seven days a week. My local pub was just around the corner from where I lived so I was always staggering about the streets in the small hours and whenever I returned home, the car was there, regardless of what time it was. It didn't take a rocket scientist to figure out that I was being watched.

I had no reason to worry because the only illegal thing that I was doing was taking base. If the police were hoping somebody was going to drop a kilo of cocaine off at the house then they were barking up the wrong tree. I might have had some dodgy people knocking on my door but I never got involved in their business.

I should have felt reassured that there was nothing the cops could pin on me but they were making me feel guilty even though I hadn't done a thing.

The coppers weren't the only people who were convinced of my guilt either. When Jack's mum found out that I had been raided, she went mental and pressurised him into stopping seeing me. Things had been fizzling out for a while but I was still gutted because he was a decent lad. It seemed as if everybody in the local area was talking about me and discussing my downfall.

The only place that I could relax was work because I was able to throw myself into it and forget that I was Aylesbury's most wanted. I loved to clean. There is something about transforming a dust-ridden mess into a surface that could pass for a mirror that is infinitely rewarding. Whilst I was working I was no longer Terry Daniels, international fugitive; I was just a regular cleaning girl. It was the only small semblance of normality in my life and I didn't know what I would have done without it.

Everything was going well at work until the day I was asked to clean an old folks' home in the nearby town of Princes Risborough. I remember thinking it was strange that I had been sent there on my own because the number one rule for cleaning places like that is that you always go in pairs so that nobody can steal things from the old people and try to blame it on the cleaner. I should have insisted on going with somebody else, but had a lot on my mind and wasn't thinking straight. This turned out to be a big mistake. I have an uncanny knack of being in the wrong place at the wrong time and this was certainly no exception.

Chapter 14

ARRESTED AGAIN

The old folks' home was filthy. I don't know who was supposed to have cleaned it before me and what their excuse was, but all the walls were covered in a thick layer of grime. The place was in a state, but I was confident that I could leave it looking spotless, so I donned my rubber gloves, picked up the cleaning material and went to work straightaway.

I worked my fingers to the bone to get the filth off the walls and did a really thorough job. It was another pay cheque in my pocket, which would allow me to drown my sorrows with speed and Malibu. I had fuelled my addiction to cleanliness; now it was time for me to feed my more destructive urges.

After spending the night getting horribly drunk and high as usual, I dragged myself out of my pit and made my way to work. I had enjoyed the challenge of the previous day's cleaning session and hoped my boss would send me somewhere similar. As I approached the office, I caught sight of a young, jumped-up looking policeman standing at the entrance. Panic immediately set in. I knew that he was there for me and felt my knees go weak. Maybe the twenty-four hour surveillance that I was under had uncovered some minor act of wrongdoing. I wanted to turn around and run but knew full well I had to face up to whatever it was I was supposed to have done.

'Are you Teresa Daniels?' the officer asked as I approached the door, a stern look on his face as if to say, 'You're for it now young lady'.

He was quite attractive for a copper but had a rude demeanour to him.

'Yeah, why? What's going on?'

'I'm arresting you on suspicion of theft. Several credit cards have gone missing from an old people's home in Princes Risborough and I have reason to believe that you might be responsible. You don't have to say anything but anything that you do say can and will be used in evidence against you.'

This was even more of a shock to me than the drug bust had been. I might have been a whiz addict and an alcoholic, but one thing I would never do is steal from the elderly. I couldn't even believe somebody would think that I could do a thing like that. It sickened me to the core.

As the copper escorted me into the back of his car, I thought, 'Is this how my life is going to go on? Am I going to spend the whole time being ferried back and forth from police stations?' I was at the end of my tether. Every other week I was accused of something else. Somebody mistaking me for a drug smuggler was one thing, but getting nicked for thieving from an old folks' home was an entirely different matter. It was the type of crime that only somebody with no morals whatsoever would commit. Did the police honestly believe that I would stoop that low? It was difficult to take in.

I was taken to High Wycombe Police Station and locked up in a dirty little cell with a toilet in the corner. By this stage I was in the depths of despair. The police were going to raid my house again. They wouldn't find anything but it was unfair on my housemates. They were caught up in my never-ending cycle of arrests, raids and interrogations. First I was a cocaine smuggler, then a terrorist, then a drug dealer and now the coppers were accusing me of robbing people's grannies. It was all too much to take.

It sounds bizarre but one of the things that really got to me was the fact that I had cleaned the old folks' home so well. I had really put my heart and soul into my work and here I was getting nicked for supposedly fleecing the place. I felt angry that I was taking the rap for something that someone else had done. I was as much of a victim as the owners of the credit cards because somebody had set me up and I was paying for their dishonesty.

'Who else was about at the time?' I asked myself, trying hard to work out who the real culprit was. I was usually very aware of my surroundings, which was probably a result of being both highly paranoid and wide-awake due to whiz. The fact that I was unable to recall anybody else being in the area made me doubt myself. I started thinking, 'Did I do it? Did I put something in my pocket by mistake?' It was ridiculous because I knew full well that I would never steal from an old folks' home but I was in a state of extreme anxiety and felt guilty even though I hadn't taken a thing.

The police phoned up my mum and told her I had been arrested.

'What's she done?' she asked, shocked that I was in trouble yet again.

The copper read the charges out.

'Oh, whatever. She hasn't done that,' scoffed Mum.

If I had been accused of something else then it's possible she might have thought that I was guilty, but she knew full well that I would never steal from old people. At least somebody could be sure of my innocence. I was caught up in a whirlwind of self-doubt. Had I started stealing things without even realising what I was doing? My brain went into overdrive, attempting to figure out who else could have snuck in and taken the credit cards.

Fortunately the law firm that was dealing with my extradition provided a solicitor, who was able to remind me how preposterous the allegations were. He had to travel down from London and wasn't best pleased with the police. As far as he was concerned, it was all a massive waste of time. He knew enough about me from what his colleagues had told him to know that I wasn't the type of person who would steal from the elderly. Now it was just a matter of convincing the Old Bill. My interview was fairly one-sided because I was unable to answer the majority of the questions.

'Who else was nearby at the time? Which other members of staff were present? Did you see anybody suspicious hanging around?'

I had been far too immersed in my job to take in anything else. When you're cleaning a room, you don't usually scan the building for potential thieves whilst doing it. You tend to concentrate upon the task at hand. To be honest, somebody wearing a black and white striped jumper and carrying a bag labelled 'swag' could have strolled into the home and I would have carried on obliviously scrubbing away.

'We didn't find anything in your house. You must have hid it pretty well', the copper told me, as if the lack of evidence was somehow proof of what a professional thief I was.

My solicitor wasn't too chuffed at this. He looked as if he was going to explode. His face went bright red and the vein in his head seemed on the verge of bursting.

'Shut up now,' he snapped. 'You've got nothing on her. Let the poor girl go.'

The officer did as he was told but couldn't resist getting a sly dig in whilst I was being released.

'If your fingerprints are found on any of the stolen things then you'll be straight back here before your feet can touch the ground,' he sneered.

This was a pretty stupid thing to say because I had been wearing rubber gloves, which meant the cards would still be print-free if I had taken them. Nevertheless the fact that he was so convinced I was guilty really got to me. Had I sunk to the level where people thought that I would steal from dear old biddies? I hung my head in shame as I left the station. The police had succeeded in making me feel as if I was the lowest of the low.

I was taken back to work by another equally jumped-up copper, who tried to slyly pick my brains during the journey.

'Who do you know in Aylesbury then?' he asked. But what he really meant was, 'Who do you know in Aylesbury who's a criminal?'

'I don't hang around with crooks if that's what you want to know,' I said. 'I'm in enough trouble as it is in Spain without involving myself in anything like that over here.'

The officer carried on trying to subtly trip me up but it was all to no avail. The minute we pulled up at the cleaning office, I thanked him for the lift and hopped out of the car. I was glad to finally be free of interrogation. It had been a very long and tiring day.

I was half-expecting my boss to fire me but he knew I wasn't the type of person who would steal from the home. He was just pissed off because he wasn't going to be paid for the work that I had done. I was relieved to have been given the benefit of the doubt but annoyed that we had both lost out on wages.

Rather than heading home straightaway, I called in at my mum's house first because I was still in a state of shock and needed a shoulder to cry on. Mum was more upset than me. She was unable to get her head around the fact that I had been accused of depriving old dears of their pension money. One of the reasons I was so worked up was that I couldn't believe that anybody could steal from vulnerable, elderly people. It was something I would never even contemplate.

Two days later, a woman was arrested for trying to use the credit cards at a garage in High Wycombe. Did I get an apology from the police for being hauled into the station and treated like the scum of the earth? Well, I think you can guess the answer to that one. I hoped they felt ashamed but knew deep down that people who are that pigheaded never admit to being in the wrong. Nevertheless justice had been served and the filth that stitched me up was now heading to jail.

The capture of the thief should have provided me with a sense of closure but I still didn't know exactly what had happened. I only had the name of the culprit to go on, which left me wondering whether she was a worker at the home or just a passing opportunist looking to make a buck. It angered me to think that some of the employees might have tried to pin the blame on me deliberately. They probably thought, 'Oh, this girl's never been here before. We'll get her into trouble and make some money whilst we're at it.' The thought of the staff at the home conspiring against me made me even more depressed. They say God only throws at you what you can handle but I was sure that one more unpleasant episode would finish me off for good. I contemplated moving back in with my mum because I didn't fancy spending another night on the couch where I had been sleeping every night since the raid, in case the police burst into my room again. The problem was that I would have had to cut down on the drugs. I couldn't have Mum finding out that I was shovelling amphetamine down my throat like it was going out of style. No, I would just have to soldier on and stick it out at my house. It wasn't as if I was spending all my time at home; I was out most nights at the parties anyway.

Even though the base now sent me paranoid, the raves were still the only thing I had to look forward to. They were full of people who were just as off their heads as me, which provided me with a false sense of assurance that I had everything under control. Some of other ravers were actually *more* off their heads. One lad in particular fell firmly into this category. His name was Bruce and he liked smoking crack. Unfortunately this was something that I remained blissfully unaware of until it was too late.

I was always wary of crack users. The problem was that it was impossible to tell who was on it and who was high on other things. Ravers tend to be quite skinny because they usually take a lot of Ecstasy. Any one of them could pass for a crackhead. For all intents and purposes, Bruce was just your average, run-of-the-mill partygoer. I had no idea that he was a slave to one of the most addictive substances on earth; it never even entered my mind.

I nearly missed out on the party where our paths first crossed. I was part way through the journey there when I got word that the coppers had turned up to try and shut down the rave.

'Stop the car,' I told my friend, the fear of ending up in another police cell almost paralysing me.

We pulled up at the edge of Royston, the small town in rural Hertfordshire where the party was being held. There was no way I was going to move until the cops had buggered off. As I waited for somebody to phone and let me know the coast was clear, a wave of fear and anxiety surged throughout my body. The panic grew progressively worse until my brain was unable to cope. The branches of a nearby tree began to morph themselves into the shape of sinister-looking fairies and cackling witches' faces. I was cracking up big time.

By this stage I was used to being pushed over the edge by paranoia and didn't see random hallucinations as anything particularly shocking. Don't get me wrong, it wasn't a very pleasant experience but I knew that I just had to ride it out. My friend didn't seem to mind sitting in the car with me. She took a lot of drugs herself so I think that she was probably in a similar state. If the men in white coats had knocked on my car door that night, they would have definitely taken us away. We remained rooted to the spot for the next nine hours, afraid to move an inch in case we somehow caught the attention of the Old Bill. I think if either of us had actually seen a copper during this period, we would probably both have had heart attacks.

By the time we finally managed to pry ourselves out of the car, it was eight o'clock in the morning and the sun was coming up. I was exhausted and had cramp in both my legs but still wanted to go to the rave. It had been a long and terrifying night and I felt as if I had earned the right to have a bit of a dance to end things on a happy note.

The minute I arrived at the rave, I started to feel myself again. Being around other people helped to calm me down and stopped me tripping out. I was soon dancing away without a care in the world. It was as if nothing had ever happened, which shows how scarily commonplace losing my marbles had become. Being paralysed with fear was no longer something that left me thinking, 'What have I done to myself?' It was now just one of those things.

As I gyrated my body to the beat, I noticed one of the other ravers staring across at me from the other side of the room. He was tall, dark-haired and had a cocky look to him, which is something that I like in men. I don't know why, but I have always had a soft spot for blokes who come across as very sure of themselves. I wondered if he was looking at me because he fancied me but didn't get chance to find out because one minute he was there, the next thing he was gone, caught up in the swaying mass of bodies. I carried on dancing the night away without giving a second thought to this mysterious, tall, dark stranger. It was only after he cropped up at the next couple of raves that I decided to say hello.

I have always been a bit of a cheeky character and have no problem talking to people I don't know. I can't remember how I first struck up a conversation with Bruce, but do remember flirting outrageously. He was very confident and I'm not exactly the shy retiring type myself so we had a lot in common personality-wise.

'I'll see you at the party next week,' I told him as we eventually parted company. He drank, he took drugs and he liked dance music so he was definitely my type.

Unfortunately Bruce's mum had other ideas. She thought that he was overdoing it and put pressure on him to give the next event a miss. This was a stroke of luck on his part, as it was a particularly awful rave. It was at a warehouse in a rundown, industrial area of London and all of the other ravers looked like football hooligans. The London parties tended to be quite moody. There was a lot of crack at them, which meant you had to be on your guard against people robbing you.

The indoor setting of the party made it even shadier because the ketamine-heads usually only went to outdoor raves. Irritating as they were, they helped to keep the vibe chilled out because it's impossible to cause aggro when you're falling about all over the place. They were also normally harmless, tree-hugging, hippie types, who wouldn't hurt a fly. The crowd at this rave seemed more likely to chop a tree down and club somebody to death with it than hug it. They looked like a cross between a violent mob of Millwall supporters and the cast of *Trainspotting*. It was one of the worst events I've been to and I was relieved when it was over. At least I had got the chance to get completely off my trolley. I then went to pick up Bruce and finish the night off with someone who didn't measure the quality of a night out by the amount of bruising on his knuckles. I was still buzzing from the base and needed somebody to natter to. He had respected his mum's wishes and sat the party out, so surely she could spare him for a couple of hours to chill out at my house.

Bruce was with a couple of his friends when I met up with him so I told him they could all come back to mine. A few of my raving buddies wanted to prolong the night so I invited them as well.

'I hope there's enough booze to go round,' I joked as I drove back to Haydon Hill.

'Don't worry,' Bruce grinned, pulling out a large bag of cocaine. 'There's always this to keep us entertained.'

I assumed that he was going to snort it. Little did I know that he was planning on cooking it into crack.

When we arrived at the house, Bruce took an empty can of Coca-Cola off the side and punched holes in the bottom. I had seen Antonio do this before. He was making a crack pipe.

'I'll be back in a bit,' he told me, heading off into the kitchen. 'I'm just going to make us all a little treat.'

For whatever reason, I was very blasé about what was happening. I figured being around a crack smoker wasn't all that bad so long as he wasn't an addict. What I failed to realise was that crack cocaine is definitely not a recreational drug. Most people who take it have a habit or are at least in the process of developing one. I should have told him to go and smoke his drugs elsewhere but I was too spaced out to think. Instead I took a seat and awaited his return.

When Bruce came back, he was holding a couple of small, white rocks of crack.

'Let's get this on the burn then,' he said, a look of craving in his eyes, as if he had been waiting for this moment all night.

He sprinkled some cigarette ash on top of the can, then laid the stones on it.

'Time to get stuck in,' he smiled, lighting the pipe and sucking in the thick, white, heavy smoke.

Everybody in the room had a puff on the can. The worrying thing was that they all seemed as if they had smoked crack before – and not just Bruce's friends, my raving buddies gave the same impression. I had known that they took drugs but had no idea they did stuff like this. It should have rung alarm bells but I just thought, 'OK, whatever.' If they wanted to take such a horribly addictive substance then it was up to them. After all, I was as high as a kite on speed so who was I to talk?

Normally people get really agitated and unpredictable after puffing on rocks but homemade crack doesn't tend to be as strong so nobody was that out of it. This made me question whether it was actually as bad as people made it out to be. My friends all looked OK. They were still exactly the same as they had been before smoking the stones. We carried on drinking and socialising until nine in the morning and then finally went to sleep. I remember thinking, 'Nothing bad's gone on. I don't see what the fuss is all about.' I had forgotten that word travels fast in Aylesbury. People cooking rocks up in my house might not have bothered me but my landlord was a little more concerned.

Bang, bang, bang!

Who was this disturbing my lie in? I got little enough sleep as it was.

Bang, bang, bang!

I dragged myself downstairs and flung open the door. It was Dora, the landlord's wife, and she didn't look best pleased.

'I've been told that you've been taking crack in my husband's property,' she confronted me.

'I most certainly have not,' I said.

By this stage I was sick to the back teeth of being accused of things I hadn't done. Looking back it probably didn't matter to her whether it was me or my friends who smoked the crack, but I was incensed that she was laying the blame on me.

'Well that's not what I've heard,' she told me.

'I couldn't care less what you've heard,' I shouted. 'I have never touched the stuff.'

I was on a comedown as per usual and didn't have the patience for her. I wanted to be left to nurse my fragile brain in peace.

A slanging match ensued and Dora slapped me hard across the face. I was shocked because she wasn't usually a violent person. With the gift of hindsight, I can see why she was so annoyed. It's illegal to let a tenant smoke drugs on your property so she was probably concerned about her husband's livelihood and angry that I was so dismissive about her accusations.

I shouldn't have been so mouthy to poor old Dora. I was a gobby little madam and probably deserved her hand across my face. We bumped into each other in Aylesbury not so long ago and I apologised for my behaviour. I said, 'I was a different person all those years ago. I don't drink or take drugs any more.' She told me she could see that just from talking to me, which shows you what a nice lady she is despite our falling out.

I was angry that I had been slapped, but fury soon converted into sadness. I knew that I would have to move out of the house and didn't want to go back to living with Mum again. It felt like taking a step backwards and besides, how could I carry on partying with a worried mother looking over my shoulder? I don't like lying to my mum and didn't fancy the idea of doing it over and over again.

The other thing that made me feel depressed was the realisation that I was going to have to quit my job because my landlord, who was also the owner of the cleaning company, thought I was smoking crack and that would make for an impossible working relationship. Cleaning was the only activity that made me feel like a productive member of society though and I was gutted that the one remaining piece of normality in my life was being stripped away.

I left it a couple of days to make the call to Dora's husband because I needed some time to prepare for giving up both my house and my job. He was surprisingly understanding when I finally steeled myself to ring him. I think he realised I was in a state and he didn't want to be too harsh. His niceness made me feel even worse about myself. I couldn't believe that I had driven such a reasonable man to send his wife round to kick off. What type of person had I become? I was destroying everything I held dear and turning everyone against me.

Now I needed to call my mum to tell her I was moving out. I was initially considering getting another place of my own but Mum insisted I come home.

'I'm so worried about you,' she said. 'You need to live with me so I can make sure you're OK.'

It was obvious things weren't going too well. I didn't want to relinquish my freedom but eventually gave in and let her persuade me to move back into my old room.

Mum was relieved to have me where she could look after me. She put my loss of weight and pale, sickly complexion down to stress about the extradition. I should have told her what was going on but knew she would go mad. Besides, she had enough to worry about as it was. No, I would have to be very secretive. She didn't need anything else on her plate.

Hiding my habit from Mum was actually pretty easy. The more drugs you take, the more deceitful you become. It's part and parcel of being an addict. Even people with serious heroin problems manage to conceal their lifestyles from their relatives. It's just a matter of thinking up the right excuses. I would disappear for days on end and tell Mum I was staying with a friend. When I was up all night on whiz, I said I had insomnia. Everything fell neatly into place.

Looking back, I feel terrible for stringing her along like that. Mum would have gone mental if she had known the truth, but would have eventually calmed down and helped me to get clean. I guess I felt that I would soon be out of her hair so there was little point in owning up. Ten years is more than enough time to kick a speed habit so at least if I got sent down, it might help to straighten me out and then I could finally live an honest life without having to lie to the person I loved the most.

The more I thought about my extradition, the more depressed I got. I was jobless, on bail for smuggling a million pounds' worth of cocaine and hooked on super-strength amphetamine; it doesn't get much worse than that. I decided that my level of unhappiness had fallen well below the normal lows that addicts get from speed so it was time to seek professional medical advice before I topped myself. I booked myself an appointment with the doctor and crossed my fingers that he would be able to pick me up out of the dark abyss that I had fallen into.

Dr McCarthy had been my doctor for as long as I could remember. He used to see me as a little girl and seemed the perfect person to pour my heart out to about how bad I felt. I considered telling him about the drugs but worried that he might go to the cops. My friends had always warned me not to let on to my GP that I took whiz in case he reported it. This was ridiculous because doctors aren't allowed to disclose information about their patients, but I was still highly paranoid so I decided to limit our discussion to my depression and anxiety.

I told Dr McCarthy about my sleepless nights and lack of appetite and he gave me a look as if to say, 'Is there something that you're leaving out?' I think he knew that I was hooked on drugs but was reluctant to force it out of me. I avoided his gaze and carried on relaying my symptoms. There was no way I was going to come clean about my habit. He could look at me like that all day.

Dr McCarthy eventually gave up trying to get to the truth and diagnosed me based upon the limited information that he had.

'You seem to be suffering from a high level of stress,' he said. 'You can't work in this state. I'm going to give you a sick note so that you can get incapacity benefit. You need to take it easy and try your hardest to relax. Do you want me to prescribe a dose of antidepressants?'

I didn't want to take any form of medication that I could possibly get addicted to. It was bad enough with just the one habit without adding Valium to my daily drug intake.

'I'll be OK without anything like that.'

'Are you sure?' Dr McCarthy asked, raising his eyebrows as if to suggest that he knew better. 'It might help you to sleep.'

Not with the mountains of amphetamine that I was pouring down my neck each night it wouldn't. I didn't want to risk mixing my drugs either. I had always been careful to only take one thing at a time. There was no telling what antidepressants would do in conjunction with speed and I didn't want to find out.

'Yeah, I'm OK,' I said. 'I'll just try to take it easy. Thanks for seeing me.'

As I left the surgery, I felt sad that I had lied to somebody who seemed so genuinely concerned about me. How was I going to get help if I couldn't even admit what was wrong? The fact that I was on the sick should have helped to reduce my stress but had the opposite effect. It only compounded my feeling of uselessness. Not only was I looking at ten years in prison but I was now forced to rely on government handouts to get by. My life had reached rock bottom and wasn't getting any better. My only ray of hope was the possibility that I might not have to go to Spain, but even if I managed to avoid being extradited, I was still an addict and most of my immediate circle of friends was hooked on crack cocaine, the worst drug of the lot.

The first time I saw Bruce smoking a rock he had seemed OK, but every time since then it was as if he was possessed whenever he got high. The atmosphere immediately turned sour and he was like a completely different person. He was always arguing with his friends and accusing them of smoking his drugs. This was probably true most of the time because they kept trying to sneak off to puff stones on their own so that they didn't have to pass the pipe on to their mates. They transformed from a close-knit group of friends into people who would stab each other in the back to get the largest share of rocks.

Smoking crack seemed anything but fun. Heroin might be more addictive but at least it chills people out. Crack makes people violent, agitated and above all untrustworthy. Once it gets a grip of someone, they won't think twice about stealing from their mates, a fact I found out first-hand when Bruce nicked all my DVDs and tried to sell them to get drug money. It's a good thing I had seen what happened to Pookie in *New Jack City* or I might have become like him. I owe a lot to Pookie and Zammo. They made me steer well clear of crack and heroin and for that they will forever have my gratitude.

Looking back, I think the only reason that I carried on knocking about with the same set of druggies was because I had become so needy that I was glad of the company. I didn't care that I was surrounded by crackheads; I just wanted people around me so that I wasn't left alone with my thoughts. After a rave had finished, I would usually chill out at one of their houses so that I didn't have to be on my own.

Although I spent a lot of time with Bruce and his friends, my family were still my main source of support. They were usually fast asleep when I returned from the parties but I could always count on them during the day. Kelly tried to take my mind off the extradition by chatting to me about other things. It was always nice to converse with somebody who didn't constantly bring up the possibility of being shipped off to Spain.

Mum was just as good to talk to. She knew that I was going through hell and did her best to reassure me that everything was going to be OK. I should have been more grateful but the base had hold of me. It wasn't quite in the same league as crack but made me moody and bad tempered and I was always kicking off about something, which must have made me a nightmare to be around.

I was particularly obnoxious in the weeks leading up to my hearing. Lack of sleep mingled with extreme anxiety and created monstrous temper tantrums. Mum had the patience of a saint. Anybody else would have thrown me out on my ear. I think what stressed me out the most was the idea that I might have my bail revoked and get remanded in custody straight after the case. It was scary to think that even the brief period of freedom whilst the authorities decided my fate might be snatched away from me.

I spent the night before the hearing going over how I would react if I was taken away in handcuffs. By the morning, I was in a right state. I prayed that even if things didn't go my way, I would at least get bail. My mum would be gutted if I was suddenly whisked away to prison. It didn't bear thinking about.

I was at the peak of anxiety during the journey to Bow Street. It didn't help that there was a load of press waiting outside the court to photo some Americans who were involved in a big fraud case. It was intimidating having to walk through a seething mass of paparazzi to get inside the building. When you're sleep deprived and on a comedown, something like that can really take it out of you. I just hoped the end result would make it all worthwhile.

The spectators' gallery in the court was also full of reporters. The Americans were facing extradition straight after my hearing and the media didn't want to miss a thing. It would have been nerve-wracking enough without every seat in the room being filled. My heart was beating so fast that I thought it would explode.

Judge Evans looked just as snooty as he had done during my first time at Bow Street. He spoke with a plum-in-the-mouth Etonian accent and had a hard edge to his voice, as if he thought that everybody who entered his court was scum and needed locking up. The prosecutor seemed a little bit more sympathetic. She had a kindly demeanour and every now and again, I caught her giving me a concerned look, as if to say, 'Am I really doing the right thing here?' Unfortunately in order to do her job correctly, she couldn't let her personal opinions come into play. She was going to try her best to have me extradited irrespective of how bad it made her feel.

My barrister spoke in detail about how unfair my trial in Spain had been. He talked about the lack of real evidence, the misinterpretation of my diary and the fact that I was denied a translator. Judge Evans didn't seem to give a monkey's. As far as he was concerned, I was as guilty as could be.

'I do not accept as truthful what she says about the lack of interpretation,' he scoffed. 'The Spanish legal authorities were clearly aware of their legal obligations to provide interpreters. The trial judge would have also understood his duty to ensure that there was no lack of interpretation such as might prejudice Ms Daniels' full involvement in the trial.'

This was somewhat ridiculous, considering that all he had to go from was his own misguided belief in the fairness of the Spanish legal system. The prosecutor didn't dispute the lack of interpretation. She argued that my trial lawyer could have explained what had gone on after the court case had finished because he spoke perfect English.

'A lawyer able to speak the defendant's own language is no substitute for a proper interpreter, interpreting the proceedings fully and simultaneously,' my barrister countered. 'In addition to this, explaining the case after it has concluded is very different to having it translated word for word as it is taking place.'

'I am committing this case to the High Court,' said Judge Evans, looking upset that he hadn't been able to order my immediate extradition. 'You are to attend a hearing on 28 January, at which point a decision will be made.'

This meant that I had eight more months in the UK. I was disappointed that I hadn't been granted the right to stay but at the same time relieved I wasn't being remanded. As I left the court, I found myself longing for the day when I would no longer have to explain myself to jumped-up toffs in wigs. I was looking forward to it all being over and never having to see another judge again.

During the months leading up to my High Court appearance, I almost worried myself into an early grave. As it got nearer to the date, I became even more nervous and upset and felt as if I was teetering on the edge of a breakdown.

I knew that this court only heard the most high-profile cases, which made it very intimidating. It didn't get more serious than this. If I failed here then I would have to pack my suntan lotion ready for Spain.

On the day of the hearing, I got the train to London with my mum and spent the journey discussing all the possible outcomes of the case. I was absolutely wetting myself. Even though I had already been to court a couple of times before, the thought of people publicly going through the intimate details of my life still made me feel extremely anxious and uncomfortable. The fact that it was the High Court made it even worse. They were probably used to dealing with the likes of Ronnie Biggs and Howard Marks. It would be a shock for them to see a frightened girl from rural Buckinghamshire standing before them.

We arrived at Euston Station and hopped on the tube to The Strand. I almost had a warrant issued for my arrest because I couldn't find the court but managed to locate it in the nick of time. It was one of the most imposing buildings I have ever seen in my life. It looked like a big white castle and had a huge arch at the front, which I could have imagined a drawbridge extending out from. The pavement outside was also swarming with protestors because there was a demonstration going on in support of fox hunting.

'Just my bloody luck,' I thought.

First it was the paparazzi, now this. It was as if the world wanted to turn out to witness my downfall.

As I navigated my way through crowds of placard-bearers and people holding toy foxes, I felt a fresh wave of fear wash over me. This was it; the day of reckoning. If I failed to convince the judges that I had got a raw deal at my trial, I could say goodbye to England. At least then I would be able to get my sentence over with. Not knowing my fate was tearing me apart. I felt as if I had waited long enough.

The High Court is a little different to the magistrates in that there are three judges instead of one. You would have thought this would have given me a greater chance of getting somebody vaguely human but no, they were all old and obnoxious with a compassionless air to them.

The hearing was very similar to the one at Bow Street. The prosecution and defence came out with the same arguments and the judges seemed just as disinterested as Judge Evans had been. They gave the impression that they had already made up their minds that I was going to be extradited.

Part way through the hearing, a representative for Fair Trials International got up and walked out of the room in disgust. He was incensed that they were paying so little attention to the points that my solicitor was making. I looked over at my mum and she looked back at me. We were both in a state of shock. I had been hoping this would be the point my fortune finally turned. How wrong I had been.

'I see there are a lot of factors to be taken into consideration,' the head judge summed up. 'You will be informed of our decision via a letter sent to your solicitor.'

I knew things hadn't gone as planned but still felt relieved that the proceedings were over. It was time for me to go home and get trolleyed to take my mind off things. It was looking increasingly unlikely that I was going to remain in the UK so there was no reason to stay sober. I figured that I might as well go flat out until my extradition.

Mum went on holiday to Tenerife shortly after the court case, which enabled me to go out every other night. I shovelled so much speed down my throat during this period that I probably helped a couple of dealers to pay off their mortgages. Terrifying highs and cataclysmic lows cycled continuously round and round as I downed bag after bag of paste. On the day that my solicitor finally phoned with my result, I had been awake for four nights in a row. My brain felt as if it had been used as a football.

'Your case has been referred to the Home Secretary Charles Clarke,' he said. 'He'll have the final say on whether you stay in England.'

The home secretary is the most senior figure that can decide on the result of an extradition case. I felt a mixture of emotions; on the one hand I was worn down by the fact that things were dragging on so long, but on the other, I felt a strange glimmer of hope. Charles Clarke could say, 'This girl's been through enough. She's going nowhere.' Then again he could well say, 'Send her to Spain immediately. She needs locking up.'

Whilst Mr Clarke pored over the details of my case, I poured mounds of high-strength amphetamine out of a plastic sealer bag. I also poured myself glass after glass of Malibu. The further I drew towards my fate, the more reckless I became. I no longer cared how much damage I did to my body. Nothing mattered any more apart from the outcome of my case.

It was August by the time my solicitor rang up to inform me of the final verdict.

'I'm sorry Terry,' he told me. 'The Home Secretary wants the authorities to go ahead with your extradition.'

I felt as if my heart had been ripped out of my chest. All of my trips back and forth to court had been for nothing in the end. It's bad enough going to prison in England but the thought of being locked up in a country where I was unable to speak the language was absolutely terrifying. This was it; I had used up all my chances. I was off to sunny Spain. Years of uncertainty had been thrust on me because of a crime that somebody else committed and now I was being jailed for it as well. It beggared belief.

Chapter 15

THE EXTRADITION

Tears formed in my eyes as I thought about everything that I would have to leave behind. My life in Buckinghamshire had gone a bit pear-shaped but still beat sitting cooped up in a cell for a decade. I had no idea how long it was going to be before Scotland Yard got back to me with my extradition date. The Spanish authorities are very unpredictable. Sometimes they can take months to make the simplest decisions. For all I knew, it could be anything from a week to a year before I heard when I was going.

If I hadn't already been taking the maximum amount of whiz that I could possibly consume, then I probably would have gone even crazier on it than before, but as it was, I carried on at a steady rate of knots. None of my drug-taking friends were particularly surprised about the outcome of my case. They had known there was a strong possibility things wouldn't go my way. Some of them were in denial and thought that I was going to be spared at the last minute, but other more realistic raving buddies said their goodbyes and wished me a hassle-free sentence.

I was going to miss my fellow ravers but the raves themselves were the one thing from the free world that I would be happy to do without. Drugs had got me into this mess in the first place. If I had never touched cocaine then I wouldn't have started knocking about with Antonio and he would have gone to Brazil on his own. Excessive partying was the cause of all my problems. It was something that my time inside would hopefully iron out.

At 10 a.m. on Tuesday, 18 October, Scotland Yard finally phoned to tell me the date of my flight. I was being extradited in two days time. It was nice of them to let me know so far in advance. I was still awake from the previous night but didn't want to waste what little time I had left so I decided to go without sleep until the twentieth. I didn't stop to consider the fact that this would mean I had to travel to Spain whilst on a comedown. Once again my impulsive, drugged-up brain had put a plan into motion without considering the consequences.

Shortly after hearing the news, I headed round to Bruce's house to say goodbye. I wasn't particularly bothered that I was leaving him behind because we never really had a proper relationship anyway. We only ever saw each other when we were taking drugs. Still, it was only right to let him know that I was off. I couldn't have him thinking I had disappeared into thin air.

Bruce seemed very blasé about the extradition and kept telling me I wasn't going anywhere. A couple of our friends were round his house at the time and they all said the same. I don't know if this was because they wanted to reassure me or whether they were genuinely convinced that I was staying, but it got me wondering if I was going to end up somehow wriggling off the hook. I wasn't in Spain yet so there was still a chance that something unforeseen could happen to prevent me from going.

There was no romantic Hollywood farewell from Bruce. We sat up taking drugs together until he fell asleep at 5 a.m. and I then headed home. Arriving back at the house felt like turning up at my own funeral. My mum and sister were trying to remain strong but both looked absolutely devastated. I spent the day chatting away to them to try and make up for how little I was going to see them over the next decade. It broke my heart to see them so upset. I would have given anything in the world to have had another week with them.

Day soon transformed into night and Mum and Kelly went up to their rooms. I wished that I could go to sleep as well but had enough base in my body to keep a narcoleptic awake. It was during this period that panic really began to set in. I was convinced that there must still be a way of avoiding extradition so I powered up my computer and started frantically browsing Spanish law websites. I didn't even know what I was looking for. Everything was written in legal jargon and I couldn't speak a word of Spanish. I had more chance of finding lions in Antarctica than I did of stumbling across a loophole that would allow me to stay at home.

At 6 a.m., I finally abandoned hope and packed my bag ready for the trip. By this stage I was spaced out and exhausted so I just flung in the first few items of clothing that I found. Four pairs of trousers and a couple of T-shirts made it in. I was going to have to spend the next ten years without knickers or socks.

I had been told to surrender myself at Heathrow Airport, where the Spanish police would escort me onto my flight. Mickey drove me there and Mum came along to see me off. None of us were in a particularly talkative mood so we sat in sombre silence for the whole journey. I was in a strange limbo between being high and coming down. Every inch of my body felt crippled with exhaustion but yet my brain was still buzzing. Travelling to Spain in this state was going to test my endurance to the limit.

Five Spanish Interpol officers were waiting for me at the airport, which I thought was a bit excessive considering the fact that I had given myself up voluntarily. One thing I have learnt about the police is that they never do things by halves. They can always be guaranteed to send in an army to do a one-man job.

I said a final goodbye to my mum then followed the officers to the terminal. My plane was just your regular, run-of-the-mill commercial airliner. They didn't have a special aircraft for transporting criminals like in the film *Con Air*. I had to share a cabin with a load of happy holidaymakers, who were excitedly chatting away to one another about what they were going to do when they arrived. I was going to a place where I would hardly get to see the sun, let alone the sea or sand, which meant my mood couldn't have been further removed from that of the other passengers.

As I fastened my seatbelt and prepared for lift off, I suddenly realised that I had no idea where I would be going when I got to Spain. Would I be locked up straightaway or would the police take me to court first? I didn't want to spend the whole flight wondering what the next step was so I decided to put the coppers to good use.

'Excuse me,' I asked the officer sitting next to me, 'what happens after we get there?'

He pretended not to understand and looked annoyed that I was asking him a question. Even if he was unable to speak perfect English, he could at least have made an effort. He was being deliberately awkward.

After a couple of failed attempts to strike up a conversation, I eventually gave in and grabbed myself a magazine to read. There was no point trying to communicate with my miserable, Spanish travel companions. It was like getting blood out of a stone.

As the aircraft left the runway, I immersed myself in the private lives of Hollywood celebrities and glamorous TV stars. It was your usual trashy gossip but helped to take my mind off things. I would have liked to go to sleep but there was still no chance of that. I was just going to have to try to relax and enjoy my last few hours of freedom to the best of my ability.

I managed to remain relatively calm for the majority of the journey but towards the end of the flight, the last of the drugs left my body and I became extremely agitated. When you're at the worst stage of a comedown, somebody could drop a pin and you would jump a mile. Not knowing where I was going next had me feeling on the verge of a panic attack.

'What happens when we land?' I asked, hoping that my Spanish friends would be a little more co-operative now that we were nearly there.

The coppers shot me a look as if to say, 'You've been quiet for the entire journey. Why are you starting up with this again?' I wasn't in the mood for their shit so I repeated the question in a louder, more aggressive tone.

'You need to calm down,' the officer in charge told me. 'You go court and they decide whether you stay in country or go home.'

There was a possibility that I would be sent home? My mental anguish temporarily alleviated as I imagined landing back in England to a hero's welcome. The coppers had given me a ray of hope.

As the plane touched down on the runway, I felt conflicting emotions. On the one hand I was pleased that there was now a faint possibility of avoiding jail but on the other, it would be a relief if I was taken straight to prison from the airport – at least then I wouldn't have to keep thinking, 'Will I go or won't I?'

'Please remain seated until the aircraft doors are open. We hope you have enjoyed your journey and that you have a pleasant stay in Spain...'

The coppers watched me with an eagle eye as I waited to get up. They looked eager to get rid of me and acted as if I was the troublemaker of the century because I had raised my voice to them. The Spanish Old Bill aren't like the police over here. If you try to backchat them, you'll be lucky not to get a slap. They weren't used to anybody giving them lip. As far as they were concerned, I was a stroppy little madam who needed passing on to somebody else as soon as possible.

A group of Guardia Civil officers were waiting at the terminal and took me to a small police station within the airport. It was filled with metal cages like the ones you see in American prisons on the telly. I was ushered into the nearest one where I sat and waited to see where I was going next.

It's impossible to eat whilst you're on speed but when it finally leaves your system, you feel ravenous. I was hoping that the coppers would bring me some food but I had no such luck. They didn't even give me anything to drink. Fortunately I was whisked out of the cage after a couple of minutes and shoved into a police van. I knew that there would be no point asking the officers where they were taking me. After a brief drive through Madrid, the van pulled up at a large, white court building, similar to the ones that I had been to in England. I was marched through the front door in handcuffs and taken to a filthy, cramped holding cell containing twenty other prisoners. I was the only English girl in there. The others were a mix of Spaniards and Romani gypsies. The gypsies all wore long, traditional skirts and leggings and had olive-coloured skin. The Spanish girls seemed like your typical petty crooks. Many of them bore the telltale signs of drug addiction and I got the impression that very few were strangers to the prison system.

None of the other inmates came across as particularly hostile. They just seemed surprised that I was there. I didn't exactly fit the mould of the average Spanish criminal. Most foreign prisoners in Spain are either North African or Latin American so I was a bit of a novelty. Some of the girls attempted to talk to me but I couldn't understand a word they said. They were probably trying to figure out what I had been convicted of.

I was eventually left alone and sat down on an uncomfortable wooden bench that stretched from one side of the cell to the other. Was this going to be what the next ten years of my life would be like? Nobody had attacked me or given me any grief for being English, but they had looked at me as if I was an alien and I didn't like the idea of having people pointing at me wherever I went.

Every now and again, a guard opened up the door and called one of the inmates out into the corridor. I hadn't got a clue where they went after this. All I knew was that they didn't come back again. As the number of prisoners gradually fell, I began to wonder when it would be my turn to leave. I was dying for a fag and desperately hungry. If nobody fed me soon then I was going to pass out.

After half an hour of sitting on my own, I decided that I was going to have to do something to get the guards' attention. I was so dehydrated that my mouth felt like a desert. It was ridiculous that nobody had offered me a drink since I had touched down in Spain. If I didn't cause a scene, I would most likely die of thirst.

'Somebody get me out of here!' I shouted. 'What the hell is going on? Why are you keeping me here so long? I haven't had any food or water. Somebody help me!'

An English-speaking lawyer was standing just outside the cells and came to see what I was making so much noise about. His name was Ricardo Perez-Clague and he was the first person I had met since landing in Spain who talked to me like a human being.

'I will go and get the officers to unlock the door,' he said. 'Please wait here and try to remain calm.'

A minute later, the cell door opened up with a heavy clanking sound and Ricardo came in carrying a slip of paper, some yoghurts and a sandwich.

'This explains why you are here,' he told me, handing over the paper. 'It says that you are being held pending transfer to Soto del Real prison.'

That was my hope of getting sent back home dashed on the rocks. The Spanish authorities had made an irreversible decision to steal a decade of my life. There was no getting out of it.

'I will leave you with this food. If at any point you need a lawyer, here is my calling card.'

I took the card and thanked Ricardo for his help. If it wasn't for him, I wouldn't have had a clue what I was waiting for. As he left the cell, I wondered how long it would be before the guards sorted my transport out. I felt as if I had been staring at the same four walls forever. It was a sensation that I was going to have to get used to.

The food that I had been given was barely edible. The bread was as hard as a brick, the cheese could have passed for rubber and the yoghurts were past their sell-by date. In ordinary circumstances I would have hesitated to feed them to a dog but I was ridiculously hungry so I wolfed them down in seconds. I was polishing off the last mouthful of rancid yoghurt when I realised that I still had nothing to wash it down with. The dry, stale sandwich had made me even thirstier and I was also beginning to get very cold, which was surprising given that the winters in Tenerife had all been fairly mild. I knew that mainland Spain had got a cooler climate but assumed that it would still be fairly temperate. I hadn't packed any warm clothes to wear which was a big mistake because Spanish winters can fall below zero degrees centigrade.

After what seemed like an eternity of sitting dry-mouthed in a freezing, empty room, I eventually curled up on the bench and tried to get some sleep. It was now three in the morning and I hadn't had a cigarette since nine o'clock the previous morning. I wanted to drift off to a place where I could dream of drinking cool, refreshing water and smoking pack after pack of fags.

I had been asleep for all of two seconds when a loud, shrill noise woke me up with a start. What on earth was this? A crazy, aggressive-looking, little woman was blowing a whistle in my ear and shouting frantically in Spanish.

'*¡Sígueme! ¡Es hora de ir a la cárcel!*'

She might as well have been saying, 'Gibberish, gibberish, gibberish.'

'What are you doing?' I asked, my head battered by exhaustion and nicotine withdrawal.

'Come on. We go prison now.'

It was strange that we were in a hurry all of a sudden, considering how long I had been waiting. The woman didn't even look like a guard. She was in plain clothes and could have been another prisoner for all I knew. I was contemplating telling her to bugger off when a load of Guardia Civil came marching into the cell and slapped a pair of cuffs on me. I knew by this stage not to try to ask them any questions. They would only ignore me so there was no point.

The coppers ushered me down a corridor and through the front door of the court.

'Get in,' an officer ordered, pointing to a van parked opposite the entrance.

I clambered aboard the vehicle and plonked myself down next to a hard-faced Spanish convict. She was dressed from head to toe in expensive designer clothing and looked very pale, which I figured must have been because she had spent a lot of time in prison. There was something about her that said, 'I'm someone important'. She was definitely a cut above the small-time thieves and drug addicts that I had shared the holding cell with. I thought it best to avoid speaking to this mysterious, well-dressed lady. I got a vibe that she wasn't in the mood to be disturbed.

The two of us sat in silence as we were driven through Madrid. After about ten minutes, we stopped off at the local hospital and the guards picked up a Filipino drug mule, who had swallowed condoms filled with cocaine. The poor girl had fallen ill and had to have the drugs surgically removed from her stomach. She looked as if she had been dragged through hell and back. The staff had obviously discharged her early from the hospital so that she could start her sentence as soon as possible. She didn't seem to me to be anywhere near fit to travel.

So there I was, sitting aboard a prison van with the hardest-looking woman in the world and a half-dead drug mule. I didn't speak their languages so there was no point talking to either of them. I don't think the Filipino girl was in a particularly good state to hold a conversation anyway. She must have been desperate to do what she did. Perhaps she was trying to earn enough to raise her family out of poverty. Whatever the motivation for her crime, I got the impression that she had already paid the price.

I tried to get some sleep during the journey but it's impossible to get comfortable with handcuffs on. My two travel companions kept looking at each other as if to say, 'Gosh, who have I ended up with here?' They were probably giving me the same look too but I was far too tired to pick up on it.

It was 4 a.m. by the time we reached the prison and I could hardly make out the building because it was pitch-black outside. I just saw the outline of a huge wall covered in barbed wire. It looked a hell of a lot bigger than an English jail. I wondered how many prisoners it held and what types of things they were in for.

I would have been absolutely terrified if I had known anything about the place that I was heading into. Soto del Real has housed its fair share of big-time crooks over the years. ETA terrorists, Colombian drug lords and even Russian mafia bosses have all been locked up there at one point or another. It is a maximum-security prison, which means that there are no petty criminals within its walls. Everybody who inhabits the jail is somebody the authorities have deemed to be a serious risk to society.

As the huge, mechanical gates opened up to let us through, I felt butterflies in my stomach. I was heading into the belly of the beast. Part of me was eager to get inside so that I could go to sleep but the more rational part of my brain was absolutely terrified.

Prisons are scary buildings. When you go inside, you feel as if any sense of dignity or individuality that you might once have had is being stripped away from you. I now belonged to the jail; I was the property of Soto del Real.

The Guardia Civil ushered us out of the van and into the reception area. It looked like the reception of a hospital and seemed to be where all the new arrivals were issued with prison numbers. None of the staff at Soto were in uniforms, which I thought was a bit weird. In English jails, the guards wear them to distinguish themselves from the prisoners so that inmates can't attempt to switch places with them. In Spain, this method of escape is a little more difficult to pull off because prisons are constantly circled by police. Anybody who manages to make it outside of the front gate is unlikely to get far. The constant police presence also eliminated the problem of people throwing drugs over the walls. There was a police station right next to Soto so nobody who looked even vaguely dodgy could have got within a hundred yards of it without being nicked.

A male and a female guard were in charge of assigning prison numbers. They kept pointing at me and laughing to one another, which confused the hell out of me. I have since found out that this was because the prison numbers in Spain begin with the year of your arrest. They were probably making jokes about the fact that mine was eight years earlier and speculating where I might have been for all that time.

The girl in the designer clothes was taken straight up to her cell after being processed. I wondered what the deal was with her. The prison staff seemed very wary of her, as if they were handling somebody who was extremely dangerous. She was definitely a person that I didn't want to end up getting on the wrong side of.

Whilst Ms Big-Time Gangster was being escorted out of the reception area, me and the drug mule were taken to a block of showers, where we were forced to strip and wash ourselves. The water was freezing cold and a female guard watched us with an eagle eye to make sure that we didn't take out any drugs that we had hidden internally. Somebody ogling me whilst I was in the shower would have usually made me feel uncomfortable, but I had been expecting to have my privacy invaded so I just took it in my stride. I was going to have to get used to being humiliated like this because it would be an everyday occurrence for the next ten years.

The drug mule remained silent for the whole time we were there. She seemed very timid and withdrawn and had a detached look in her eyes, as if she had suffered from such an immense trauma that nothing mattered anymore. I couldn't help but think that prison wasn't the best place for her. They should have at least allowed her some more time to recover in hospital.

Rather than handing us back the clothes that we had arrived in, the guards issued us with bright orange jumpsuits, presumably so that they could have a laugh at our expense. I looked like a giant satsuma. We were then escorted up a flight of stairs to the induction wing, which is where inmates stay on their first night inside. The idea is that it gives them time to get acquainted with prison life before they move onto the main wing.

Our cell was cramped and claustrophobic. It had a bunk bed at one side and a shower at the other, which seemed to randomly alternate between being freezing cold and boiling hot. I was tired, upset and dehydrated so I headed straight to bed without bothering to try and chat to the drug mule. She did the same, presumably attempting to drift off in order to forget about what she had just been through.

As I lay and tried to get to sleep, the reality of the situation began to hit home. I was in a foreign country, locked up in a place where nobody cared if I lived or died. I still hadn't been given anything to drink and didn't fancy drinking shower water. My throat felt like I had gargled a pint of sand and I couldn't stop shivering from the cold. Was I going to come out of the other side of this a stronger person or would it leave me irreparably damaged? Only I had the power to determine the answer.

Chapter 16

LIFE IN SOTO DEL REAL

I can't talk to anyone about what's going on. I feel so alone and useless. Please God, I hope someone outside of here is trying to help me because I feel like I'm going mad. I have no rights in here – none at all. Today I feel sick with nerves. I really don't know how much more of this uncertainty I can take. I'm cold, tired, anxious, nervous, depressed, and worried about everything. It's been five days since I left England and still no contact with my family or the outside world.

Diary entry from 24 October 2005

'*Buenos días. Es hora de desayunar.*'

I tried to blot out the booming voice of the guard and the heavy, metallic clanking noise that accompanied it but eventually gave in and prised my tired eyes open to see what he wanted. It was 7 a.m. and I had barely slept a wink. My mind and body were still wracked with nicotine withdrawal so I was particularly irritable. The noise had been made by a hatch in the door being opened and two steel trays of coffee and croissants being shoved through. At least now I would be able to rehydrate my arid throat so that it didn't feel as if I had just swallowed a cactus.

As I perched on the edge of the bed and sipped my coffee, it suddenly struck me that I would soon have to leave the cell and face the other prisoners. Would I be a novelty like I had been in the holding cell or would there be other English people in the prison? I didn't fancy the idea of being unable to communicate with anybody for the next decade. It would no doubt send me totally loopy.

I was just finishing off my last mouthful of croissant when the door slid open and a tall, dark-haired convict came striding into the room.

'Hello there. How are you finding things in Soto then?'

'You're from England,' I gasped

'You noticed then?' he joked, plonking himself down next to me on the bed. 'The screws sent me to translate for you when you go to see the doctor, which you'll be doing in a bit. They need to check out everybody coming into the prison but there wouldn't be much point in them asking you questions in Spanish when you can't speak a lick of it, would there?'

By this stage I was grinning from ear to ear. I can't even begin to describe how good it felt to have a fellow Englishman to talk to. I hadn't had a proper conversation for twenty-four hours, which meant I spent the next ten minutes firing off as many questions as I could think of at him.

'What are the other prisoners like? Are there any other English girls here? And how come you're on the women's wing?'

'Whoa there, slow down a bit,' he chortled. 'You're going to wear me out. The other cons are mostly OK, but it's a prison so there's bound to be a few wrong 'uns. There are quite a few English girls and they look after their own so you'll be all right. And the guys and girls are mostly kept separate but it's not that strict. We get to see the girlies at the gym so it's not like in England, where you come out forgetting what they look like. Oh and by the way, my name is Jeff. It was nice of you to ask!'

In my hurry to pick his brains about the prison, I had forgotten to ask him anything about himself.

'What did you do to end up in here then, Jeff?' I smiled back.

'Got involved with drugs, same as most people in Soto,' he told me. 'You do the crime, you do the time, eh? It's a bit of a rough old gaff to be banged-up in though. They give you nothing and lots of it and you still have to fight for your fair share of it.'

Jeff went on to explain that Soto was the largest prison in Madrid, with a population of just under 2,000. Some of the inmates were men, some were women and there was a mother and baby wing for girls who had given birth behind bars. I wondered what type of a future a kid who was born in a place like that would have. One thing was for certain; it sure wouldn't be a bright one.

After clueing me up on every aspect of prison life, Jeff told me that it was time for me to see the doctor and escorted me out of the cell. He took me down a flight of stairs into a small office, where a little, beady-looking Spanish bloke was sat behind a desk.

'*¿Tiene algún problema de salud?*' the bloke asked me.

'He wants to know if you've got any problems with your health at the moment,' Jeff translated.

'I've recently recovered from an aneurysm,' I replied, unsure of whether to direct my answer towards Jeff or the doctor. 'I sometimes have problems sleeping too and get very anxious and depressed. I've had a bit of a headache since I came into the prison as well, which might be down to stress.'

'*Es alérgico a algún medicamento?*'

'He wants to know if you're allergic to any medication.'

'Yes paracetamol,' I answered. 'It can make me really ill.'

The doctor didn't seem to be taking note of anything that I said. He gave me a quick look over and then told me that the check-up had finished. I had a feeling that I was on my own if I fell ill in Soto. This guy seemed completely disinterested to the point where he could hardly wait to get me out of the room.

'OK you're allowed a phone call now,' Jeff told me as I shuffled out of the exit back into the hustle and bustle of the prison. 'They've got a funny rule where you can only use your free phone call to ring Madrid numbers though.'

Was he being serious? Mum would be worried sick if she didn't hear from me. She didn't even know what prison I was in. This was even more worrying than the fact that I was clearly going to have to go without proper healthcare for the next decade.

'I'm going to have to ring the British Consulate then,' I sighed.

It was as if the governor of the jail was determined to make things as difficult as possible for the foreign prisoners. Jeff took me to another office, where a guard stood over me whilst I dialled the number. I told the woman on the other end of the line to ring Mum as soon as possible to let her know where I was.

'OK we'll do that for you,' she assured me. 'We'll also send somebody to the prison to check up on you. They'll make sure that you're being treated OK.'

As soon as I hung up the phone, the guard escorted me out of the door and took me down to the cafeteria, where I was given a tray of food and sent back to my cell. My meal – a piece of ham, a potato and a bit of slimy salad – looked vaguely edible but not particularly appetising. I was going to have to get used to eating lettuce that a slug would have turned down. If the state of the medical care was anything to go by then the staff at Soto didn't see the prisoners as being worthy of anything above the minimum standards that were required for survival.

I had just finished the last bite when the door slid open and another guard came bowling in.

'Come,' he told me. 'You go to main wing now. Get your things.'

It was nice of him to give me so much prior warning. I grabbed the few belongings that I had and trailed behind him through a door into a bigger, noisier section of the jail. He escorted me to a cell, shoved me inside and then walked away as if I didn't even merit talking to.

There was a girl already in the room who could have passed for Skeletor's stunt double. She was as skinny as a whippet with a scruffy, feral look to her, as if the need for taking copious amounts of crack and heroin had long since overtaken her need for basic personal hygiene.

'Hi, I'm Terry,' I told her. 'It looks like we're going to be living together.'

'No lo entiendo.'

'Do you speak any English?'

'¿Hablas español?'

Oh well. I was still exhausted from the previous day's journey so I abandoned any vague hope that I might have had of developing a rapport and sprawled out on my bed. The thought entered my head that I should probably stay awake in case my new cellmate rifled through my pockets whilst I was asleep, but I had nothing worth stealing so I figured she could search away until her heart's content. I was so tired that she could have probably stolen my left arm without disturbing my sleep.

I woke up the next morning feeling freezing cold and soaking wet from head to toe. The cell had a damp mist in it that had coated everything in a fine layer of condensation. I hoped that it was water, not evaporated junkie sweat. My heart was beating ninety to the dozen and for some reason I felt more anxious than I had done at any point since entering the jail. I knew that this would be the day I had to go out onto the wing and hoped to God that Jeff was right about there being other English girls there. If it was just a load of druggie Spanish girls and me, then I had a feeling that I was going to be spending a lot of time on my own.

Sure enough, shortly after I had finished my morning shower, a guard in came to tell us that it was time for association. This was the moment of reckoning; I was about to enter a world of muggers, thieves and murderers. I nervously edged my way out of the doorway and scanned the wing for anybody who looked likely to be English. I saw a lot of South Americans and Eastern Europeans, but all of the other girls apart from them were definitely Spanish. I was on the verge of having a panic attack when I heard a broad Northern accent and turned around to see a group of seven pale-skinned British girls chatting away in English.

'Thank heavens for that,' I thought to myself.

'Excuse me,' I approached the nearest Brit, who happened to be the Northern one.

'You lot are from England, aren't you?'

I wanted to make doubly sure, just in case my mind was playing tricks on me.

'Yeah of course,' she told me. 'Are you the new girl? Adriana told us you'd be landing on the wing.'

'Yeah I am,' I said, 'but who on earth is Adriana?'

'She was on the bus with you on the way here – mafia girl, quite smartly dressed. We got a message from her that an English girl had come here with her. She told us to look after you and make sure you're all right.'

Wow. I had known the hard-looking girl from the bus was somebody with a bit of clout but had no idea that she was Soto's answer to Tony Soprano. It was nice of her to put in a good word for me. Maybe things weren't going to be so bad in this place after all.

'Everybody helps their own here,' the Northerner explained to me. 'Adriana wanted to make sure that you got in with the Brits. She said you looked as if it was your first time behind bars. Stick with us lot and you'll be OK.'

The other girls seemed equally friendly and kept asking me if there was anything that I needed. I got the sense that the English cons all banded together for protection because they were so badly outnumbered by the other nationalities. I soon learnt that the Northern girl was called Karen and that she had been caught with a massive stash of guns and drugs. She was definitely no angel, but treated me with respect so I tried not to think about her crime.

'What's your cellmate like then?' she asked me. 'Do you get on OK with her?'

'She can't speak a word of English,' I told her. 'We've hardly spoken since I moved in with her.'

'Well that doesn't sound too good. Stella here is on her own at the moment. I could ask the screws to move you in with her if you want?' she suggested, pointing to the girl standing next to her.

'Yes please, that would be brilliant,' I told her. 'Otherwise I'm going to be sitting in the corner every night, wishing I could talk Spanish.'

Karen grabbed a passing guard, gibbered something to him in Spanish and then gave me the thumbs up.

'Sorted. Get your stuff, you're moving.'

I wondered if the other inmates would be as helpful as the English girls had been. Karen and her little crew couldn't have been nicer to me if they had tried. As I transferred my things across from one cell to another, I glanced over one last time at the Spanish junkie and breathed a sigh of relief that I wasn't going to have to spend another night with her. She looked like Gollum from *The Lord of the Rings*.

Stella seemed glad of the company. She was in for forgery, which I didn't see as being too bad a crime, and came across as kind and good-hearted. I still took people at face value. This would prove to be a big mistake because in prison, nobody is what they seem to be. The girls who come across as being the friendliest can often turn out to be the biggest nutters going.

I relied upon Stella to get the low-down on the way the prison worked.

'The main groups in here are the South Americans who are mostly drug mules and fraudsters, the Eastern Europeans who are mostly pickpockets, the ETA girls and the other Spanish girls,' she explained to me during our first night in the cell together. 'ETA is like the Spanish version of the IRA. They think that an area of Spain called the Basque Country should be a separate country. Most of the girls are only in for helping their boyfriends though, they aren't proper terrorists. The other Spaniards are nearly all junkies and aren't too fond of the

English. They're probably a bit pissed off because there's so many of us over here.'

'Is there anybody that I need to be wary of then?' I asked her.

'Yeah the guards,' she laughed. 'Get on the wrong side of them and you'll really know about it. The staff here aren't like the ones you get in English prisons. They don't give a shit if you live or die, especially if you're foreign.'

'I gathered that from when I went to see the doctor,' I told her. 'I told him I was having trouble sleeping and that I needed something for my nerves and he completely ignored me.'

'You want to ask a guard to sort you out another appointment next time we're let out,' she advised me. 'I wouldn't bank on getting anything though. The health care here is awful, especially if you aren't Spanish. As far as they're concerned, we're just a burden on them. The key is persistence though. You need to pester them until it's easier for them to give you what you want.'

Stella and I chatted for a couple more minutes and then a guard came to our door to let us know that we were allowed out for association. This was my chance to try and get some medication sorted.

'Excuse me, do you know if it would be possible to see a doctor?' I asked him, being as polite as possible in the hope that it would increase the chance of him co-operating.

'*No entiendo.*'

I was sure that he had at least understood the word 'doctor'.

'Doctor,' I repeated, 'I need to see a doctor.'

He eventually got bored of pretending that he didn't know what I was asking him and promised to book me an appointment. I felt annoyed that he had used the whole 'I no speak English' routine on me to try and get out of bothering. For all he knew, I could have been seriously ill. If I was diabetic or had chronic asthma then his reluctance to help me could have been life-threatening. Even criminals deserve access to healthcare when they're sick.

I was called for my appointment over the prison loudspeaker system later on that day whilst I was standing in the queue for dinner. By this stage my head was killing me so I prayed that I would be able to get some painkillers. This time it was just me and the doctor. Jeff wasn't there to help me out, which meant I had to communicate as best I could without being able to speak a word of Spanish.

After five minutes of watching me pointing at my head and screwing up my face to indicate that I was in a lot of pain, the doctor eventually handed me some paracetamol-based headache pills. It was nice of him to issue me with medication that I had specifically told him I was allergic to.

'I can't take these,' I told him. 'No paracetamol. I am allergic.'

'*¿Qué? Tome estos analgésicos.*'

'No paracetamol. I can't take paracetamol.'

¿Qué? ¡Tome las píldoras!'

I carried on repeating myself until he put the pills back in his drawer and handed me another packet of tablets. There were no instructions with them so I didn't have a clue what they were or how many of them to take. This looked as if it was the best that I was going to get though so I thanked him for his help and asked if he could give me anything to help me get to sleep at night.

'*¿Qué?*'

'Insomnia. I need something for insomnia.'

'No. *Usted no puede tener nada.*'

I understood the word 'no' but had no idea what his reason for refusal was. He was seemingly willing to prescribe me pills that had the potential to make me seriously ill but not to give me sleepers. There was no point kicking up a fuss though because he probably wouldn't have even understood what I was saying if I did, so I thanked him for his time and headed back to the wing.

By the time I got to the canteen, dinner had finished and everybody was being locked up in their cells. I was going to have to go hungry for the night, which wasn't really all that bad a thing because the food was disgusting. I opened up the door to my cell and almost tripped over Stella, who was kneeling prostrate on a rug with a piece of cloth tied round her head whilst chanting loudly to herself in Arabic.

'*Subhana Rabbi al-A' la...*'

'What on earth are you doing?' I asked her, trying to stifle a giggle.

She looked absolutely ridiculous.

'Shh!' she told me, 'I'm praying. I converted to Islam a while back so I do this a couple of times a day.'

I had seen her eating a big slab of ham when I first came into the prison; what was the point in her being a Muslim if she was going to follow certain parts of the religion but wilfully ignore others? The girl in the cell next door was a proper Muslim from Morocco and the contrast couldn't have been greater. Stella didn't know the first thing about Islam. She was just one of those girls who embrace religion the minute they get locked up because they've got too much time on their hands. Still, if it prevented her from getting bored then at least that was something. I sprawled out on the bed and let her get on with it, immersing myself in my thoughts and attempting to blot out her crazy wailing to the best of my ability.

I mentioned Stella's spiritual awakening to Karen during the following day's association and was told that she had originally started claiming to be a Muslim because Islamic prisoners were given a special feast at the end of Ramadan.

'She just wanted some more food at first but now she's really into it,' Karen smiled. 'That girl's a little bit on the nutty side though. She's hooked on painkillers and does a lot of crazy stuff. Mind you, most people in here have their vices.'

The majority of people behind bars are addicted to one thing or another so I figured painkillers were a fairly harmless craving. I had been addicted to coke then booze then speed so it would have been hypocritical of me to pass judgement on her. What I didn't realise was that her addiction had reached its upper limits. She would do whatever it took to get a fix, even if it meant hurting other people.

I first became aware of the true extent of Stella's problem when we were locked away behind the door just under a week after I had moved in with her. She started off by pacing around the room, looking extremely agitated, then came straight out with it and asked me if I had any painkillers. I told her no because I needed them for my headaches and she went absolutely ballistic.

'I know you've got some,' she snarled at me. 'You'd better give me one or you and me are going to have a major falling out.'

'I would if I had any spare,' I attempted to placate her, knowing full well that she would bully me out of every pack I got if I gave in to her. 'You'd be better off seeing the doctor and getting some of your own.'

Stella's face went beetroot red and she balled her hand into a fist.

'Cellmates are meant to share. You'd better give me one.'

I was just about to tell her no again when she lunged forward and gave me an almighty crack to the side of the face. I stood there rooted to the spot in stunned silence, unable to believe that she had actually hit me over a headache pill. It wasn't as if I had been deliberately awkward; I genuinely needed every last tablet for the pain. As soon as the reality of what had happened sunk in, I burst into tears. Maybe the other inmates could handle being punched for no apparent reason but I wasn't used to violence and felt very scared and upset. I might have mixed with petty criminals in the outside world but none of them had ever been particularly aggressive towards me. This was a worrying reminder that I was now living in a place where disputes were settled using fists.

Stella remained completely unrepentant and sat on her bed sulking, looking as if she was waiting for the slightest provocation so that she could go nuts again. Luckily a guard opened up the cell for association a couple of minutes later and saved me from a second attack.

'I need to get out of here,' I told him, tears streaming down my face.

I knew that there would be drastic consequences if I grassed Stella up for attacking me so I made out that we had had a blazing argument. The guard agreed to put me in with another English girl, which was a huge relief. My new cellmate was very sympathetic and told me that she wasn't at all surprised by what had happened because she knew exactly what Stella was like.

'She's a ticking time bomb, that girl is,' she said. 'One minute she's all sweetness and light and the next thing she's throwing a wobbler. You'll be a lot better off in here with me. And don't worry, I don't want any of your aspirin. It's not really my thing.'

I smiled and wiped the tears from my eyes. This lady had injured her leg and needed crutches to get about the place so even if she did turn out to be a nutter, she was still unlikely to pose much of a threat. Her name was Rochelle and she was inside because her husband had been caught smuggling drugs across from Holland. In Spain, the Guardia Civil will often nick the relatives of people who have committed a crime under the logic that anybody who was close to the guilty party must have been aware of what was going on. Sometimes whole families will be locked up because a single member has broken the law.

Rochelle seemed as if she really was a top bird. She was very down to earth and sorted me out with fags, which was a lifesaver. This helped to cheer me up a bit and made me feel as if I could at least relax within the confines of my cell even if the rest of the prison was full of loonies. I was fortunate to be in with one of the few good eggs.

Me and 'Chelle had a right laugh together. We had a similar sense of humour and the days passed quickly now that I didn't have to share a cell with somebody who spent the whole time kneeling on a rug and yelling, 'Allahu akbar'. I wouldn't have had any problem with Stella's prayer routine if she had been a proper Muslim, not somebody who spent all day praying to Allah and then tucked into a slab of pork at dinnertime.

It was a good thing that I had Rochelle there to look after me because the British Consulate didn't show their faces until a week into my sentence. They had promised that they would send someone to see me straightaway and I had been relying on them to tell my mum which prison I was in. They kept me waiting for a week without so much as a phone call to the jail to let me know what was going on.

On the day that a Consulate representative finally turned up to see me, I was escorted into one of the prison visiting rooms and told to take a seat in front of her. She was very apologetic for not turning up earlier and explained that she had only just found out which institution I was in from her employers.

'I thought you'd been flown straight over to Gran Canaria to serve your sentence there,' she told me. 'If I had known that you were here, I would have driven to the prison straightaway. Your mother's been on the phone and I've let her know that you're in Soto. Fair Trials International rang us as well. They should be writing to you soon.'

'Do you know if I'll get flown over to Gran Canaria then?' I asked her. 'Am I going to go to Salto del Negro, where I was locked up when they first arrested me?'

'I'm sorry, I can't tell you that,' she said. 'I can't give you any information about which prison you'll be moved on to. That's not what I'm here for; my job is to make sure you're OK and that you're getting treated properly.

'Well I do have one concern about things here,' I told her. 'I've recently had an aneurysm and I'm getting awful headaches. I've been to see the doctor but he doesn't seem bothered. The last time I went, I didn't even have a translator with me so he probably didn't have a clue what I was on about.'

'That doesn't sound too good,' the lady said, frowning. 'You're entitled to the same level of medical attention that the Spanish inmates get. I'll have a word with the prison staff and see if I can get them to buck up their ideas a bit.'

'I have to borrow cigarettes because I haven't got any cash either,' I told her. 'Is there any chance that you could ring my mum and tell her to send some money in for me?'

'Sure,' she said. 'That shouldn't be a problem. Once again I'm sorry for the delay. Good luck in here. If there's anything else you need then don't hesitate to contact me. Hopefully we'll be able to get somebody here a lot quicker next time.'

I thanked her for her help and we both left the room. She was escorted out of the prison and I was ushered back to my cell.

I didn't want to have to wait until Mum received the message and sent some money over to me before I got to speak to her. Calls were expensive though, and I had no cash on the phone card that they had issued me with when I came into the prison, so the only other alternative was to ask to borrow a card from one of the other inmates. Karen was always giving me coffee and cigarettes so I figured that she would be the best person to approach. She was all too happy to lend me hers.

It was nice to hear Mum's voice again. She was trying to remain positive but I could tell that she was suffering just as much as I was.

'Think of your time in Soto as being like a package holiday,' she told me. 'The food's crap and the accommodation's crap but you've just got to make the best of it.'

That brought a smile to my face.

'I should be visiting you this weekend,' she said. 'I could only manage to sort out a glass panel visit though.'

There are three types of visit in Spanish prisons; family visits, conjugal visits and glass panel visits. Family visits take place in a private room with chairs and a toilet in it. The guards leave you completely unattended until your time is up, which gives some of the more drug-orientated inmates a chance to get things passed across to them. Conjugal visits are something that most inmates in British prisons would die for. They're visits where you're left alone with your visitor in a room with a double bed and a bath in it. The idea is that there will be less sexual attacks in the prison if the inmates are given the opportunity to have some 'quality time' with their partners every couple of weeks. Glass panel visits are the worst of the three types. Rather than having face-to-face contact, inmates are forced to speak to their visitors from behind a screen.

The prison staff had been unable to sort a family visit out for the weekend at such short notice so a glass panel visit was going to have to do. I would have liked to have given Mum a hug when I saw her but it was still a damn sight better than phoning her from overseas. The visit wasn't the only good news that she had for me either; Fair Trials had rung to tell her that they were looking for a reputable Spanish lawyer and petitioning to have me released on grounds of ill health. They had highlighted the fact that the stressful conditions of life behind bars could trigger another aneurysm and argued that the only humane thing to do would be to set me free as soon as possible. They were right as well because although I had been stressed out by my drink and drug problem whilst in the outside world, it was nothing compared to the anguish of being separated from my family and friends. Some people might think that taking amphetamines every night was a lot more unhealthy than being locked up; but for me, doing whiz was a side effect of being told that I was facing time in prison. I had managed to get my addictions under control at one stage and they had only started up again when Interpol turned up to tell me that there was a strong possibility that I was going to get shipped off to Spain.

'I hope it works,' I said to Mum. 'I'd love to talk to you for longer but I'm using somebody else's phone card so I'm going to have to get off now. I can't wait to see you this weekend. Love you.'

'I love you too,' she told me. 'Take care in there and remember to stay safe. See you soon Terry.'

I felt better for speaking to her. It reminded me that there were still people out there who cared about me even if the screws at Soto didn't give a toss. When I told the other English girls about our conversation, they were pleased that things were looking up but warned me that the Spaniards would be unlikely to allow me to walk free without a fight. The general consensus was that once you had been convicted it was very hard to get released from prison before the end of your stint.

That night, I went to sleep feeling hopeful that I could still eventually be released. Soto was the type of environment where any medical condition that you had was likely to be amplified tenfold. The prison was a stressful, noisy, dirty place that could re-ignite my haemorrhage and put my life in danger. Fair enough, taking drugs and drinking had posed a high level of a risk when I was back in England, but I hadn't suffered from the crippling headaches that I was experiencing in Soto. They made me constantly on edge in case something was wrong.

The fact that there was now a chance of being set free should have made me more relaxed but I awoke at 5 a.m. the following morning feeling as if my head was about to explode. It was throbbing unbearably and every now and again a shooting pain went through it. The minute the door was unlocked, I rushed over to the prison nurse to beg her for some aspirin. She was dishing out methadone to the heroin addicts at the time and didn't take too kindly to being disturbed.

'*No entiendo,*' she shouted, along with some other things that didn't mean anything to me.

By this stage I had learnt that '*no entiendo*' meant 'I don't understand.' I had heard it repeated to me so many times by the guards that it would have been impossible for me not to pick it up. The word 'aspirin' is the same in Spanish as it is in English though so I knew that she was lying.

'Aspirin,' I repeated. 'I need aspirin for my head.'

'*No entiendo el inglés!*'

I was the verge of going berserk and shouting my head off at her but somehow managed to restrain myself and walked back to my cell. So much for the lady from the Consulate having a word with the governor. The only thing that prevented me from breaking down and crying was the thought that I would be able to see my mum in a couple of days' time. The Spanish authorities had other plans though. I wasn't even going to be in the same prison by the time the weekend came.

Chapter 17

TOPAS

This is a maximum-security prison. There are a lot of people on methadone. One girl is schizophrenic but there's no room for her on the medical wing. Let's just hope her medication is working. I'm not sure if the plastic knife that they have given me to eat with will be any good for self-defence!

Diary entry from 16 November 2005

I was chatting to Rochelle outside our cell when the announcement came.

The prison tannoy system wasn't very clear but I could still make out my name. It sounded as if they were saying that I was being transferred to another jail. Surely I must have misheard the announcer though. They wouldn't ship me out before my visit, would they? If they did then it would mean that Mum would arrive at the prison only to be turned back at the gate because I was no longer there.

'Tell me that didn't mean what I thought it meant,' I said to 'Chelle.

'You're being sent to Topas,' she told me. 'You'll be setting off tomorrow. That's another rough old nick. You'll need your wits about you there.'

This was the final straw. We were about to be banged up for the evening so there was no time to ring Mum and tell her not to come. I knew full well that the prison wouldn't try to contact her either. The thought of her turning up at the wrong jail made me so angry. What right did they have to mess her about like that? Tears welled up in my eyes and I felt my face go red with rage.

'I can't believe they're doing this,' I cried. 'They're going to let Mum come all this way for nothing. It's going to be weeks before I see her now. What has my mum done to them? She's never broken a law in her life so why are they punishing her?'

'Don't cry,' 'Chelle told me. 'It isn't your fault. They should have pushed it back a couple of days 'til after the visit. You're right it isn't fair but I'm sure your mum will understand.'

I appreciated her efforts but nothing she said could make me feel any better. I spent the next eight hours crying my eyes out on my bed. Rochelle was brilliant and did her best to comfort me but it was all to no avail. I carried on sobbing well into the night and by the time I nodded off, my bedding was sopping wet with tears. God knows what the guards must have thought when they woke me up for my transfer. It looked as if somebody had turned a sprinkler on in the cell.

'I'm going to miss you,' 'Chelle told me as I was marched out of the door clutching a bin bag full of my belongings.

'I'll miss you too,' I sniffled. 'I'll write to you and let you know how I get on.'

It felt just as intimidating leaving Soto as it had done coming in. There were guards and coppers everywhere, patrolling the perimeter and reminding me what a dangerous place I had been living in. The screws handed me over to a Guardia Civil officer, who bundled me into the back of a prison bus and slammed the door shut. There was a mental-looking Romanian pickpocket in there, who was guaranteed to make my voyage all the more delightful. Her skin looked filthy and she kept twitching and fidgeting as if she was coming down from drugs.

It was a four-hour drive to Topas so I passed the time by gazing out of the window at the scenery. I remember thinking, 'Wow, I didn't know Spain could be so green.' It was strange to see vast expanses of grass growing in such a hot country. The wide, open spaces reminded me of Wingrave and made me feel homesick.

As we journeyed on through the picturesque countryside, the realisation hit me that this could be the last time I saw trees and fields for the next ten years. If I had to do the full decade then I would probably forget what a tree looked like by the time they let me go. The greenery gradually grew sparser and signs of civilisation began to reappear as the bus approached Ávila Prison. I was hoping that they were planning on dropping the Romanian girl off there but it soon became apparent that we were picking somebody up. A skinny, little, blonde-haired girl was waiting outside the jail, ready to be herded onto the bus.

Our new passenger was German and couldn't speak Spanish or English. Anyway, I wasn't feeling too chatty. The image of Mum being told that I was no longer in Soto still dominated my thoughts. Those bastards probably wouldn't even explain to her that I had been moved. She would no doubt be left wondering where I had disappeared to until I managed to borrow a phone card from somebody in Topas and fill her in on what had happened.

After several awkward hours of sitting in silence, attempting to avoid eye contact with the Romanian, I finally caught sight of the prison and felt a shiver travel down the base of my spine. The building had the same air of menace to it that Maghaberry had. Giant stone walls towered above the main body of the jail, hammering home the fact that it was somewhere that nobody could ever hope to escape from. Guard towers poked their heads up from above the parapets at regular intervals, as if to emphasise how much of a risk the inmates behind those stone walls posed. Everything about the place screamed 'danger' at 1,000 decibels.

Topas is one of the harshest prisons in Western Europe. Famous inmates have included serial killer Rodríguez 'Old Lady Killer' Vega, who sexually assaulted and murdered sixteen elderly women in the space of a single year; Islamic terrorist organiser Mohamed Achraf and former ETA leader Eugenio 'Antxon' Etxebeste. The jail housed a total of 1,600 inmates, 1,500 of which were male and 100 female. Roughly half were foreign nationals, which meant that there might be some other English girls in there.

The minute we got inside the prison, the reception staff were upon us, bawling in our faces and throwing their weight around. I had no idea what they were so worked up about. They kept shouting at the German girl, who stood there ignoring them with a vacant look in her eyes, as if she didn't know what planet she was on. The next thing I knew, she had been dragged into a side room and beaten all over her body with a baton. I remember thinking, 'OK, this place is hardcore.' I had only been in the prison for a matter of minutes and somebody had already been battered to within an inch of her life.

The poor girl was brought back into the room with huge, dark-purple bruises adorning her skin. I later learned that the reason that she hadn't responded to the guards was because she suffered from schizophrenia. She had been away with the fairies and couldn't understand what they were saying. The Spanish prison authorities really had a lightness of touch when it came to dealing with mentally ill people. The way they looked at things, there was nothing that a baton round the head wouldn't cure.

'*¿Hablas español?*' one of the screws asked me.

'No sorry,' I told him, 'I'm English.'

'OK wait,' he said.

He left me in the care of the other two guards, who were still shouting hysterically, whilst he went to fetch an English prisoner to translate for me. The lad that he came back with was a tall, dark-haired drug dealer from London. He seemed nice enough as convicts go and offered to take me to the wing and let me use his phone card so that I could ring the Consulate.

'That would be a massive help,' I told him. 'I owe you one for this.'

My new translator motioned to one of the guards to take us further into the prison and the guard escorted us through a set of electronic doors into a large room filled with crooks of every race, creed, colour and nationality. It was as if the criminal underworlds of Africa, Europe and Latin America had converged together under one roof. Bulgarians, Venezuelans, Colombians, Romanians and Brazilians casually milled around the place, going about their daily business. One thing was for certain: nobody was going to single me out because I was a foreigner.

The guard walked me straight over to the phone and waited whilst I keyed in the Consulate's number. I prayed that the staff had rung Mum up to tell her not to bother visiting but knew full well they wouldn't have. The second I heard a voice on the other end of the line, I started firing questions off.

'Did you know that I was being transferred? Did you let my mum know? Does she still think I'm in Soto? She's visiting me in two days and if you haven't told her then she's going to come across from England for no reason and I won't be there and she'll have wasted her journey...'

'Calm down,' the Consulate woman told me. 'I'm sorry but we haven't been able to get the message out to your mother. We have only just found out about the move ourselves.'

'Well there's no point doing it now then,' I sighed. 'She's probably already on her way to Spain. You've got no idea what you've put her through. You need to send somebody over to the prison as soon as possible because I don't know how I'm going to hold up now that I'm not going to get to see my mum.'

I had a feeling that I would be unable to cope with life in Topas and wanted somebody to voice my concerns to. The prospect of being able to talk things through with somebody who was genuinely concerned about my plight had been the only thing that had kept me functioning. Now I would be lucky to avoid going the same way as the German girl.

I hung up the phone and told the guard to take me to my cell, resigning myself to the fact that there was now no chance of the visit taking place.

'Come,' he said. 'I show you your room.'

By this stage, I was used to being locked up in cramped conditions so I didn't bat an eyelid at my tiny, claustrophobic digs. I was more concerned about the fact that my new cellmate was the Romanian from the bus. Something about her made me feel incredibly uneasy. She was the type of person that I would have crossed the road to avoid if I was in the outside world. I didn't like the idea of spending hours each day locked up with her but didn't want to risk complaining and getting a baton round my head so I kept my feelings to myself.

The guard left the cell unlocked because we had arrived part way through association so I made the brave decision to venture out onto the wing to try and find some other English cons. By this stage I had been in three different jails so being the new girl wasn't half as stressful as it had been when I first got locked up. The other prisoners stared intently at me but didn't seem particularly aggressive. They were probably just trying to figure out what I was in for because I stood out from the crowd.

As with Soto, most of the girls in Topas looked quite rough. A good number of them were wearing black, which is how Spanish widows dress. Most of them were only in their forties so their husbands must have passed away quite young. Maybe their fellas had all been involved in crime and died a violent death or maybe it was the pain of losing a loved one that had driven these girls to break the law. Whatever the case, I got the impression they had lived hard lives.

Staring soon progressed to walking across to get a better look and within the space of a few seconds, a crowd of inmates had surrounded me, chattering excitedly away and asking questions in Spanish. Some of them were gypsies, some were South Americans. I hadn't got a clue what they were saying so I just repeated 'no lo entiendo' over and over again.

I was on what must have been my fiftieth 'no lo entiendo' when I spotted a skinny, black girl pushing her way through the crowd towards me.

'Come on, out the way,' she shouted. 'Give the poor girl some room to breathe.'

She spoke English! There were other Brits in there amongst the hordes of Latinas and Eastern Europeans after all. She spoke with an accent that sounded like a cross between London and Spanish, presumably because she had been in Topas for so long. I would be sure to attract some funny looks if I went back to Buckinghamshire talking like Manuel from *Fawlty Towers*.

'Are you OK there? It's good to see another English girl in here. There aren't too many of us in this nick.'

She looked like a drug addict but seemed friendly enough.

'Yeah I'm holding up all right,' I lied. 'What's it like in here then? It seems quite grim from what I've see of it.'

'It's like a lunatic asylum. The guards are animals, the food is terrible and we get so many people overdosing and trying to kill themselves that I've lost count of them. If you're not Spanish, they won't give you a job so you've got nothing to do and no way of getting any money.'

This didn't bode particularly well.

'My name's Katie by the way. What's yours?'

'I'm Terry,' I told her. 'Pleased to meet you, Katie.'

'Likewise. I didn't mean to scare you; it's just better to tell things how they are. I'd be lying if I said it wasn't bad in here but I'll help you out if you need anything and try to make things easier for you. You smoke?'

I nodded enthusiastically and she handed over a couple of cigarettes.

'The only good thing about this place is that there are blokes as well as girls. We're mostly kept separate but there are times when we're allowed to mix. You want to get yourself a boyfriend; it'll help you pass the time. I got married in here, believe it or not. Eh, they'd never believe that in an English prison, would they? Can you imagine the look on their faces if you told them?'

Spanish jails got more bizarre by the day. Quite a few inmates get married. I guess prisoners who are doing long sentences don't want to have to wait until they're released before they start the hunt for their soul mates.

Katie told me that the prison was divided up amongst the various different nationalities.

'The Latin Americans are mostly drug mules or prostitutes,' she explained. 'They tend to come from shanty towns in places like Venezuela and Brazil. Then you've got the Romanian pickpockets, the Bulgarians who are mostly in for credit card scams, the Africans and the Spanish. Most of the Spaniards are either ETA girls or gypsies. The ETA girls are all very friendly but some of the gypsies might be a bit off with you. They've got a thing about English girls who live in Spain who can't speak any Spanish.'

I wanted to butt in and tell her that I was only over there because the police had flown me back across to serve my sentence, but stayed quiet and listened. She seemed to enjoy sharing her prison knowledge with me and I was eager to lap up every last nugget of information.

I chatted to Katie until it was time to be banged up again and then retired to my cell to spend the night with my good mate the Romanian. There was no point attempting to make conversation because I might has well have chatted to a brick wall. For all I knew we could have got on really well if we had both spoken the same language, though I severely doubted it.

The only advantage that Topas had over Soto was the temperature of the rooms. My cell was very cosy, which meant I actually got some sleep for once that night. I drifted off, cursing to myself about everything that the Spanish authorities had put me through. First they took my freedom, then they had deprived me of the opportunity to see my mum. It was difficult not to feel extremely bitter towards them.

I spent most of my second day in the prison alone in my cell reading some books that Katie had lent me. The wing was crowded, noisy and unwelcoming, especially given how antisocial and depressed I felt. The fact that I was unable to speak Spanish made me feel so isolated. Prison is the loneliest environment that you can imagine and being locked up in a foreign country is even worse than being inside in the UK. My appetite had completely disappeared so I didn't eat any of my meals. All that I could think about was how worried my mum would be when she found out that I was no longer in Soto. The only crime that she was guilty of was caring about her daughter, yet she was being made to suffer more than anyone.

I awoke the following morning to the sound of people shouting through the windows to the men on the wing opposite. When you're in prison, you're bombarded with non-stop noise from the minute you wake up until you go to sleep at night. Yelling, banging, slamming and screaming fill your every waking moment. It wasn't what I needed on the day that my mum should have been visiting and made me want to pull the covers back over my head and pretend that I was still asleep.

I managed to drag myself out of bed and over to the shower, where I closed my eyes and let the warm water flow over my face, hoping that it might somehow wash away the pain of being locked up. Part way through soaping myself, I heard the cell door slide open and had to run and grab a towel to cover myself up before a Spanish prison guard poked his head into the room.

'Teresa Daniels, *visita.*'

Eh? Had Mum found a way to come and see me after all? I almost threw the towel up in the air in my excitement but just about managed to rein myself in before the screw was treated to a free peepshow.

'OK give me a minute,' I told him, attempting to stay calm but feeling like a kid on Christmas Eve. 'I'll be out in a second.'

I quickly put some clothes on and rushed out of the door. I should have known Mum wouldn't let me down. She was the best mum in the world.

The guard ushered me down a corridor into the glass-panel visiting room. As I drew close to the divide that separated the inmates from their relatives, I saw Mum waiting for me on the other side with a smartly dressed, middle-aged bloke I'd never seen before. I was over the moon that she had made it and felt like running over and hugging the glass screen.

It was a bit weird having to talk to my mum through a divide but I was so relieved to see her that I soon got over it.

'How on earth did you track me down?' I asked her, my voice shaking with emotion. 'And how did you organise a visit here at such short notice? I knew you wouldn't give up Mum. I had a feeling you'd come.'

Mum was beaming from ear to ear. She had obviously been missing me as much as I'd been missing her.

'Well we've got the *Daily Mirror* to thank for that,' she said. 'I got in touch with them after the guards at Soto told me you'd been moved and promised them an exclusive if they could find out where you were and get me in to see you. Tom here's covering the story for them.'

'That's great,' I told her. 'It's about time the world knows what it's like in here. I'm not sure how long I can cope in this horrible place. I've seen a woman beaten horribly by the guards, nobody speaks a word of English and the food's inedible.'

Tom scribbled down everything that I said in shorthand then asked a couple of questions about daily life behind bars in Spain. I told him about the lack of medical attention, cruel, unsympathetic staff and the constant threat of violence. The prison governor would no doubt be pissed off that I had slagged off his jail but what more could he do to me? Nothing that he conjured up could possibly be worse than the conditions that I was already living in.

'It sounds horrendous,' Mum told me once I had finished describing the prison. 'I'm doing everything that I can to get you out of here as soon as possible. We've had a fundraiser for you in the village and made quite a bit of money. Dr McCarthy's writing to the prison to tell them that too much stress could make your brain start bleeding again, so hopefully that should make them treat you with a little bit more respect. Everybody at home misses you like crazy. Kelly sends her love and Emma hasn't been the same since you left.'

Hearing about how the community back home were rooting for me made me proud to be from Wingrave, but also made me feel a little bit sad because I wished that I was still there, getting on with my life. The visit only lasted forty minutes, which seemed to go in the blink of an eye. Before I knew it, I was saying a tearful goodbye to my mum and hanging up the receiver on the phone. Mum looked heartbroken and blew me a kiss from behind the glass.

'I love you too,' I shouted, as the electronic visiting-room doors slid open to let me out.

I was pleased that I had got to see her but gutted that I would have to wait at least another week until my next visit. It was back to the world of psychos, lowlifes and scumbags for the time being. I hoped the guards would take steps to improve my treatment after reading the article in the Spanish language version of the *Mirror* but had a suspicion that it might make them even worse than they already were.

Prison life was more tense than usual over the next couple of days as I braced myself for the screws to drag me off and baton me for giving their nick a bad name. Fortunately a girl from Holland asked me if I wanted to move in with her so I didn't have to spend any more time cooped up with the Romanian. The Dutch girl had been best mates with Rochelle in Soto and spoke perfect English so I said yes straightaway.

My new cellmate was called Sara and she had been caught smuggling coke across from Venezuela. She was short and fat but seemed relaxed and good-natured. She also had a television which was a lifesaver in the evening when there was nothing to do apart from sit and stare at the walls. Inmates were allowed to buy tellies from the jail but very few were able to afford them so it was a bit of a luxury. None of the programmes were in English but watching somebody speak a language that I was unable to understand still beat counting down the seconds until the next association.

Two days after my visit, I got word from Mum that the article had been published in the *Mirror* under the headline, 'Save my innocent girl from jail hell'. Tom had described my trial as being 'shambolic' and highlighted the fact that my family wouldn't have even known what prison I was in if he hadn't helped to track me down.

'A MUM pleaded yesterday for her daughter to be freed from a grim Spanish jail where she faces 10 years for drug-running. Mum Pat said: "My poor daughter is totally innocent but now she's looking at the prospect of being in jail until she's 42. I can't stand to see her in that horrible place." And in an emotional reunion, Terry begged: "Please help me get out of here. I can't take it much longer."'

I was pleased that the world was finally getting to know the truth and even more made up that none of the guards had kicked off about it. If they had read the piece then they were keeping it to themselves because nobody had said a word to me.

'That's not the only good news that I've got for you,' Mum told me. 'The BBC have rung. They want to do an interview with you about your case over the phone tomorrow. People are finally starting to sit up and take notice, Terry. The more publicity we can get the better 'cause then they'll see what a joke this whole thing is and maybe you'll get let out.'

'I'll do it,' I told her. 'There's no way I'm giving up a decade of my life without a fight.'

My interview with the BBC went without a hitch and before I knew it, Radio 5 Live and *Look East* were ringing Mum up, asking if she would be a guest on their shows. All of the British journalists covering the story seemed sympathetic to my plight. If the Home Secretary had shown an ounce of compassion and reacted the way they did, I wouldn't have been sent down in the first place.

The flurry of media attention got citizens up and down the country interested in my case and before I knew it, I was receiving up to thirty letters a week. My mum also got random people posting cash to her, which was brilliant. It was heart-warming to know that they were concerned enough about my plight to dip into their wallets.

Things were starting to look up for me on the wing as well. I managed to befriend some of the ETA girls, who were all lovely. Their politics reminded me of my time in Northern Ireland, which made me feel a bit uncomfortable, but none of them were really proper terrorists. They all seemed to have fallen victim to the Guardia Civil's love of banging people up for being in the wrong place at the wrong time. Anybody who knocks about with criminals is automatically a villain in the eyes of the Spanish police. If you're unlucky enough to be there when somebody gets raided then the betting is that you'll be hauled off to jail with them.

Over the weeks I grew particularly close to a girl called Andia, who had been given a five-year sentence after being caught with an ETA boy in her house. Quite how that merited such a lengthy stint inside, I will never know. She could speak a little bit of English and made sure that none of the other inmates gave me any problems. The ETA girls were at the top of the prison hierarchy. All of the other groups were constantly competing for lesser positions of power but nobody ever challenged Andia and her friends. They were the one faction in the prison that was completely untouchable.

I also became pally with an African woman called Mama Rosa, who was arrested in Gran Canaria with six million pesetas on her. The police had no proof whatsoever that it was earned through illegal means, but locked her up for eight years anyway under the logic that it must have been drug money. Her sentence never got her down though; she was always smiling and gave me a big hug whenever I saw her. Nobody ever had a clue what she was on about because she didn't speak a word of Spanish or English so most of our conversations included a lot of gesturing and pointing at things. She couldn't read or write either, which must have made it difficult for her to keep in touch with anybody outside of the prison. If I was her, I probably wouldn't have been able to cope but she seemed to hold up OK.

My two other closest friends were a Brazilian cocaine smuggler called Elizabeth and a transsexual drug dealer called Adriano. Adriano was one of the prison's biggest characters. She was part way through her transformation from female to male and looked like a bloke with a woman's body. Years of drug abuse had made her teeth fall out and she was as eccentric as they come, but very good-hearted and a laugh a minute.

Elizabeth had deliberately got herself pregnant whilst working on the male wing so that the Spanish government would let her stay in the country. Questions should have been asked about how this was allowed to happen but nobody seemed to care. She had eight kids back in Brazil so you would have thought that she would want to return home to see them, but the conditions in the slum that she was from were so horrific that she was willing to sacrifice her family for the chance to get away. I didn't judge her for what she had done because at the end of the day, I hadn't been through what she had been through and didn't know her life. She was one of the few genuinely pleasant people in the prison so I was glad of her company.

Although I tried my hardest to get on with everyone, the gypsies were hard work at first. They thought that I was rude because I talked to people in English and hadn't bothered to learn Spanish. I actively resisted picking up the local lingo to begin with because the way I saw it, I had been taken overseas against my will and didn't see why I should have to adapt to a country that I didn't belong in. I hated the Spanish and everything that they stood for, so the last thing that I wanted to do was start speaking like them.

Most of the other Spanish prisoners were hardcore addicts, who I wanted nothing to do with. Their world was no longer of any interest to me because I had stopped taking drugs the minute I entered the prison system. Seeing their track-mark-covered bodies and wiry, skeletal frames was like an advert for staying clean. It made me think, 'Thank God I stopped taking whiz before I got to that stage.' I felt sorry for some of them but others were prolific offenders, who I thought should have used their first few jail sentences as a wake-up call and sorted themselves out. Being honest, I don't think I had the understanding of drug addicts' circumstances that I now possess. I have since worked as a drug counsellor and learnt that even the most dedicated quitter can end up relapsing.

Drink was just as readily available as drugs so I still had the odd tipple every now and again. There were two ways that inmates could get hold of booze. They could either bribe the guards to bring a bottle of whisky in for the equivalent of £50 or drink homebrew made by fermenting fruit. The homebrew smelt disgusting so I usually stuck to the whisky. By this stage Mum had sent some money over for me but I still didn't have enough to splash out on luxuries like that so I usually relied upon people giving me a sip of theirs.

I had to keep my addictions hidden from the authorities because anybody who had suffered from any kind of drug or alcohol abuse was prescribed methadone and normally ended up getting hooked. Meth is only meant to be given to heroin addicts but I had seen the nurses dishing it out to everybody from alcoholics to crackheads. They didn't reduce the dosage either, which meant that the inmates still had drug habits but were just addicted to meth instead of whatever it was that they were on before. A Spanish girl I knew had entered the jail with a minor cocaine habit and ended up a fully-fledged meth-head. She tried to go cold turkey at one stage but only lasted two days.

The side effects of methadone are just as unpleasant as those of illegal drugs. Some girls had no teeth because it had rotted them away. Others were forced to eat liquidised food because the drugs had given them serious problems with their stomachs. Technically they had had the choice to refuse the meth but when you land in prison with a crippling drug habit, you're likely to take anything that you can get your hands on. The morality of offering recovering addicts such a harmful and addictive drug is questionable to say the least. It was yet another example of the Spaniards' haphazard approach to caring for their prisoners. They didn't worry if people managed to get clean or not, just as long as they were able to make out that they were taking steps to try and rehabilitate them.

Heroin was also rife within the jail and every couple of weeks, I heard the clanging of the metal trolleys that they used to cart people off who had overdosed. Sometimes the guards would give OD'd inmates a glass of sugary water to rehydrate them and then leave them in their cells. More often than not, the addicts would be dead by the next morning. Life was very cheap in Topas. The medical care was non-existent. One time I went to the doctor to tell him that I felt depressed and tired all the time and he advised me to boost my energy by eating more chocolate. And there was me thinking that they were meant to tell you to eat an apple a day!

Another time I cut my finger and asked one of the guards for a plaster. She came back with a piece of Sellotape. God knows what she would have given me if I had broken my arm. I probably would have had to wrap it in a dishcloth.

The mentally ill inmates were the ones who suffered the most from the poor quality healthcare. There wasn't enough room for them all on the medical wing, so vulnerable prisoners with schizophrenia and psychosis were bunged in with the rest of the riff-raff. Some girls hadn't got a clue what day of the week it was. They should have been in hospital, not locked away with muggers, armed robbers and murderers.

Then there were the AIDs cases. Prisoners would come in looking healthy and in shape and leave dying on their feet because they had shared a syringe. One of the Spanish inmates got brain damage as a result of the virus and went from being quiet and reserved to smashing up her cell and randomly kicking off on other girls within the space of a few months. It was blindingly obvious that there was something wrong with her but yet she still didn't get moved off the wing. Violence was perfectly normal in Topas. The guards expected it and usually ignored it.

The fights were never one on one; they were always massive brawls. The female prisoners would fight like men and pummel each other to within an inch of their lives. There was at least one fatal stabbing whilst I was in the jail and countless brutal beatings.

A lot of the fights involved two big, hard Russian birds, who spent every waking moment looking for a scrap. One of them was in for murder and the other was a drug dealer with a mouthful of gold teeth, which presumably meant that she had earned a bit of money from her crime. They were both incredibly tough and loved to show off their fist work. All they ever did was drink and batter people.

I did my best to stay away from the more aggressive girls in the jail because my haemorrhage meant I was especially vulnerable. A single punch could trigger another aneurysm and put me back in hospital. It didn't take much provocation to start a fight in Topas, though. Sometimes the other prisoners would kick off for no reason at all. One day I was chatting away to someone on the wing when a nasty, rough-looking junkie with track marks all over her arms and legs came sidling up to me. She stood there for a couple of minutes giving me the evils and then suddenly lunged across and slammed my head into the wall.

'Speak Spanish!' she shouted, as the other inmates dragged her off me. 'You are in Spain now. You need speak Spanish!'

The attack made me feel jittery for weeks afterwards. I saw the junkie girl whenever I went out on the wing so there was no getting away from her. The guards should have been on hand to protect me but all they cared about was how much money they could hustle up by exploiting their positions. If they weren't selling whisky to the alkies, they were stealing food from the kitchen.

The screws weren't the only members of staff who were on the take either; the prison governor was the most bent of the lot. He had been sacked from the last jail that he worked at for siphoning off money and there were rumours that he was doing the same in Topas. The word about the wing was that he had put a non-existent person down on the books as 'sub-medical director' so that he could embezzle prison funds. With such an unsavoury character in charge of the guards, it was little wonder they were fleecing the place for all that it was worth.

The governor was also incredibly two-faced. A couple of weeks after my interview with the BBC, he invited me into his office and told me he was going to make my time inside as easy as possible, presumably as a way of making sure I didn't bad-mouth him to the media. This would have been all well and good if I hadn't found out from Fair Trials that he had spoken to the Spanish government behind my back and advised them not to pardon me because I wasn't ill enough. The way I saw it, he shouldn't have acted all pally-pally with me when he knew full well that he had done something that was likely to extend my stay in jail. I had known that the prison staff were not to be trusted, but still felt betrayed and let down. Now the chances of being released were even slimmer than before.

The governor's backstabbing antics sent me spiralling further into depression and I started going for days without eating. Sometimes my stomach would be horribly painful because I was so hungry and I would go to sleep dreaming about food. Looking back, I think this was a form of self-harm. Starving myself was the only way that I could express how awful I was feeling.

I also suffered terrible bouts of anxiety. Some nights I would lie awake, unable to get to sleep because I was so full of dread, other nights I would have horrendous nightmares. There were rumours going round the wing that the guards would let themselves into girls' cells and rape them whilst the other inmates slept, which left me paralysed with fear whenever I thought about it.

As well as having to deal with anxiety, depression and hunger pains, my head was also still cripplingly painful. Sometimes it was so unbearable that I could hardly move and had to spend all day in bed. After pestering the doctor time and time again to examine me more thoroughly, I eventually managed to persuade him to arrange for the Guardia Civil to take me to the local hospital. This proved to be a thoroughly humiliating experience because I was escorted there in handcuffs by gun-toting Old Bill. Mothers pulled their children back away from me and old ladies clutched their purses tighter to their chests as I walked past them in the waiting room. I felt as if the prison authorities had deliberately engineered my appointment to be as degrading as possible so that I wouldn't ask for any more trips outside the jail.

The doctor at the hospital was even worse than the one at Topas. Upon reading my notes, the first thing that he did was signal for me to get inside a CAT-scan machine, which was a little bit worrying because I had been warned specifically not to have a CAT scan by the doctor who did my coiling. I had a metal plate in my head where they had repaired my skull and had been told that scanning it could cause it to heat up and explode. Refusing to budge was completely out of the question though because I knew full well that the coppers would beat me up if I did. They might even shoot me if I kicked up too much of a fuss. Nobody spoke a word of English so attempting to explain to them that I could die if I had the scan would be a pointless exercise. I was just going to have to get in the machine and hope that they realised something was up and stopped before it was too late.

As the scan began, I closed my eyes and braced myself for my skull to blow up. Maybe it would be less painful than having to go back to Topas anyway. It would mean no more junkies, no more being treated like an animal by the guards, no more rubbish food, no more having to listen to hours of people shouting across the wing to one another in Spanish...

'¡Parar! Hay un problema.¡Detenerlo ahora! ¡Parar la TAC!'

... no more being crammed into a space the size of a rabbit hutch...

CLANK!

... but I was still almost jumping for joy when the whirring of the machinery came to a halt – so maybe life was worth living after all.

'There is problem. We cannot do scan,' the doctor told me. 'We no able to proceed.'

By this stage I no longer cared about my headaches. I was so relieved to be alive that I had forgotten all about them. The relief didn't last long though because it was quickly replaced by rightful indignation. If the prison had sent somebody along with me to translate then none of this would have happened. The guards had needlessly endangered my life just for the sake of being awkward. I felt frustrated but was unable to show any signs of anger in front of the police for fear that they would take it as an act of aggression and beat me with their truncheons. The whole thing sickened me and made me long to return to a world where life was actually worth something. The screws would have probably preferred my head to have blown up so that they had one less foreign prisoner to worry about.

The only slight silver lining was that I had some good news waiting for me back at the jail when I returned. The British Consulate had written to ask if I wanted them to authorise a transfer to an English prison on grounds of ill health, which meant that even if I didn't get my pardon, there was still a chance of serving my sentence in my own country. After what I had been through at the hospital, I didn't need to think twice about the answer. It was a total no brainer.

The letter stressed that the transfer would be reliant upon Interpol agreeing to send an officer to accompany me on my flight. There was a good chance that the move wouldn't come to fruition but the fact that there was even a faint possibility of landing on British soil again still made me feel a lot more optimistic. Things were starting to look up. As I lay in bed that night, I closed my eyes and imagined what it would be like to talk to other prisoners and know exactly what they were saying when they answered. It would be like heaven on earth after spending months surrounded by people speaking Spanish at a million miles per hour. I just hoped that it would actually happen. After all, I was due a bit of luck. Fate owed me a good turn and I was hoping he'd pay up.

Chapter 18

UPS AND DOWNS

Well it's the day of my little sister's wedding. I told her that I would have done anything to be there and that I love her with all my heart. She told me not to get down and to try and be happy for her. It was one of the hardest phone calls I've had to make. I just wish I could stop crying. My heart is breaking. I still can't believe I'm missing my little sis's big day.

Diary entry from 29 July 2006

The months went by and I heard nothing about my transfer. Every day I crossed my fingers and hoped that there would be some news in the mail. I had no idea when my reply was likely to arrive, so it was just a matter of playing the waiting game. In the meantime, I was going to have to make the best of things and adapt to life in Topas as well as I could. Now that I felt a little bit more upbeat, I was no longer as stubborn and decided to make an effort to learn as much Spanish as possible. It was difficult at first but the other inmates helped me out and before I knew it, I could put together basic sentences. When you're around Spanish speakers 24/7, you learn their language a lot faster than you would in a classroom, which meant that I could soon speak enough to get by.

The gypsies saw that I was making an effort and became more sympathetic. They stopped giving me the evils on the wing and started helping me out instead. They even gave me a coat when I was cold during the winter. I think they respected the fact that I was trying hard to fit in even though I shouldn't have been there.

The public back home in England were just as supportive. Every other day I got a letter telling me how unfair my trial was or how much everyone was rooting for me. The local papers constantly highlighted my situation and John Bercow bombarded the Spanish government with letters pleading for my freedom. The biggest boost to my case came when the *Mirror* managed to find Antonio and got him to agree to an interview. He backed up my story one hundred per cent and even offered to sign a document to say that I was innocent.

Antonio was living on the Spanish mainland with his parents when Tom found him. His wife had been so furious when he was arrested that she had filed for a divorce and told their kids that he was dead. He had only spent six years in jail and served two of them in an open prison where he was allowed out for two days a week. It was blindingly obvious that he had grassed somebody up to get a shorter sentence. It was his second time inside for smuggling so why would the authorities have been so lenient to him if he hadn't thrown somebody's name into the mix? He was not only a low-life criminal but also one that dragged everybody else down with him.

'Terry is totally innocent. I can't believe she's in prison for a crime I committed,' he apparently sobbed down the phone during the interview. 'She knew nothing about the drugs. She will be going through hell in prison. She will be like a little bird in a cage full of tigers.'

It was all very well Antonio crying and making out that he was remorseful but at the end of the day, I wouldn't have been in prison in the first place if he hadn't tricked me into going to Brazil with him. I was glad that he was letting the world know that I was being made to suffer for his actions though. It was sure to help the case for my pardon and might encourage Interpol to agree to take me back to Britain.

I couldn't wait to see the story in print and hear the public's take on it. Tom sent me a copy and told me that it would be published in the paper within the next few weeks. Every time I spoke to Mum, I asked her if it had been in yet. Then, after days of sitting on the edge of my seat, I got a letter from the *Mirror* saying that Antonio had been in touch again. He had retracted his story and claimed that I had been in on the smuggling operation from the start. I couldn't believe the cheek of him. One minute he was bawling his eyes out and the next thing I knew he was trying to make out I was guilty. I felt like punching a hole in the wall.

Luckily Tom remained unconvinced by Antonio's fairy stories and didn't incorporate them into the article. The *Mirror* eventually pulled the piece though, which was a major disappointment. Antonio had clearly got cold feet about having his interview made public and lied through his teeth so that the paper wouldn't put it out.

The other girls on the wing all rallied round me when they heard what had happened. Andia and her friends were particularly sympathetic and suggested that I started going to the outside exercise area with them to help take my mind off things. This was one of the few parts of the prison where the men and women mixed freely with one another. She told me that an Irish lad called Aidan from the men's wing always went out there and pointed out that he would be a good person for me to get to know, seeing as we hailed from neighbouring countries.

You needed to apply for permission to be allowed out for exercise and I had put off filling out a slip until this point because a lot of sex offenders knocked about out there. Rapists and paedophiles inhabit separate wings in most British prisons but in Spain they are allowed to mingle with the general population and don't seem to get much stick. Sex crimes are a lot less taboo in Spanish nicks. Nonces are frowned upon by the other prisoners but very rarely get attacked, which is in stark contrast to the sex cases in English jails, who aren't even one hundred per cent safe when the guards are there.

'Will I be OK out there?' I asked Andia. 'I've heard that lots of nasty people go out to exercise.'

'You will be with us,' she told me. 'We won't let anything happen to you.'

'OK I'll do it,' I said. 'I'll put an application in this afternoon.'

It took a week for the guards to get back to me and tell me that I was allowed out. To be honest I was almost hoping that they would say no. It was scary enough on the wing and there were only women there. The idea of rapists and kiddie fiddlers milling about the place made me feel sick to my stomach.

The first thing that struck me when I stepped out of the door was how different the exercise area was to the yards in English prisons, which are small pieces of concrete with little room to actually exercise in. This one looked like a school playing field. There was a running track around the outside and a football pitch in the middle, with groups of people stood around chatting on it. Nobody came across as particularly predatory but I couldn't help noticing a few faces that I had seen on the news. I recognised a woman who had made the headlines for a horrendous crime against a little girl. Her and her husband had been abusing their daughter and the woman had thrown acid into the daughter's face to try and prevent her from going to the police. The evil cow was walking round the field with her husband as if they were just your average, carefree couple.

'What are you looking at?' Andia asked me, sensing that I was becoming increasingly agitated.

'It doesn't matter,' I told her. 'Let's go and find this Irish boy.'

I wanted to get away from those two sick people as quickly as I could. I had associated with characters who were on the fringes of criminality before I came to jail but never willingly mixed with anybody who had done the kind of evil things that those two abominations had done. As far as I was concerned, they could no longer even be considered human. They were vile monsters and I was glad that they had ended up in Topas. I just hoped that they were finding it as difficult as I was.

'Look there he is,' said Andia, pointing across the field to a tall, well-built lad, who looked as if he spent all day in the gym.

Aidan was definitely in shape. He could have given Popeye a run for his money and had the kind of twinkle in his eyes that only our friends from across the Irish Sea can have. The only problem was that he was clearly a Catholic; I could tell from the makes of clothes that he was wearing. Irish Catholics refuse to wear brands like Reebok or Lonsdale that incorporate the Union Jack into their logos and tend to avoid clothing made by British companies. How was he going to take to an English Protestant? Would it be a problem for him or had he left all that behind him when he came to Spain?

'Hi I'm Terry, pleased to meet you.'

I was bracing myself for a torrent of sectarian abuse.

'Nice to meet you too,' he grinned. 'I've heard a lot about you.'

'All good I hope?' I asked him.

'Of course,' he told me. 'What brings you to a place like this then?'

I didn't want to bore him with my life story so I summarised the events of the last few years in as few words as possible, which must have taken a good fifteen minutes.

'Jeez, it sounds as if you've had quite a time of it.'

'Yeah not half,' I laughed. 'What about you then? What are you in for?'

'Kidnap.'

Wow. I hadn't been expecting anything as serious as that.

'I didn't do it though,' he hastily added. 'The boys in blue fitted me up.'

If we were in England I would have probably thought 'Yeah, right' but given how corrupt the Spanish Old Bill were, he could well have been telling the truth.

'Join the club,' I laughed. 'So are you out here every day?'

'Yeah,' he told me. 'You should come out for a chat more often. You're all right for a Brit, you know.'

I smiled and told him that I would meet him in the same place tomorrow. Over the next few weeks, our friendship quickly progressed into a jailhouse romance. He was quite shy and reserved but had a cheeky side to him, which was very endearing. I should have learnt my lesson from the first two Irish boys, but he seemed quite well rounded to begin with. The first sign that our relationship was going to be problematic came when I asked him what part of the country he was from.

'A place called Tallaght in County Dublin,' he told me. 'It's a good Catholic area. They don't like you Brits round those parts.'

'Why's that then?' I asked him.

'A lot of people support the IRA. I don't blame them either; they've done a lot for our country.'

Oh dear. Now I had been out with UVF, UDA and IRA sympathisers. At least nobody could accuse me of political bias.

'What about you then? Where did you grow up?'

'A little village called Wingrave,' I told him. 'It's not a bad place to live. Nice and quiet. Near to Aylesbury too, where there are plenty of good raves to go to.'

Aidan raised a single eyebrow and gave me a disapproving look.

'You're not into all that shite are you? What do you want to go out polluting your body with drugs for every weekend?'

I should have guessed that somebody who was so into health and fitness would be militantly anti-drugs. I tried to explain to him that I had stopped taking them but he seemed disgusted that I had ever gone near them in the first place. Our lifestyles before we came to prison couldn't have been more different. We were like chalk and cheese. The only thing we had in common was the language that we spoke.

Aidan was obsessed with the gym. He spent every waking moment working out and got incredibly moody when he missed a session, which led me to believe that he was probably using steroids. He had a fiery temper and would often work himself up into a rage for no reason at all. I should have ended things the minute I realised what he was like but felt as if I needed someone there to comfort me when I was down. I even put in for a conjugal visit with him, which turned out to be a very foolish move. It made me feel like a sordid prostitute going to a cheap hotel for sex. I think it might have been OK if he had been somebody who I really loved but he was such a moody character that it was difficult to know how I felt about him. There were times when he could be kind and compassionate and it wasn't as if we were always at each other's throats. On the day of my sister's wedding, I was glad that he was there to act as a shoulder to cry on. It would have been awful going through that alone. Missing out on the most important event of her life had me on the verge of a breakdown.

I phoned Kelly up at eleven o'clock on the morning of the wedding and told her that I would have done anything to be there with her and that I loved her with all my heart. I should have been the chief bridesmaid but yet there I was, reduced to being told what her dress looked like over the phone. All of the other prisoners did their best to cheer me up and even the guards were nice to me but I was still horrendously upset. As it approached 2 p.m., the time the ceremony started, I closed my eyes and pictured Kelly walking down the aisle as all of the guests marvelled at how beautiful she was. I would have given my right arm to see her say 'I do'. Aidan was full of sympathy and did his best to make things as easy as possible. It was at times like this that I was really glad of his company.

After the wedding, I became even more determined to get out as soon as I could. I didn't want to miss out on any more events like that; just the one was bad enough. It had been almost a full year since I had entered the prison and I still hadn't seen the lawyer that Fair Trials had told me they were sorting. I knew they wouldn't let me down but the tension was still killing me.

It was October 2006 by the time my solicitor finally came to see me. She seemed very down to earth and had a sympathetic face, which was a breath of fresh air after being locked up with nothing but hard nuts for so long. Her name was Mari and although she was Spanish, she spoke perfect English.

'It's good to finally meet you,' she told me. 'I must say, your case is a very unusual one. If you had been tried in England, you would never have been convicted but I'm afraid our legal system isn't quite the same as yours. The diary entries that were used in evidence were not translated by official translators. They shouldn't have even been accepted by the court, but seem to have slipped through unnoticed.'

This was news to me. I asked her to translate the prosecution's account of what I had said and was shocked to learn that vast sections of it bore no resemblance to what I had originally written. One of the translations read, 'Right now I'm sitting at the airport, very bored and a bit worried, dreaming about what I'll do with the money. I feel this will be a long fucking night but if everything turns out right, I'm having a party tomorrow.' They had completely reworded what I had written and added a random F-word to make me seem rough and uncouth, as if I was the type of person who would willingly accompany a crackhead on a smuggling trip. I very rarely swear and certainly did not include that word in my diary.

Another entry read, 'Cheer up. This is our last day in this shitty place. The goods did arrive so we can have a party and get stoned.' I'm not in a third-rate gangster film and don't say things like 'the goods did arrive'. I don't use the phrase 'stoned' either. They had twisted things around and added bits to put across a false image of me. Until then, nobody had brought what they had done to my attention. If I had known about all this during the trial then I could have pointed it out to the judge and he might have dismissed the diary entries as evidence.

'Are you going to write to the government and tell them this then?' I asked Mari, hoping that it might be grounds for them to re-open the case.

'That's not how things work here,' she told me. 'If they think that you are criticising the Spanish justice system then your pardon will be less likely to be successful. The best thing you can do is to collect as many supporting letters from influential figures as you can. The more the government sees that people are supporting you, the greater the chance you will have of being released.'

So what she was basically saying was that they can give you an unfair trial in Spain and then penalise you even further when you complain about it being unfair. It sounded ridiculous to me but if I had to keep my mouth shut to get out then I was just going to have to bottle up everything that I wanted to say until I was released. I had a feeling that I still had a fight on my hands, but felt a damn sight better off now that I had got the chance to sit down and discuss my case with someone in the know.

Mari gave me a new lease of life. The fact that she thought I was actually likely to get a pardon changed the way I looked at being inside. Topas was no longer somewhere that I would have to endure for years on end; it was just a momentary stop-off point before I cleared my name and got on with my life.

The following month, I got an even better piece of news. The British Consulate had written to let me know that my transfer to England had been approved. This was it; I was on my way back home. Even if my pardon didn't come to fruition, I was still going to get to spend the majority of my sentence in a place where everybody spoke English and I got proper medical attention. Aidan had just been told that he was being transferred back to Ireland too so we would both be out of there before we knew it. Now it was just a matter of sitting tight and waiting for Interpol to sort out the arrangements for my flight.

Mum was ecstatic when I spoke to her on the phone later that day.

'I'll tell you what, it'll save me a fortune on flights,' she joked. 'It means you'll get to see the new arrival too.'

'What new arrival's this then?' I asked her, wondering what the hell she was going on about.

'Kelly's pregnant.'

OK wow. That was unexpected.

'You're going to have another little niece or nephew.'

I had missed Kel's wedding but there was no chance that I was going to miss the birth of her child. It's a lot easier to get moved to an open prison in England than it is in Spain and non-violent offenders are often released early with a tag on their leg, so if Interpol hurried up with my transport then it was likely that I would get to witness a new member of the family being brought into the world.

From that moment onwards, nothing seemed to bother me. I was no longer fazed by my headaches, the relentless noise or the threat of attack from other prisoners. It was as if I was floating around the prison in an impenetrable bubble. Topas was a horrible, morbid place but I would only be there for a little while longer. Soon I would be holding my sister's baby in my arms in good old Buckinghamshire.

It took a good few months for my bubble to finally burst and send me crashing back to the ground. I was sitting on the wing writing my diary when it happened.

'*Perdone* Teresa, I'm sorry but your boyfriend is leaving for Ireland tomorrow. I thought you might want to say goodbye to him. There is a room free for you both if you want time alone.'

I didn't know what to say. I had known this day was coming at some point but still felt shocked by the suddenness of it. For all his faults, Aidan was the one person in the prison who I knew that I could rely upon when I needed someone. Life in Topas wouldn't be the same without him. We'd had our ups and downs but I was still going to miss him like crazy. It was nice of the guard to be so understanding. At the end of the day, prison guards can be bad or good, just like everybody else and this guy was definitely one of the nicer ones.

My last moments with Aidan were spent hugging him and telling him I didn't want him to go.

'It's OK,' he tried to comfort me. 'Being apart will only make us stronger. I'll write to you the minute I touch down in Dublin.'

'Promise?' I asked him, drying my eyes and attempting to stop sniffling.

'Of course,' he told me. 'I'm not big on writing letters but I definitely will.'

I hugged him even tighter and buried my face in his top. Looking back though, things probably wouldn't have worked out between us even if we'd stayed in the same nick. He was an Irish Catholic from a rough, sectarian neighbourhood and I was an English girl who didn't give a monkey's about a person's politics or religion. Our relationship was doomed from the start.

The next couple of days were very difficult but I soon got used to Aidan not being there. Prison is a stressful, draining environment and it had been nice to have somebody there to help me through it; but being on my own was a positive thing in a way because it forced me to learn more Spanish. I had started relying on Aidan to fill in for me whenever I had trouble making myself understood but now that he was no longer there, there was no safety net. It was a case of either trying hard to remember the words that I was looking for, or no one knowing what I was on about.

The weeks flew by and before I knew it, it was my turn to say farewell to Topas. As usual, they left it until the evening before the transfer to tell me that I was moving so I only had a couple of hours to say goodbye to my friends. The other girls were sad to see me go and wished me the best of luck.

My Spanish ordeal wasn't over yet. I would still have to stop off at Soto for a couple of weeks whilst Interpol got things ready for my flight. This was the final hurdle before my repatriation. I only had to last a few months tops in there and then I was off to sunny England.

I was hugging Adriano and saying goodbye to him/her when two skinny, rough-looking Spanish girls staggered into the room, shouting their heads off and spilling homebrew everywhere.

'Great,' I thought to myself, 'this is just what I need on my last day in here.'

The guards usually turned a blind eye to inmates drinking alcohol because they had normally sold it to them in the first place, but this time they seemed to have had enough and dragged the culprits off the wing. Five minutes later, the two drunkards came back covered from head to toe in bruises and shaking uncontrollably. The screws had taken them to the medical wing, handcuffed them to a hospital bed and beaten them senseless.

'God almighty,' I thought to myself. 'I'm glad I'm getting out of here.'

Chapter 19

RETURN TO THE ASYLUM

'Somewhere out there looking out my window, daydreaming of how nice it could be to be free...'

'Looking out my window' by the Rat Pack, a song that sums up to a tee how I felt during my sentence.

'Teresa Daniels?'

Was it that time already? I had got a terrible night's sleep. I spent the whole time wide-awake, buzzing about the transfer. Even the journey between prisons was something to look forward to. When you're locked up, every day is the same so any slight hint of variety is a welcome change. The guards' sadistic treatment of the alkies would have normally upset me but all that I could think about was stepping off the plane onto English soil. The incident only served to remind me what a sick and twisted place I was about to leave behind.

There were a couple of other prisoners with me on the bus but I was too busy looking out of the window and picturing myself enjoying life in the free world to pay them much attention. We passed through a sleepy little Spanish town and I saw people sitting outside cafes, sipping their drinks and soaking up the sun. Soon that would be me if I got either let out with a leg tag on or moved to an open prison.

I was hoping that life in Soto would be easier now that I knew a bit of Spanish but the guards put me in with an Austrian who only spoke German, so my newfound language skills didn't make any difference whatsoever. She seemed nice enough but didn't understand a word I said to her. Some of the ETA girls were still in the prison but the mix of nationalities had changed and there were now a lot more Vietnamese and Jamaicans in there. The atmosphere was very different too. Tension between the different ethnic groups had increased dramatically and the wing was like a powder keg.

The Yardies were all very tough girls but seemed OK to get on with. The Vietnamese came across as quite sly so I made a mental note to stay away from them. They were delicate, dainty little things, who didn't seem particularly aggressive or violent but gave the impression that they were not to be trusted. It was obvious from the outset that the two groups didn't get on well with one another so I kept myself to myself and tried to remain neutral. The last thing I wanted was to end up getting involved in a fight and have my trip back to England cancelled at the last minute because I was categorised as a security risk.

Sure enough, a few days after I had arrived, the tension in the prison came to a head and there was a vicious brawl between the Vietnamese and the Yardies. Before seeing them going at it, I would have expected the Jamaicans to win without breaking a sweat, but the Vietnamese girls were actually surprisingly hard. They seemed to be highly skilled in martial arts and did all kinds of crazy flying kicks. The Yardies shunned the fancy stuff in favour of brute force and threw wild uppercuts into their tiny rivals' faces. Before long, chairs and tables were being chucked around the place and the wing had descended into a full-scale riot.

The maddest part of the fight came when the smallest of the Vietnamese girls flew across the room and put a huge, muscle-bound Yardie on her backside with a kick that Bruce Lee would have been proud of. I thought, 'OK remind me not to piss off any of the Vietnamese lot whilst I'm in here.' They were getting the better of girls at least twice their size.

The guards eventually managed to get the situation back under control and separated the two warring clans, much to the relief of the other inmates on the wing, who had been crapping themselves in case they got caught in the crossfire. There had been fights every other day in Topas but nothing that even remotely resembled this one. It was the talk of the wing for days to come and taught the Jamaicans a valuable lesson never to underestimate an opponent. The Vietnamese might have looked as if a strong breeze would blow them away but they were some of the toughest girls I've ever seen.

That night I prayed that nothing else like that would happen whilst I was inside. I was paranoid that I would get dragged into something that might jeopardise my transfer. All that it would take for me to be marked down as a troublemaker would be for somebody to attack me and the guards to presume that I was the aggressor. Interpol would refuse to transport me overseas if they thought that I was likely to kick off so it was in my best interest to stay on everyone's good side.

As I lay there trying to get the fight out of my head, I heard a loud banging noise coming from the cell next door followed by a blood-curdling scream. What on earth was going on? If our neighbours were having an argument then they needed to tone it down a bit because it was the middle of the night.

The noise continued for a good ten minutes before suddenly stopping and plunging the wing back into silence. It was soon replaced by the sound of heavy footsteps and concerned voices. I got up to have a look through the food hatch and saw a group of screws crowded round our neighbours' open cell and our neighbour standing sobbing uncontrollably on the landing. This didn't look too good; they never opened anybody's door during the night unless there had been a serious incident. My return to Soto was turning out to be more eventful than the rest of my time inside put together.

A couple of minutes later, a load of paramedics came rushing across the wing towards the cell and the guards motioned them inside. The screws didn't always call the medics in when someone had overdosed so I knew that something major must have taken place. My suspicions were confirmed when a guard came out of the cell pushing a newspaper trolley with a dead body wrapped in sheets on it. No wonder the girl from next door was so upset; her roomie had topped herself in front of her.

I spent the rest of the night sitting wide-awake, feeling as if my heart was about to beat out of my chest. Why hadn't the guards taken the girl to hospital when they first discovered she wasn't breathing? For all they knew, she could have been unconscious and they could have saved her life. It took them long enough to get the paramedics on the wing as well. The way the bloke had wheeled her out of the room reminded me of somebody casually pushing a luggage trolley along at the airport. None of the screws seemed in the least bit bothered that a girl had lost her life. It was just part of the job to them.

One of the ETA girls had heard the entire thing unfold and told me the full story when our cells were opened up next morning.

'It is sad,' she said. 'The girl was caught smuggling cocaine and given a twenty-year sentence. She didn't even have a large amount either. I think they wanted to make an example of her. Her family disowned her and said they wouldn't visit her so she took some pills and put a plastic bag around her face. She was blue when they found her. It's such a shame. She was so young as well.'

There were a lot of things that didn't add up about this story. Why would she have taken the pills and then suffocated herself before they took effect? And what was her cellmate doing whilst she was sitting there with her head in the bag? I would imagine that it takes a while to die from lack of oxygen.

'It must be awful for the girl that she was sharing with as well,' the ETA girl went on. 'It's the fourth time this has happened to somebody who was in with her. I think she must be cursed or something.'

The dead girl's roomie was in for killing her husband and looked a nasty piece of work. She was a creepy French bird who hardly spoke to anyone. The thought entered my head that she might have drugged then killed the other girl but I held my tongue and kept it to myself in case it wasn't true. It doesn't pay to gossip about other people in a place like Soto. She had looked genuinely upset when I saw her outside the cell but then again it's easy to turn on the waterworks, especially if you've had a lot of practice.

The more I thought about it, the more I became convinced that the death was the result of murder rather than suicide. The cells were tiny so it would have been impossible for somebody not to hear their cellmate dying. What better place would there be for a killing to go undetected than Soto? The guards didn't even view the death as suspicious. They just got on with their jobs as if it hadn't happened. The other inmates didn't seem too fazed either. I was the only one who was at all bothered.

The prospect of sharing a wing with a serial killer chilled me to the bone. I spent even more time than usual in the safety of my cell and started having trouble sleeping. The image of that poor girl's corpse being wheeled out will remain with me until my dying day. They could at least have used a hospital stretcher. A newspaper trolley is no place for a dead body. It was as if they were determined to deprive the girl of her dignity even after she had passed away.

'Roll on England,' I thought to myself.

Even Topas had been better than the nuthouse that was Soto. I just had to keep repeating to myself that it would all be over soon.

Interpol took two full weeks to finalise the plans for my flight. One of the screws broke the news to me on the wing and I literally jumped for joy.

'Make sure you have your bags packed for 8 a.m.,' the guard told me. 'You might not be called then but that's the earliest they could come for you.'

The earlier the better. I like to have a lie-in as much as the next girl does but the less time I had to spend in that crazy place, the happier I would be.

My final night in Soto was so cold that I had to sleep wearing a jacket. As I drifted off, I looked back on my time in Spanish prisons and reflected on everything that I had been forced to endure. Wherever they sent me to in England was going to be a walk in the park compared to what I had already been through.

'Bye bye Spain,' I whispered to myself. 'Soon you will be ancient history.'

Chapter 20

BACK TO SUNNY ENGLAND

So the day has come, the day I thought would never come. I've been here nineteen months and one week exactly. I'm a little nervous but I'm trying to be as calm as possible. It will be a long old day but it'll be worth it in the end. So my diary, I'll see you in England.

Diary entry from 3 May 2007

On the morning of my transfer, I put on my smartest clothes and made sure that I looked my best. It was going to be the first time since my extradition that I got to spend the day around people who weren't criminals and I didn't want them to see me looking scruffy.

A Spanish copper drove me to Madrid Airport, where I was handed over to two English Interpol officers. The first thing that struck me about them was how different they were to the Spanish Interpol who had accompanied me on the plane to Spain. They were a lot more friendly and relaxed and talked to me as if I was their equal.

'You must be the infamous Terry Daniels,' joked the male officer.

He was a tubby little Londoner with a typical, good-natured, Cockney sense of humour.

'I'm so glad to see you,' I told him. 'I've never been so pleased to see a copper in my life.'

Being in the company of an authority figure who actually treated me as if I was a human being was a huge culture shock after a year and a half of seeing inmates getting dragged away and battered for saying a word out of turn. I had a good old chinwag with the Old Bill until my plane arrived and then boarded the flight with an officer on either side of me.

'I have to warn you that there's still a chance we won't be flying today,' the female copper informed me as I made my way down the aisle.

Was she being serious? We were on the plane, what could possibly stop us now?

'The staff all have to agree that they're comfortable with transporting a convicted criminal. Most of them are OK with it, but one of the hostesses isn't all that sure. She thinks that you might be a psychopath.'

Charming! If I had to go back to Soto with my tail between my legs because some stupid stewardess had got it into her head that I was Norman Bates then I wouldn't be too pleased.

'Can't you have a word with her?' I implored the copper. 'Tell her what I'm like and that I'm not some violent lunatic!'

'I'll see what I can do,' she told me. 'I'll be back in a sec.'

Two minutes later, the copper came bowling towards our seats with a big grin on her face as if to say, 'Don't worry, I've sorted it'.

'She says she doesn't mind you being here just so long as she gets to stay at the other end of the plane. She doesn't want you gouging her eyes out with a plastic spoon because the airline food is crap.'

I wiped a bead of sweat from off my head and fastened my seatbelt. The cabin crew talked us through the safety procedure and the plane began to taxi up the runway. I had made it. I could almost taste the rain and feel the icy chill of English weather on my skin.

The flight back home was a world away from how the one to Spain had been. I excitedly chattered away to the officers for the entire journey, telling them all about my arrest and how I had ended up being extradited. They seemed fascinated by my case and listened intently as I described every last detail to them.

'I feel scared being on a plane with somebody as unlucky as you,' the little Cockney bloke chortled. 'I hope it doesn't crash-land or get struck by lightning.'

The banter continued until we landed in Heathrow, where I was made to wait until everybody else had left the plane before being cuffed up and walked across to an unmarked police car.

'Right get in, you're off to Holloway,' the female officer told me. 'They're going to wonder where you got your tan from when you get there.'

I had heard that Holloway was a rough old nick but felt confident that I would fit in OK. After surviving the likes of Maghaberry and Topas, I was no longer fazed by the prospect of entering a jail with a bit of a reputation to it. It was a case of been there, done that, got the mental scars to prove it.

The police spent the short trip from the airport to the jail winding me up and trying to convince me that I was going to be sharing a cell with a big, butch lesbian called Betty. We had a right laugh together and I almost forgot that I was heading to a place that housed some of the most dangerous women in the country. Holloway might not have been as bad as the Spanish prisons that I had been in when it came to the treatment of the prisoners, but the residents there were just as violent and deranged. The difference was that I was now accustomed to life behind bars and had got used to mixing with shady characters.

As we pulled up to the jail, the gates opened up to let us through and I thanked the coppers for the lift. They wished me luck and handed me over to a big, fat, jolly-looking female screw, who walked me into the reception area. Entering a prison for the first time is always a bit intimidating no matter how many jails you've been in and Holloway was certainly no exception. Weaselly, beady-eyed, smack-rats milled around the place and Yardies gibbered away to one another in incomprehensible patois. Worse still, the hardest, butchest girl I've ever seen in my life was checking in at the same time as me. She looked like a big, burly, shaven-headed bloke.

A closer inspection revealed that this manly-looking creature was not only unrecognisable as female, but was also covered in vomit. Congealed lumps of sick plastered her clothing and a thick crust of mucus and stomach acid had formed around her mouth. She was obviously on the bad end of some heavy-duty drugs.

After waiting patiently for a good ten minutes whilst the man-woman drooled puke everywhere and repeatedly fell asleep on the desk, it was finally my turn to be processed. The receptionist must have had the patience of a saint. If the he-she had come into a Spanish prison in the state that it came into Holloway, it would have been beaten over and over again until it sobered up and then probably beaten some more for good measure. I gave the desk staff all the information that they asked for and then followed another female screw down a corridor onto the induction wing.

There were nine other girls on induction with me, most of whom were drug addicts and low-level criminals. It was supposed to be four to a cell but there was only one other girl in the room that I was allocated to, which was a turn up for the books. My new cellmate seemed to be taking very badly to life behind bars and lay sobbing on her bed all day. I figured she might not want to talk to anyone so I left her to get on with it. It was sad to see her so distraught but when you're sharing a cell with someone, you have to give them space when they feel down. If I had been upset about something, the last thing that I would have wanted was for someone to pry into my business by asking why I was crying.

The following morning, I was woken up early and told to pack my things because I was moving onto the main wing. Prison life is full of uncertainty; you're never in the same place long enough to settle and soon get used to upping and leaving your digs all the time. It's still always nerve-wracking moving in with a new set of people, like starting a new school as a kid.

The minute I set foot on the wing, a load of druggies and fruit loops were all up in my face, asking me where I was from and what I was in for. As with Soto and Topas, the inmates didn't come across as particularly aggressive or hostile, just very curious. They seemed to have no concept of personal space though. Two of them followed me all the way to my cell, gibbering away incessantly about nothing in particular until a guard shooed them away.

The guard unlocked the door for me and motioned me inside, which was a bit of a relief because I didn't think I had the energy to deal with any more over-zealous junkies. My cell had four other cons in it, none of whom were English. There were two Bulgarian pickpockets, a Jamaican drug dealer and a short, fat Pakistani girl, who was in for fraud. This was just my luck; I had spent ages sorting out a transfer to England so that I would be around other English-speakers and here I was, stuck in a room with every nationality under the sun.

None of my cellmates were people that I would have mixed with in the outside world. The Bulgarians couldn't understand a word of English and kept calling me Diana for some unknown reason, which soon became incredibly wearing. The Pakistani and the Jamaican were both crackheads so all they really cared about was drugs. Most of the prisoners in Holloway are transferred to another jail shortly after arriving though, so I knew I wouldn't be in with them for very long.

Holloway was a lot less multicultural than Soto and Topas, but still contained a lot of foreign nationals. Most of them were from Jamaica but there were also quite a few Bulgarians, Polish and Vietnamese. The Vietnamese were all in for growing marijuana. They looked very weak and frail but I knew better than to do anything that could possibly provoke them after seeing their martial arts display in Soto. I didn't fancy being kung fu-kicked across the wing so I tried my best to stay on their good sides.

Literally all of the English prisoners were on either crack or heroin. They were always cutting themselves as well, which was something that I had never seen in any of the other jails that I had been in. Most of the girls had scars all over their arms where they had slashed them over and over again with homemade prison shanks. It's strange because no one in Spain had any noticeable blade marks on them. I don't know if this is because British prisons have more of a culture of self-harm or what, but it was horrible to witness and hammered home what difficult lives these girls had.

Fortunately I was able to arrange a visit soon after I arrived at the prison, which provided me with a momentary respite from seeing people getting rushed to the hospital wing after slicing themselves up. My visits in the Spanish jails had taken place in a private room but this one was in a large hall full of tables and chairs. I had been dying to share my excitement at being back in UK with my sister and my mum and spent the whole time telling them how great it was to be on English soil. Seeing them reminded me how much I longed to be back home, where I would be free to chat to my family whenever I wanted.

Two weeks after touching down in Holloway, I got word that I was transferring to HMP Cookham Wood in Kent, which I saw as another step towards freedom. The other girls on the wing told me that you got longer visits and more time out of your cell, which sounded good to me. I hoped that it was the last time I got moved before I was released though because I was sick of being shipped out the minute I got used to a jail. The constant change was like a form of torture. It meant that I was never fully able to relax.

The transfer bus that took me to Cookham was like a limousine compared to the buses that they had in Spain. The seats were comfy, we didn't have to sit cuffed up and we were even given a packed lunch to eat. It would have been a pleasant journey if the screws hadn't stuck a paedophile in with us. The minute the other girls got onto it, they started shouting and screaming their heads off, calling her every name under the sun.

'You're dead when you get off this bus,' bellowed an angry Cockney bird. 'You're not even going to make it to the wing.'

Luckily for the paedo, we were all in separate compartments so none of the other prisoners were able to get at her. I wondered why they had decided to put a sex offender on a bus with regular criminals. The nonces had their own separate unit in Holloway and were usually kept well away from the general population. I hoped the same was true of Cookham.

Upon arrival at the prison, our compartments were unlocked and we were escorted one by one into the building, the nonce being saved until last to prevent her from being attacked. I was taken straight to the main wing and shown to my cell, which was even smaller than the ones in Holloway had been. My new cellmate was a crazy Jamaican woman with no teeth and a swollen stomach. She was as skinny as a rake and had a hairdo that could have passed for a particularly poorly-made bird's nest.

'Hi I'm Terry,' I told her. 'It looks like we're going to be sharing.'

'Yeah you got lucky,' my new roomie told me. 'This place is full of 'nough monsters. You did well to avoid being in with a wrong 'un. Kiddie fiddlers, child killers... they've got 'em all in here.'

This didn't sound too good. Was that why they had stuck the nonce on the bus with us? Was Cookham Wood reserved for sickos and sex offenders? I wasn't sure if Bird's Nest Head was telling the truth at first so I quizzed some of the other inmates when I got out on the wing.

'There's your answer for you,' a grizzled old heroin addict from London told me, pointing over to a mousy-looking, brown-haired girl, who was surrounded by an army of screws. 'That's Sarah Whittaker.'

'Not *the* Sarah Whittaker?' I asked her.

I had read about this evil woman in the papers. She had left her little children wallowing in their own faeces and dying of starvation whilst she went out boozing and living the life of Riley. One of her kids was found with maggots crawling about in his nappy and was under half the weight of the average child his age when the police found him.

'Yeah,' the smackhead told me. 'It's full of celebrities in here. See that woman over there?'

She was pointing towards a big, black woman with horrible, cold, evil-looking eyes.

'That's Marie Kouao.'

Although not quite as notorious as Sarah Whittaker, this was another name that had been plastered all over the news. The sick monster had beaten her niece with bicycle chains and hammers and forced her to sleep in a rubbish bag in an unlit, unheated bathroom. The little girl eventually died of hypothermia.

It made my mind boggle that such intensely evil people were allowed to walk around the jail unhindered. Sarah was escorted everywhere by a group of guards but the other nonces were left to their own devices. Over the course of the next few weeks, I was forced to mix with all manner of freaks and perverts. People who had killed and molested their own children were in with the general population and would often lie and claim that they were serving time for fraud. Occasionally one of them would appear on the news and get stick from the other prisoners but they were usually left alone.

Sometimes the most innocuous-looking inmates turned out to have committed the most disturbing crimes. I remember seeing two quaint, little old ladies walking around the wing together and thinking, 'I wonder what they're in for'. I later learnt that one of them had burnt her grandchildren to death so that she could get out of looking after them to go to the bingo, and the other was a paedophile. Cookham was like some weird twilight zone where demons walked around the place in the guise of regular human beings.

The girls who weren't nonces all seemed to be plastic gangster types. They acted like rebellious teenagers who thought that they were cool because they were always in trouble. There was even more self-harm than there had been in Holloway. Some girls barely had an unmarked patch of skin. They were scarred all over their bodies, with huge slashes down their arms and legs. I didn't know how they could do it to themselves. I'm far too vain to cut myself. If I fall over and graze my knee, I worry that it will mess up my legs, so the chances of me mutilating myself because I'm having a bad day are slim.

The one redeeming feature to the prison was the fact that we were allowed to make phone calls to inmates in other jails. This was brilliant because I hadn't spoken to Aidan for ages and missed him almost as much as I missed my family. We had been writing to one another but it wasn't the same. When I rang him up, I was surprised at how much stronger his accent had got since he had been back in Ireland. It was so thick that I could barely work out what he was saying. He kept going on about all the things that he had planned for us when we got out of jail but to be honest, I wasn't sure if I wanted to carry on seeing him after I was released. I liked him a lot but was he really someone that I had a future with? We were two very different people with conflicting views on life.

The more I thought about it, the more I made up my mind that I was going to have to say goodbye to Aidan at some point. He had the same anger in him that I had seen in Jamie and I didn't want to make the same mistake twice. He had treated me well whilst I was in Topas but seemed far too mixed up for me to have a relationship with him in the outside world. When I got out, I wanted to start afresh and put behind me everything that had happened in Spain. Aidan would be a constant reminder of my time inside, which wasn't what I needed. Staying away from him was going to be difficult but I knew that it was for the best.

Thinking about the changes that I needed to make when I was released made me wonder what was going on with my pardon. I hadn't heard anything from Fair Trials for a while and the tension was killing me. The longer I went without any word from them, the more anxious I got.

Just as I was beginning to think that everybody had forgotten me, I got a note to say that I needed to attend a meeting that would determine whether or not I was eligible for transfer to an open jail. Prisoners aren't usually considered for open conditions until they've served the majority of their sentences so I had a feeling that John Bercow had pulled a couple of strings to fast track things for me. If I was successful then I would be able to put in for a home visit. The thought of spending a day outside the confines of the prison made the hairs on my arms stand up. It would be my first taste of freedom.

On the morning of my meeting, a million different thoughts were flying round in my head. What if I got turned down and told that I was going to have to stay in Cookham until the day of my release? I wasn't sure how much longer I could put up with being surrounded by wannabe bad girls and creepy sex offenders. The month that I had already spent in there was bad enough as it was.

The assessment only lasted a couple of minutes. I was asked some questions about what I planned to do when I got out of jail and was then told straightaway that I was getting my transfer.

I couldn't believe that it had been so easy. I was off to a place called HMP East Sutton Park in Sutton Valance near Maidstone. It would only be a matter of time before I got to tuck into one of Mum's gorgeous roast dinners and sleep in my own bed. My stint in hell was finally coming to an end.

Chapter 21

MURDER AT HOGWARTS

We were having our tea when it all went downhill. We noticed a paramedic car and a cop car in the little car park by the gate and they then started to cover it all with tape. After about half an hour, one of the governors came in to tell us that one of the prison teachers had had her throat cut. We are all very traumatised.

Diary entry from 12 September 2007

'Pack your bag,' the screw told me. 'You're off to your cushy open nick. Don't overdo it on the caviar and make sure that your shoes are clean so you don't dirty the red carpet on your way in.'

Funny guy. By this stage I had come to realise that a jail is a jail and that there is no such thing as an easy prison. I had expected British nicks to be a walk in the park but although they were a damn sight better than the ones in Spain, they were still quite gruelling so I knew not to expect anything too great from East Sutton. It was also the fifth time I had been shipped from one jail to another within a two-month period so changing prisons had now become extremely repetitive.

It was lovely looking out of the bus window as we were driven to the prison. East Sutton Park overlooks the Weald of Kent, which is an area of fields and woodland that stretches out for as far as the eye can see. Gazing out at such a vast expanse of countryside was like a breath of fresh air after being cooped up in a tiny little cell for so long. It made me feel alive again.

The prison itself was equally impressive. It was the spit of Hogwarts from the Harry Potter films. Big, archaic-looking stone chimneys stuck up from the roof, making it look more like a National Trust property than a prison, and there were no fences or walls. There weren't even any bars on the windows.

'I could get used to this,' I thought to myself as we drove up to the entrance, past the well-kept lawn and rows of pretty flowerbeds.

The inside of the jail was equally impressive. There were proper carpets on the floor and luxurious leather sofas dotted around the place. The prisoners were just as scruffy and drug-addled as ever but I suppose you can't have everything.

Instead of cells, the accommodation in the jail consisted of large dormitories with seven beds in each. My dorm was huge, with a fireplace and posh bay windows in it. Holloway had prepared me for sharing with a lot of people so I wasn't bothered about rooming with six other girls. So long as none of them snored too loudly, I would no doubt settle in just fine.

My other roomies were all fairly chilled out. They were a range of different races and ages, which was to be expected because prison is a real melting pot. Crime crosses all boundaries and villains come in every shape and size there is.

The other girls were intrigued by my story and seemed to think that I was some kind of big time gangster because my sentence was so long. They were all coming to the end of theirs and couldn't get their heads around the fact that I had been moved to an open jail with so long left to go.

'You won't get a home visit until you've done three quarters of your time inside,' a skinny, Afro-Caribbean girl warned me. 'You won't get to work outside the prison until you've had the visit either.'

Ah well. It still beat Cookham Wood. I'd take a prison that looks like a stately home over a prison that looks like a prison any day of the week. As soon as I had got the introductions out of the way, I headed off to the dining room to get myself some food. I had arrived just in time for dinner and a day of travelling had given me quite an appetite.

The food was a huge improvement on the slop that Cookham Wood had served. It still wasn't a patch on Mum's but then again, not much really is. Most of the other inmates seemed to have been in the jail for quite a while and chatted loudly to one another as they ate but one girl sat in total silence with her eyes fixed firmly on her meal. She was a delicate little Chinese thing, who barely seemed old enough to watch a fifteen-rated movie, let alone do anything worthy of being sent to prison for.

'Are you all right there?' I asked her.

She looked up at me with a blank expression on her face. I knew how hard it was to be a prisoner in a foreign land so I slowly repeated the question and enunciated my words more clearly so that she would understand. She nodded her head, looking nervous, as if she wasn't used to people making the effort to communicate with her.

'I no speak English so good.'

'You speak it better than I speak Chinese,' I laughed. 'My name's Terry. I just got in today. And yours is?'

'Chan. I in for fraud and money launder.'

She might not have known much English but she had still proven that she was familiar with the standard prison conversation. The next question after, 'What's your name?' was always, 'What are you in for?'

Chan seemed very innocent compared to the other girls in the prison and had an endearing vulnerability to her. Talking to her reminded me of the conversations that I'd had with Mama Rosa because neither of us had a clue what the other one was on about but I still enjoyed her company.

'I'll tell you what,' I said. 'I'll make it my mission to teach you English whilst you're here. It'll give me something to do and you'll find it a lot easier to fit in when you know what everyone else is saying.'

'OK I like,' she nodded. 'I like a lot.'

Over the course of the next few weeks, Chan and I spent every evening together, going through useful words and phrases. Teaching her made me feel as if I had a sense of purpose. Life inside is very boring and monotonous so any goal that you can work towards is guaranteed to make your time less soul-destroying. She picked the language up very quickly and could soon speak enough to get by.

I also enrolled in classes of my own in the hope that it would count in my favour when the government made the final decision as to whether or not I was going to get my pardon. I did maths, first aid, health and safety and a course called CLAIT, which stands for Computer Literacy and Internet Technology. Learning new things was fun and I got to stand outside and have a fag with one of the English teachers during the break. It was nice to speak to somebody intelligent for a change. Her name was Louise and she was well spoken, polite and always had something interesting to say.

I had hoped that all the good work that I was doing would speed along the process so that I'd get out before Kelly had her baby but alas, it wasn't meant to be. On 5 August 2007, I received the news that her waters had broken and she had been rushed to hospital. Later that day, I rang home to check on her progress and was told that she had given birth to a beautiful baby boy. He weighed a whopping 8 pounds and was as healthy as could be. I was disappointed that I had missed out on yet another important chapter in the Daniels family history but also over the moon that we now had another new addition to the clan.

That night I thanked God for the precious gift that he had given us and prayed that I would be able to see the baby soon. I knew that East Sutton was the last prison that I would be in before I was granted my freedom and couldn't wait to hold my little nephew in my arms. I just wished that the government would hurry up and make their decision.

As the days went by, I became increasingly impatient. Seeing the other inmates going out to work was a constant reminder of the outside world. In English prisons you do half of your sentence inside and the other half on license so it would only be another couple of months before I got my home visit but I still wasn't sure that I could wait that long.

The only thing that I enjoyed about being inside was seeing Chan's English getting better and better. She progressed from hardly saying a word to being able to casually chat away to the other prisoners within the space of a few weeks. It was amazing how fast she could learn vocabulary. She would have probably ended up one hundred per cent fluent if she hadn't been deported part way through her sentence. We were in the middle of a study session when it happened and neither of us had any idea what was going on. One minute we were going through some phrases and the next thing she was being cuffed up and escorted out of the door.

Poor little Chan had tears streaming down her face as she was ordered into the back of a prison van. The authorities had given no prior warning that they were going to come for her. I was going to miss her terribly. I just hoped that she had a safe journey to China and enjoyed her life back home.

In the days that followed the deportation, I grew increasingly lethargic and spent more and more time in bed. It's difficult to gain the motivation to prise yourself from under the duvet when you know that there's nothing productive available for you to do. I was still doing my classes but they were only a couple of days a week, which gave me an excess of spare time to fill. Prison life was so boring that it was hardly worth waking up in the morning – although if I had known what was about to happen next, I would have relished the lack of eventfulness. Sometimes things can get a little bit *too* interesting.

The first sign that there was something wrong came when I looked out of the window and saw an ambulance and a squad car pulling up in the car park. The police came to the prison to question people every now and again so I thought nothing of it until a copper jumped out with a roll of yellow tape and started cordoning off the grounds. I had seen them doing this before on *CSI Miami*; it was what they did when there had been a murder.

Within seconds, everybody in the prison was discussing what might have happened and speculating as to who could have been killed. It reminded me of the morning after the supposed suicide in Soto. There was the same frantic, tension-driven atmosphere, with everybody gossiping and whispering to one another.

An hour and a half later, the prison governor came in to give a harrowing announcement.

'I'm sorry to have to be the one that breaks the news to you but earlier today, a member of the teaching staff lost her life in the prison car park.'

I just prayed that it was no one that I knew.

'Ms Evan's death is being treated as suspicious...'

Oh God. Not Louise. I had been laughing and joking with her just the other day. She was the nicest, kindest person that you could imagine. I might have expected something like this to happen at Holloway or Cookham Wood but East Sutton was meant to be a minimum-security prison. It was hardly the type of place where you would expect anyone to get killed.

'The police have requested that everybody remains locked in the prison until they finish gathering evidence. You will also all be questioned at some point. I know that this is likely to be a difficult time for all of us. Louise was a popular teacher and I'm just as shocked and upset as anyone.'

It was as if drama followed me wherever I went. The scary thing was that for all I knew, it could have been one of the girls from my dorm that was responsible. I felt as if I had stumbled into a scene from the film, *Scream*. The other inmates all looked absolutely mortified. Some of them were crying and others were holding their heads in their hands. One thing was certain: if the murderer was a prisoner then she wasn't going to be very popular when the police solved the case. Louise was a much-loved figure and we were all gutted that her life had been cut short in such tragic circumstances.

We spent the remainder of the evening glued to the window, trying to figure out exactly what had happened. By this stage, there were so many police there that we could hardly see for blue. It wasn't long before the press were on the scene either. They managed to conceal themselves in a hedge and were just getting ready to take pictures of us when I spotted them. I had accidentally put my top on back to front that morning and prayed to God they hadn't got a snap of me. The last thing that I wanted was for the image of me wearing a topsy-turvy jumper to be plastered all over the papers.

'Over there,' I shouted, pointing a quivering finger towards the hedge. 'Get them out of here.'

The guards were on the scene in seconds, chasing the cheeky buggers around the grounds. It would have been quite an amusing scene if the presence of the paparazzi hadn't demonstrated how easy it was for outsiders to get close to the prison. If the murderer was still nearby then he would have no problem striking for a second time. I just hoped they caught him as soon as possible so that my heartbeat could return to its normal strength and speed.

The footage of the screws shooing the cameramen out of the prison was broadcast on the news later that night.

'East Sutton Park was regarded as a model prison up until this evening,' the newsreader announced. 'Then, as she walked to her car after a day of teaching English to the prisoners, forty-eight-year-old Louise Evans was stabbed forty-three times and left to bleed to death. There were no witnesses and no CCTV cameras.'

This was all too much. It was like something out of a slasher flick. Some of the inmates sobbed quietly to themselves and others sat expressionless in a state of shock. My heart went out to Louise's family. It couldn't have been easy for them to hear that their relative had died in such a nasty way.

I was glad that I was in a dorm and not a single cell that night because I wouldn't have slept a wink if I was in on my own. Every time I closed my eyes, I saw images of crazed knifemen hiding in hedges. I kept thinking about Louise as well. The news report had said that she had two daughters. If my mum had died like that, it would have no doubt haunted me until my dying day. I said a silent prayer for all Louise's friends and relatives and asked God to look after them in their time of need.

The following morning, we were taken out of the dorms one by one and interrogated by the police. They didn't bother driving us to the station; they just interviewed us on a bench outside the prison, which I didn't think was very professional. The officer who questioned me talked down to me as if I was a lower form of life because I was a prisoner. It was the last thing I needed after hearing that somebody I knew had died and had me on the verge of tears.

The police have an amazing knack for making you feel guilty even though you are one hundred per cent innocent. I went back to the wing thinking, 'Damn, I must be a really bad person for him to have treated me like that.' The copper doing the interview had been completely insensitive and seemed more interested in upsetting people than he was in doing his job.

We spent the rest of the day cooped up in our dorms because there were still forensic investigators milling around outside. Every time the news came on, the room fell silent and we listened intently for updates on the case. The newsreaders repeated the same details during the first few bulletins but then, later that evening, the identity of the murderer was finally revealed.

'Police are looking to question Keith Prest, the ex-boyfriend of murdered teacher Louise Evans, who was stabbed to death in the grounds of HMP East Sutton Park in Sutton Valance near Maidstone yesterday evening. Officers have warned that he should not be approached under any circumstances, as he may be a danger to himself or others.'

The moment I saw Prest's photo, I knew straightaway that he was guilty. He had the same cold, uncaring look in his eyes that I had seen on the faces of the wrong 'uns on the wing in Cookham Wood. I was relieved that none of the prisoners had played a part in the killing, but at the same time furious that a man who had once claimed he loved Louise thought he had the right to commit such a horrific act of violence just because she had the common sense to try and distance herself from him.

The police eventually apprehended Prest and charged him with Louise's murder. The spineless rat attempted to kill himself but unfortunately survived and was sentenced to a minimum of seventeen years in prison. He had been stalking and harassing Louise in the build-up to the killing and thought that if he couldn't have her, nobody should be able to. The detective in charge of the case described him as a 'nasty, vindictive, controlling beast of a man', which I thought was very apt. I hoped that his time inside would be just as depressing and soul-destroying as mine had been.

Louise's death took away what little motivation I had left to get out of bed in the morning. The only thing that kept me going was the thought of my home visit and even that was a constant source of worry. Lots of girls went off the rails after getting their first taste of freedom. They couldn't handle it and ended up absconding and getting sent back to closed conditions. I just hoped that I would have more self-control.

A month after the murder, I was told that I was eligible to schedule my first trip back home. I felt excited but scared at the same time because I knew that I would be classed as an absconder if I was five minutes late returning to the jail and transferred to a high-security prison. I still had to wait a couple of weeks whilst the prison finalised the visit, which gave me just enough time to work myself up into a state of panic. What if the car broke down on the way back to the clink? It might destroy my chances of getting the pardon. Then there was the demon drink to think about. Would I be OK if I had a glass of wine with my meal or would it set me off on another epic bender? This was really my most serious concern because I would be gutted if I became an alcoholic again after everything that drink and drugs had put me through. I wanted to get a second opinion so I booked myself an appointment with the prison drink and drug counsellor to see if she thought I should risk it.

The counsellor advised me that a single drink could very easily topple me.

'It's against the prison rules to consume alcohol whilst you're on home leave but that's got nothing to do with me,' she said. 'I've seen hundreds of girls go out with the intention of just having the one and come back hardly able to walk though. You need to think about your priorities, Terry. Is it really worth chancing it?'

She was right as well. There had been evenings when I convinced myself that I was only stopping by the pub for half an hour and ended up spending all night there. This time things would be different though. I wasn't going to put my sobriety on the line for the sake of a measly glass of wine. I made a pact with myself never to have another drink again. Up until this point I had assumed that I could revert back to being a recreational drinker but the counsellor made me realise that once you have crossed the line and become an alcoholic, there is no such thing as having a quiet drink with friends. It's usually all or nothing so it made sense to stay one hundred per cent booze free.

Now that I knew I wasn't going to lapse back into drunkenness the minute I got home, I started to feel a little less anxious. Despite my nerves, I was still made up at the prospect of being able to go to sleep in my own bed. It was all that I could think about in the days leading up to my visit. I had just about managed to mentally prepare myself and clear my head of negativity when the prison governor called me into his office to tell me that he had some bad news for me.

'I know how much this visit means to you but I'm afraid we're going to have to cancel it.'

I felt as if he had punched me in the face. How could he casually cancel something as important as that at such short notice? It was like the visit at Soto all over again.

'The media have got word of it and it's getting too much attention. Unfortunately prison protocol states that in these circumstances, it would be impractical to grant you temporary release.'

I knew he didn't make the rules but couldn't help but feel angry with him. It wasn't my fault that the press were interested in my case. Why couldn't anything ever be straightforward? A random complication always seemed to get thrown into the mix whenever things were looking up.

'Don't worry, we can reschedule it for next week,' the governor continued, attempting to placate me. 'We'll keep it quiet so that nobody knows about it. It hasn't been cancelled to punish you, you know Terry? It's for your own safety.'

I couldn't understand his logic. How was the media taking a few photos of me going to endanger me? A week is an eternity to wait when you are that hyped up about something. The date change also meant that I would be on tenterhooks, wondering whether or not the visit was actually going to happen.

The next seven days were fraught with tension and unease. What if the media got wind of the new date? I wasn't sure if I could handle any more disappointment. Every night before I went to bed I closed my eyes and prayed the visit would go ahead without a hitch.

When the day finally arrived, I felt so nervous that I thought that I was going to throw up. It was looking as if it was definitely on but I was now in such a state that I was playing through every possible way that my trip home could end up going badly in my head. I kept imagining being late back and getting dragged off to serve the rest of my sentence in some grim maximum-security prison. I had spent enough time in those places in Spain and didn't fancy landing in one over here.

This time there was no cancellation. The governor even came into my dorm to wish me luck before I left the jail. Mum was waiting in the car park and looked over the moon to see me.

'This is the beginning of the end, Terry,' she told me. 'Soon you'll be coming home for good.'

I really hoped that she was right because temporary freedom didn't feel at all like the real thing. The knowledge that I could have my pardon application torn up and thrown in the bin if I put a foot out of place was still very much at the forefront of my mind. I couldn't drink or enter a licensed premise, I wasn't allowed to gamble or set foot in a bookies and I had to remain at my address from 7 p.m. onwards. The first two criteria would be easy enough to stick to but what if I was forced to leave my house for some reason? Most people wouldn't have thought twice about it, but given my history of misfortune, I could picture the police turning up the minute I put a foot out of the door. I was just going to have to stick pedantically to the rules. It wasn't worth risking losing everything for a minor breach.

As we pulled up into our street, I felt a knot of tension forming in my stomach. I should have been looking forward to eating proper food and getting a good night's sleep but felt as if another disaster was lurking on the horizon. The governor had ruined my visit by postponing it. The uncertainty that he created had made me far too nervous to enjoy the occasion.

I had been granted a full weekend at home, which sounded like a long time when I was first told about it but now seemed too short to fit in all the things that I wanted to do. Emma was off to her school disco on my first night back so I would only be able to see her on the Sunday. It was just a case of making the best of the two days that I had.

It felt weird setting foot in the house again after being away so long. All sorts of memories came flooding back to me, some good and some extremely unpleasant. I remembered all the fun times that we had had there as a family; but also the days after Dad's death and the deep, dark depression that I fell into in the build-up to my extradition. Mum had bought a Christmas present for me every year since I had been arrested so I opened them all up, thanked her and then sat at the table, ready for the feast fit for a king that she had prepared for me. We had chicken, rice and fajitas for the main course, my all-time favourite, followed by Toblerone cheesecake for dessert. Yummy!

I had got so used to eating rubbish that I had almost forgotten what a decent meal was like. I devoured both courses in two minutes flat and then reached over for another slice of cake.

'I'll tell you what Mum, I bet they won't be having that in East Sutton,' I smiled, cheering up a bit now that I had got to stuff my face.

The combination of stress, excitement and an extremely full stomach made me feel exhausted so I finished off my last mouthful, heaved my way upstairs and plonked myself down on my nice, warm, comfy bed. You barely get a minute to yourself in prison so I laid there basking in the silence for a while before going to sleep. This was how life should be lived. Human beings weren't meant to be crammed in a dorm like battery chickens. Being locked up in prison again was going to be like moving from a penthouse to a cardboard box. I just hoped it wouldn't be too long before I could come home for good.

The following morning, I was woken up by the sound of Emma's angelic little voice firing a million and one questions off at Mum. Kelly had brought her round to spend some time with me and the cheeky monkey wanted to know why I was home so soon. Kel had told her that I was in hospital because she didn't want her to know I was locked up so Mum had to think on her feet.

'She's been allowed out for a visit,' Mum said. 'She'll be better soon but until then they're only letting her out for a few days at a time.'

I felt as if she was telling the truth in a way. Prison had been like a spell in a detox centre. It had helped me to get over my various addictions and cleanse my mind of youthful rebellion. If I hadn't gone in when I did then I probably would have carried on boozing and taking whiz, which would eventually have either sent me insane or made me seriously ill. I had matured to the point where life in the fast lane no longer appealed to me. Give me a clean bill of health over a weekend on the tiles any day of the week.

I spent the remainder of the day having my brains picked by Emma, cooing over the new baby and catching up with the latest gossip from my sister. All of my conversations took place at a million miles per hour because I wanted to cram as much as possible into my last day of freedom. Mum cooked a lovely Sunday roast and we all sat around the table together, just like when I was a kid. It would have been the best home visit that I could have possibly asked for if the fact that I had to go back in less than twenty-four hours hadn't been hanging over me. It's difficult to enjoy something when you know it's going to be so short-lived. I felt as if I was counting down the minutes until it was time to head back to jail.

The day passed by in the blink of an eye and before I knew it, my visit had come to an end.

'Don't worry, Auntie Terry will be better soon,' I reassured Emma. 'Not long left to go now. Be a good girl for Mummy whilst I'm away.'

I gave her a hug and said goodbye to Kel. A couple of hours later, I pulled up into Hogwarts again, ready to resume my spell in purgatory. All in all, the visit had been an overwhelming success. The fact I hadn't done a runner the minute they let me out would no doubt be another string in my bow when it came to the final decision on my pardon. I had a feeling that they wouldn't have granted me temporary release so quickly if they weren't planning on freeing me soon anyway.

Being surrounded by constant noise 24/7 was even more grating now that I had experienced the peace and quiet of home. I had been hoping that my visit would reinvigorate me and give me a new lease of life but I still felt just as lethargic as ever. As the days dragged on, I wondered whether anybody was still chasing up my pardon. I hadn't heard anything for ages so I decided to give Mum a ring and tell her to get onto Fair Trials. The minute I got through to her, she started yelling excitedly down the phone.

'It's come Terry! It's all over. You've made it! You're free!'

Oh. My. God. This was the moment I had been waiting for. My ordeal was finally at an end. No more rushed trips home where I spent every second worrying that something would go wrong; I was coming back for good.

'I can't believe it,' I shouted. 'I've done it! And I couldn't have done it without you, Mum.'

'It's only a partial pardon but it still means you're free,' Mum told me. 'They've reduced your sentence from ten years to six so under the rules over here, that equals three in prison and three out on license. You've already served three years inside so now they need to release you. You'll have to see a probation officer every week for a couple of years but at least you won't be in jail.'

It's impossible to be partially innocent. To me this showed that the Spanish government had realised they had made a mistake but were reluctant to fully own up to it. It beat another two years inside though so I was just as happy as Mum. I still needed to wait until it was all finalised before I could leave the jail – and an apology for stealing three years of my life would have been nice – but I was ecstatic nonetheless.

On the day of my release, the entire wing gathered in the reception area to bid me farewell. The other girls all gave me a kiss and a cuddle, which made me very emotional. I had met some good people inside. They were the only thing about East Sutton that I was going to miss. Even the guards had all turned out to see me off. It hammered home the contrast between British screws and Spanish ones. The ones in Spain would have probably given me a few licks with a truncheon as a goodbye present.

As I stepped out of the prison door, I stopped for a second to reflect upon everything that I had been through since my arrest in Gran Canaria. Over the course of the last decade, I had been in seven jails in three different countries, mixed with everyone from shoplifters to multiple murderers and survived addiction, depression, anxiety, and two near-fatal haemorrhages. My new-found freedom marked a brand new chapter in my life. The days of drink, drugs and excess were well and truly over; I now yearned for a quiet, trouble-free life. After being released from both Salto and Maghaberry, I had ended up carrying on as I left off but this time there was too much at stake. If I put one foot out of place, I would be going straight back to jail, which would totally destroy me. Mum was waiting for me in the car park so I flung myself into the car and yelled, 'Drive before they change their mind!'

My passport to hell had finally expired. And one thing was for certain: I sure wasn't renewing it.

Chapter 22

LIFE ON LICENSE

So how did this story end?

Although I was over the moon that I could now socialise with people who weren't criminals and no longer had to share a room with six other girls, being free wasn't all it was cracked up to be. Don't get me wrong, after witnessing everything from violent prison brawls to dead bodies being carted out of cells, I was relieved that I was back in the sleepy little village that I had grown up in, but being on license was just as nerve-wracking as my home visit had been. I barely left the house for fear of accidentally breaking the law. I wasn't planning on doing anything illegal so I technically had nothing to worry about but kept thinking, 'What if I'm accused of something that I haven't done again?' The idea of having to do the time that I had spent in prison all over again scared the living daylights out of me so I spent weeks on end in my room, only venturing outside to go to my probation meetings.

I got on well with my probation officer but couldn't help thinking that seeing her was totally pointless. The idea was that she would keep me on the straight and narrow and prevent me from committing another offence, but seeing as I wasn't guilty in the first place, she might as well not have been there.

The other thing that really got to me was the fact that I no longer had a group of mates to knock about with. All my friends were still going to raves and taking stupid amounts of drugs, which meant that I had no choice but to cut them off. But where was I going to find replacements? Raving had been my only real interest and there was nothing to fill the gap. I tried to arrange to meet up with one of the people who had got in touch with me after reading my story in the *Mirror* but my license conditions made it impossible. I was banned from staying anywhere overnight and he lived all the way down in Newcastle.

Aidan wanted to meet up with me but I wasn't allowed to leave the country either and he refused to come to England. He got quite angry when I told him that I wasn't willing to break the rules and hasn't spoken to me since. He would have been a nightmare to go out with in the outside world so I'm glad that we aren't talking, although I still wish him the best of luck with whatever he is doing.

The fact that I had got so used to being in jail made it even harder for me to kick-start my social life. I had become very institutionalised and no longer felt comfortable going out. Even a quick trip to the shops left me feeling emotionally exhausted and extremely panicky. Other people's attitudes didn't help either. When I went to sign on at the job centre, the woman behind the desk was very rude to me and made it crystal clear she didn't like ex-cons. I tried to voice my concerns about how hard it was going to be to find a job with a criminal record but she was totally unsympathetic and told me that it wasn't her problem.

The reality of the situation is that it is almost impossible to gain employment if you've been in jail. I might have had a pardon but the offence was still down on my record, which blighted any chance that I might have had of getting a well-paid job. I was still determined to do something productive with my time though, so I started doing voluntary work for a charity that helped people with drug problems. I thought, 'What better person is there to offer advice to addicts than somebody who has been through what they're going through and managed to get clean?'

I loved helping people turn their lives around and managed to get an NVQ in drug counselling. The training that I received helped me to understand my own addiction. I identified the things that triggered my cravings and learnt about the harm that drugs and alcohol can do to the body. One of the most interesting pieces of information that I picked up was the fact that you can grow dependent on the chemical that your body produces when you mix alcohol with cocaine to the point where you become aggressive when you take one substance without the other. This explained the times when I had got really narky when I was able to drink but couldn't get hold of any coke. It was crazy to think that I had abused drugs for so long without knowing the full extent of their effects. I couldn't believe that I had been so stupid.

Providing advice to addicts was just as enlightening. I learnt a lot about myself through hearing about their problems. Some people might have looked down on them but I knew exactly what they were going through. I think drugs and alcohol are the real passports to hell. If you have an addictive personality, they can create a world of problems. I felt as if I had finally found my calling; it was now my job to prevent other people from following the path that I had foolishly taken.

My criminal record still stood in the way of doing it as a proper job, unfortunately, and the job centre weren't happy about me spending my time doing something that I didn't get paid for. They started really getting on my back about it so I had to quit, which I was gutted about.

My Jobseekers advisor scared the living daylights out of me. She was so stern and abrupt that I dreaded going in to see her. There was only one thing for it: I was going to have to beat the odds and get myself a job. I decided that the only way that I was going to have any success was if I approached somebody who was familiar with the circumstances surrounding my arrest. The landlady at my local pub was friendly with my mum so I figured she was the perfect person to try. She had been following my story and was aware of how unfairly I had been treated.

The landlady agreed to take me on as a glass collector, which filled a big gap in my life. Unemployment and depression are a deadly combination so I will be eternally grateful to her for helping to take me out of the deep, dark hole that I had fallen into. Now that I had a job, I became a little bit more confident and started going out of the house. It was the first step to recovering from the host of psychological afflictions that life behind bars had left me with.

I finished my license period in April 2011 but still haven't managed to fully shake off my anxiety. Prison has irreparably damaged me. It has destroyed my self-confidence and left me with a permanent stain on an otherwise spotless record.

There have been positive as well as negative consequences though because I think I would have almost certainly carried on taking drugs if I hadn't been locked up.

The biggest test of whether I was off the drink and drugs for good came when Mum was diagnosed with breast cancer. I had always gone off the rails when faced with a family crisis like that in the past, but this time I managed to remain sober and faced it full on rather than attempting to blot it out with alcohol and amphetamines. It was a major scare after what had happened to Dad so I was over the moon when the doctor delivered the news that her treatment had been successful and she was going to be OK.

Gaining the ability to keep my head during a crisis wasn't the only silver lining to my imprisonment. My case also highlighted the inadequacies of the UK's current legislation on extraditions. Fair Trials have used what happened to me as evidence that the system doesn't work. They recently put forward their argument in the Court of Human Rights, complete with a huge photo of me in the background to illustrate their point. Hopefully the injustice that I was forced to suffer will make things easier for people who are arrested abroad to get a fair trial. If I can prevent a single person from going through what I went through then I will be satisfied that my incarceration wasn't all for nothing.

Another good thing that came out of being locked up was my friendship with John Bercow. He really took a shine to Mum and me, and even invited us as his guests to The Queen's Garden Party in July 2010. I am probably the only person convicted of drug trafficking who has ever been allowed into the grounds of Buckingham Palace. It was a once-in-a-lifetime opportunity and I would like to say a big thank you to John for making it happen. He could have easily dismissed me as a lowlife criminal and refused to have anything to do with me, but he fought my corner until the very end and then continued to support me even after I had been released.

The kindness of people like John has helped me to come to terms with the fact that my life is never going to be the same again. A lot of people might assume I hate the Spanish people after everything that they have put me through, but strangely enough I don't harbour any resentment towards them whatsoever. It wasn't the normal, everyday Spaniards who were to blame for my imprisonment; it was their rotten, crooked legal system. I still love Tenerife and even returned there earlier this year to lay some ghosts to rest.

I was understandably nervous in the build-up to my trip back to the island and kept worrying that the Spanish coppers might try to fit me up again. The terms of my pardon stated that I would be locked up for another decade if I committed another crime in Spain within fourteen years of my release. Visiting my old haunts was something that I knew I had to do though because I hadn't got to say goodbye to anyone when I fled back to England and I wanted to gain some closure.

Tenerife looked just as beautiful as I remembered it being. The sun was shining, people were milling about in their bikinis and there was a lovely, carefree atmosphere. Being able to speak Spanish gave me a stronger connection with the place and allowed me to soak up more of the culture. I met up with the Silvas family, saw some of my old workmates and even paid a visit to Veronicas. The holiday passed without a single bit of trouble and helped to put my mind at rest that what had happened in Brazil was finally behind me. I will never be able to fully erase the scars that the Spanish government inflicted on me but I am determined not to let them ruin the rest of my life. After all, I've got my freedom, my health and my family so what more could I possibly ask for?

PHOTO APPENDIX

Terry and her gramp, an irreplaceable figure in her happy childhood

Young and free – Terry, age 21

Good times – Terry and her sister enjoying a first taste of Tenerife

Terry and family in Tenerife, 1996 – from left to right: Mum, Terry, Dad and Sister

Riding high – Terry enjoying
some Spanish night-life
with her best friend

A cheerful Terry back at work after
the year of her first arrest

Terry and her father in Tenerife
in 2000, shortly before he was
diagnosed with cancer

Scarred for life – the result
of Terry's brain operation
in 2001

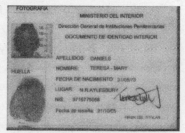

Terry's prison ID cards

Putting on a brave face whilst
incarcerated at Topas Prison, 2006

A guardian angel – John Bercow
MP (centre) with Terry and her
mum at Parliament

Standing tall – a radiant Terry at
the Buckingham Palace garden
party in 2010

Prisoners Abroad is the only charity providing welfare and practical help to British people in prisons throughout the world. Every year we care for over 1,700 people just like Terry who are held thousands of miles away from their homes and their families. We help them get food, clean water, medicine and bedding. We help people stay in touch with their families and send books and magazines to alleviate the damaging isolation and loneliness of imprisonment. Innocent or guilty, convicted or awaiting trial, we simply work with the people who need us.

Since 1978 we have been there for thousands of Britons, helping them survive in terrible circumstances in prison overseas. We also provide vital services after release, making sure that homelessness and destitution aren't the only options facing someone who has returned to the UK with nothing.

You too can help by making a donation. Without the support of people like you we simply could not do the work we do and many people like Terry would have nobody at all. You can reach people that the rest of society has forgotten, people who are truly desperate. Even a small donation can go a long way and make a huge difference to someone in an overseas prison.

You can find out more about our work and make a donation at:
www.prisonersabroad.org.uk

Alternatively please call us on **020 7561 6835** or write to us at:
Prisoners Abroad
89-93 Fonthill Road
London N4 3JH
United Kingdom

Registered charity number: **1093710**

Every year, thousands of people find themselves in nightmarish situations like Teresa's, after being arrested in a country other than their own. Many are imprisoned for months or years before their trial even begins with no comprehension of their rights and no legal aid to help them pay for a lawyer or interpreter, simply because they are a foreign national.

Fair Trials International (FTI) is a unique human rights charity that exists to help defend the fair trial rights of those who find themselves in this terrifying predicament. We seek to ensure their access to a reliable local lawyer, effective consular support, and vital information to enable them to enforce their right to a fair trial.

We became involved in Teresa's case only after her appeal had failed. We obtained proper translations of court documents and evidence, which revealed that her conviction had been based in part on badly translated documents. We continued to support Teresa after she was transferred to the UK on medical grounds and petitioned the UK Government and Spanish authorities on her behalf, until she was ultimately granted a royal pardon.

To find out more about how you can make a donation or fundraise on behalf of FTI, please visit:
www.fairtrials.net/support_us/fundraising

With your support we will continue to fight individual cases of injustice and will campaign for fair trials all over the world.